A LONE STAR ARISES IN TEXAS

The Struggles that Led to a New World

A LONE STAR ARISES IN TEXAS
The Struggles that Led to a New World

Translated and interpreted by
© 2021 Stephen A. Engelking
ISBN: 978-3-949197-68-0

Based on the German "Kampf um Texas" by Friedrich Hertneck (1941)

Texianer Verlag
Tuningen
Germany
www.texianer.com

Cover Picture: Sam Houston at San Jacinto
(PD-US)

Table of Contents

THE SPANISH FRONTIER PROVINCE 5

CONQUISTADOR MOVEMENTS 11
- The Odyssey of Cabeza de Vaca 16
- Hunting for Fairy Tale Kingdoms 30

FRONTIER PROTECTION 47
- Fort Saint Louis 55
- Monks as Frontier Guards 70
- Juchereau de Saint Dénis 80
- Redskins under the Fleur de Lis 91

INTERLUDE 105
- Missionary Work in Texas 113
- Athanase de Méziéres 126

AMERICAN NEIGHBORS 143
- The Travails of Revolution 150
- Jean Lafitte, the Buccaneer 157
- The Buccaneering Campaigns of James Long 166

AMERICANIZATION 175
- Open Borders 180
- Stephen Austin, the "Father of Texas" 186
- Mexican Suspicion 199

THE FIGHT FOR FREEDOM 211
- Resistance 214
- The Alamo 220
- The Victory at San Jacinto 229

THE REPUBLIC 241
- Sam Houston, the "Raven" 244
- The Lone Star 256
- Crusader and Troubadour 264
- The Road to the Union 273

AN ATTEMPT AT GERMAN COLONIZATION 281

The »Mainz Adelsverein«..286
A New Homeland...314
RANGERS AND RANCHES...**323**

INTRODUCTION

THE SPANISH FRONTIER PROVINCE

Texas is well known to everyone as the setting for Indian tales and Wild West romances and most have also heard of the oil wells and sulfur pits, cattle herds, and cotton fields that secure it a place in the world economy. But who knows anything about the fact that in the vast areas that stretch between the Mississippi and the Rio Grande deep into the Plains, historical events as charming as they are significant to have taken place, that Texas also has a place in world history?

And yet it does! Texas has by no means led an insular existence far removed from the course of great events, but has stood in the midst of the force field of the manifold political tensions which determined the development of the North American continent. Against the backdrop of its wildernesses and prairies, an eventful, colorful and turbulent historical spectacle unfolded, telling of the doings and activities of many men and nations, of a world full of wild, harsh sounds, shrouded in the air of an adventurous romanticism known only to the colonial and frontier era of North America. The curses of Spanish soldiers and the prayers of Spanish monks are mixed with the voices of

French rangers and the war cries of Indian horsemen until all these sounds are drowned out by the ax-blow of Anglo-Saxon pioneers who penetrate the fertile plains and valleys of the country with the strength of rolled-up shirt-sleeves.

This happened, however, at a time when there were no drilling rigs to extract the "liquid gold" from the earth and no ranches over whose endless expanses saddle-firm cowboys drove uncounted cattle. Whoever wants to know the history of Texas has to wander back into the distant past, into centuries before weather-hardy ranchers had torn the soil from the wilderness and daring rangers[1] had chased away the peace-disturbing Redskins and desperadoes.

At that time, the battle for North America was still raging, the Western European powers were scrambling for their colonial empires in the New World, and the young Anglo-American nation was advancing in impetuous expansion across vast tracts of land as far as the Pacific Ocean. The historically important period for Texas lasted from the beginning of the 16th century, when Spanish conquistadors sought the riches of fabled cities in those inhospitable lands, to the middle of the 19th century, when Anglo-Saxon settlers rose up in armed revolt against Mexico. What preceded it during the millennia before the white man came and disputed the Indian's hunting grounds is shrouded in a darkness that can only be sparsely illuminated by ethnological research. That which followed, the decades since Texas has been a part of the United States, merges into mere territorial incidents of limited interest to a European observer.

However, during the centuries that intervened between these periods, Texas witnessed a moment of world history. The lands to the north of the Gulf of Mexico were also one

---

1 "Border riders," members of a Texas constabulary force.

of the sites that saw struggles for the political shaping of North America. This battle is usually followed only on those fronts where France and England clashed and one forgets how long Spain defended its old possessions in the southwest with tenacious energy. On this southwestern front, which stretched from Florida up to California, Texas formed by far the most important section and it can add a new dimension to the history of North America if it is viewed from the perspective of a Spanish frontier province, on whose soil decisions were made that were as serious as those of the Spanish, decisions that weigh as heavily as those fought out in Canada or the Mississippi Basin, decisions that answer the question of how it came about that Spain-Mexico, which once owned most of the space over which the Star-Spangled Banner now flies, was so completely pushed out of North America.

It was not due to colonization that the Spaniards decided to settle in North America. Primeval forests and wildernesses could not excite a nation to which Mexico and Peru offered everything it expected from colonies. It was not until the French and English advanced deeper and deeper into the interior of the continent from the east coast and increasingly threatened the border of the "Indias" that Spain also laid hands on large areas of this hitherto neglected part of the world. Certainly, the desire of Franciscan and Jesuit fathers, eager to convert, to open up new mission fields, did its part to extend the Spanish empire further north. But in fact, Texas and the other provinces that the Spanish established on North American soil over time owed their creation to strategic considerations. They spread out as a multi-layered defensive belt in front of the treasury of Mexico, forming, in itself only weakly manned and fortified, a huge "glacis" in which enemy attacks from the east and north could be stopped.

As a Spanish frontier province, Texas played a role in the battle for North America as a protective wall against Mexico. Here, Spain brought the French attacks on the Central American silver mines to failure and halted the Anglo-American advance for decades. But when, after 1821, Anglo-Saxon pioneers were given the opportunity to settle in Texas, the fate of Latin North America was sealed. Before the Mexicans knew it, their frontier province was overrun, and their countermeasures only sparked passionate resistance from American frontiersmen. The end was a revolution that put an end to Mexican rule over the lands between the Sabine and the Rio Grande, and tore the most important link from the chain of the former Spanish North American front. For ten years Texas was an independent republic, until in 1846 its inhabitants succeeded, against all odds, in joining the lone star of their state flag to the ring of stars of the North American Union. The Mexican-American War of 1846/48, with all its results and boundary changes, is nothing but the logical consequence of the Texan events. And is it so far-fetched to associate with them also the terrible tragedy of the War of Secession? The controversy in which parts of the Union slavery should be admitted and in which not, flared up anew with such vehemence over the Union of Texas and the land gain of the Peace of Guadalupe Hidalgo, that passions were finally discharged in a murderous fratricidal struggle.

The history of Texas is marked at every turn by the great events that shaped the political face of North America. It faithfully reflects them in all their phases and even ultimately points the way to their development. It shows the construction and grandeur, decline and collapse of the

Spanish Empire, the paths and goals of French colonial policy, the unrestrained expansionism of the Anglo-American frontier and the desperate struggle for existence waged by the prairie tribes against the palefaces. But what brings the Texan past especially close to us Germans is that dream which was cherished around the middle of the last century: to make a German colony out of the lands north of the Gulf; and even if this dream did not come true, we will not forget the tens of thousands of our countrymen who found a new home in Texas.

FIRST CHAPTER

CONQUISTADOR MOVEMENTS

The West Indies became the Spanish gateway to the New World. The trade winds and ocean currents that had driven Christopher Columbus's three caravels into the middle of the Antilles in 1492 set the same course for the ships that dared to sail through the watery deserts of the Atlantic Ocean in the footsteps of the bold Genoese. Soon, year after year, hundreds of men from Andalusia and Castile landed on the shores of Espanola, now Haiti, where the first settlement had been established as early as 1495. From there, Puerto Rico, Jamaica and Cuba were occupied in quick succession between 1508 and 1511.

The Spanish began to explore the mainland almost simultaneously with the conquest of the Greater Antilles. The islands were a disappointment for a large part of the voyagers to America. In the hastily and meagerly built colonial towns, a strange mixture of knights and lansquenets, officials and monks, merchants and settlers, adventurers and those fit for the gallows had come together, jostling and rubbing, harassing and repressing each other in feverish restlessness and rampant selfishness. Many of these men did not want to know anything about the hardships that the development of a country entails, no matter how luxuriant the harvests the tropical sun elicited from the soil. Had they come here to work? Indignant and scornful, the hidalgos in particular, who were already forbidden any economic activity in their homeland by a strict chivalric conception of marriage, rejected such an imposition. What moved them, what excited them, was the one desire, the one covetousness: to seize goods of fortune, to find treasures such as India held.

But the "Indias" that had been reached were not the India that had been wanted. There were no precious stones in the Antilles to be used in the diadems of kings, in the jewels of noblewomen or in the altarpieces of the church; no silks to be used to make colorful garments for the male sex; no spices for which the European palates craved to make up for the monotony and poor preparation of food; no fragrances to make up for the too sparing use of baths. The only thing the islands had to offer to the Spaniards' lust for booty was some gold sand in the riverbeds. The Indians were forced to wash it out. The peaceful Aruak had hardly resisted the white invaders; now they were ruthlessly and brutally exploited as cheap work animals.

The 5 million Marks worth of yellow dust extracted annually from Espanola failed to satiate the Spanish hunger for gold. "The adventurers who went to America," wrote a contemporary, "dreamed of nothing but gold, and gold they sought, gold they extorted from the natives, gold they were given to satisfy them, gold jingled in the letters with which they sought to gain prestige at court, and gold was what the court demanded and desired." So they sailed out of the West Indian ports toward unexplored regions of the New World, hoping to find more productive mines somewhere. In the medieval idea that the closer a country was to the equator, the richer it was, the conquistadors first turned south to the Caribbean coast. They gained a firm foothold on the Gulf of Darien. But what did the little bit of gold sand that was found there mean compared to the mountains of glistening metal that their over-ambitious minds had led them to believe?

One day, in 1513, the boundless expanse of the Pacific Ocean spread out before one of the gold seekers who had ventured into the sweltering jungles of the Panamanian Isthmus. In full armor, sword in hand, Balboa strode deep into the rolling waves to plant the banner of Castile as a sign that henceforth the Spanish King was master of these waters and of all the lands they washed. This was a great gesture but it concealed a grave disappointment. The Spaniards had long since realized that the areas Columbus had discovered for them were not part of Asia. They had clung all the more to the belief that they were at least near Cathai and Zipangu, Marco Polo's China and Japan. Now, in view of the new sea, it dawned on them how far away still lay that Orient which was the goal of their longing. There could be no question of renunciation! Should Spain, the stronger nation, leave the richer Asian field to the Portuguese alone and be content with the poorer American one? Even if one had always encountered coasts that prevented further travel, no one doubted that there was a way from the "Indias" to India, an east-west passage. And the cosmographers imaginatively drew the passage, which no one had seen yet, on the world maps and thus contributed to the fact that the rumors about its existence did not cease until the 18th century.

In 1519, when all searches for the "Strait of Anian", as the passage was called, perhaps in reference to Anam, remained futile on the Caribbean coast, the governor of Jamaica sent four ships north under the command of Alonso Alvarez de Pineda. There and back, the squadron sailed the long distance from Florida to Panuco, not far from present-day Tampico. They carefully explored the numerous bays that punctuate the uniform shoreline, carefully recording their location on a parchment. For forty days, Pineda and his men rested on the delta of a great river that poured huge masses of water into the gulf. Rio del Esplritu Santo was its name; today it is called Missisippi. Otherwise, Pineda did not know how to tell much of significance on his return home. His report was as dull as the flat Texas coast, barely rising from sea level, which he was the first European to see. In any case, he had not discovered the "Strait of Anian". Nor was there any talk of gold discoveries. It seemed as if it was not worthwhile to continue to bother about the lands north of the Gulf.

If, nevertheless, Florida and Texas very soon reappeared in the Spaniards' field of vision, it was for other reasons. Not all the men who set sail were chasing hoped-for treasures and following imaginary routes. Many had a more real goal in mind. They raided the Lesser Antilles and the Bahama Islands, dragging their brown inhabitants away with them to be sold as slaves to gold panners and plantation owners in the big islands. There was a growing shortage of Indian labor in the West Indies. For the Aruak, contact with European "culture" proved fatal. They succumbed to the yoke of forced labor no less than to the foreign diseases brought by the whites, for example measles, not to mention the cruelties committed against them. Bishop Las Casas had not yet raised his voice to stop the extermination of the natives in the name of the Christian religion and economic logic, nor had those protective laws been enacted that later brought such honor to Spanish Indian policy.

CONQUISTADOR MOVEMENTS

Juan Ponce de León, who had become the governor of Puerto Rico in gratitude for the bloodhounds he had used against the defenseless inhabitants of the island, heard a strange tale from the slave hunters who were looking for their victims in the Bahamas. Somewhere in the north, it was said, lay the island of Bimini, shining with gold and pearls, where the legendary fountain of youth could be found. Thus, Ponce set out to take possession of this wonderful land. Sailing in a northwesterly direction, he came upon a coast that presented itself in such flowery splendor that it was given the name Florida. However, since the Indians were too hostile and Ponce's troops too weak, the conquistador was unable to land anywhere. He returned home unsuccessful and other military duties kept him so busy that he was not able to pursue his plan.

Then an event occurred that sent the Spaniards into a frenzy of happiness and transformed the almost despised and cursed America into a land of unlimited possibilities: Hernan Cortes discovered and conquered Mexico. This was the beginning of the great era of the Conquista. Dozens of daring conquistadors equipped expeditions to penetrate the wildernesses of the New World and imitate Cortes. Even Ponce de León could no longer be restrained. In 1521 he sailed again to Florida and this time he succeeded in getting ashore. However, during the very first battles with the Indians, he was struck by a lethal arrow. His crew, deprived of their leader, abandoned the expedition and embarked.

Where the conquistador fell, others took his place. Ponce's death was just one more incentive to draw attention to the lands on the northern shore of the Gulf. It was speculated that the governor of Puerto Rico had taken secret knowledge of a second Mexico to his grave and that secret had to be uncovered. What did the interior of Florida hold, to which Indian kingdoms did the Rio del Esplritu Santo lead, what lay beyond the coast of Texas? The Spanish conquistadors pursued this question and did not rest until they knew the answer after extraordinary marches and exertions and an admirable effort of willpower and perseverance. Yet the one who led the first platoon into these lands was Panfilio de Narváez.

The Odyssey of Cabeza de Vaca

In his "Historia de las Indias", Oviedo, the earliest chronicler of the New World, relates that he had strongly warned the Cuban landowner Narváez, who had come to him for advice in Toledo in 1525, against the planned conquest of Florida. Oviedo had spent enough time as an official in the colonies to know the dangers of the Americas; he knew from the relevant reports how many a conquistador had run blindly to his doom. Nevertheless, the immigrant visitor turned a deaf ear to his well-meant words. He thought it was a foregone conclusion that—just as it had been in Central America—a silver-rich Indian land was waiting behind the swampy lowlands of the Gulf Coast to be discovered by its conqueror. Narvaez belonged to those people, writes Oviedo with a shrug of the shoulders, who can only be taught by severe strokes of fate, just like donkeys, who only pay attention after the third blow of a stick.

Narváez had gone to the West Indies as a twenty-year-old in one of the first waves of colonists and had so distinguished himself in the "pacification" of Jamaica, as the bloody subjugation of those peaceful natives was shamefully called, that he was given military command during the occupation of Cuba in 1511. Generous allotments of lands and Indians rewarded his services in arms and made him one of the island's most prosperous inhabitants. Had he been less avaricious for vainglory and gold, he could have ended his life quietly and safely as a wealthy hacienda owner. Ambitious as he was, he allowed himself to be tempted to take on the task on his own initiative and on his own account of forcibly capturing the man who had conquered Montezuma's treasures. Narváez landed at Vera Cruz together with a considerable force of troops. But Cortes bribed his rival's soldiers and, when it came to battle, Narváez was left fighting alone with a small band of loyal soldiers until one of his eyes was knocked out. He was held prisoner by Cortes for three years, three years in which he endured terrible humiliations and had to witness the great conquistador's happiness at close quarters, whilst being filled with hatred and envy. Finally, however, he was free again in Cuba with his wife who had worked hard all this time and had collected many barrels full of gold dust. A year later Narváez went to Spain to apply to the imperial court for a piece of America that he would conquer for the crown and himself.

Narváez was well received in Spain, bringing with him what the Council of the Indies needed most: impeachment material against Cortes, who had become too powerful for the emperor and should therefore have his rights curtailed. In return, Charles V signed a state document authorizing the Cuban to "discover, conquer and settle" the lands between the "island" of Florida and the Rio de las Palmas, now Soto de la Marina in northeastern Mexico. This sounds very grand, but in reality meant quite little. As in other conquistador treaties, this conferral document explicitly stated that Narváez was to bear all the costs of the conquest and that the Crown was not obligated to do anything. "Their Majesties," Oviedo bitingly notes, "put virtually no fortune or money into the new discoveries, but only paper and fine words, and they said to the Capitanes, 'If you do what We wish, We promise you this and that,' or 'Our thanks are assured to you.'" Why should the Spanish rulers also take a risk when there were speculators enough willing to risk their goods and lives for so uncertain a cause as a campaign into the American wildernesses? The stipulation that one-fifth of the spoils belonged to the king ensured that the crown did not take the short end of the stick anyway.

At that time it was easy in Spain to recruit soldiers and colonists for an American enterprise. Since the news of the discovery of Mexico, people from all walks of life dreamed of making their fortune in the Indies. Only a few suspected what it was really like over there, what hardship and suffering, adversity and death awaited them and the ignorance of the others was unscrupulously exploited by the conquistadors. It was, as Oviedo expresses himself, so to speak, a large-scale catch of fools. "And Narváez caught many," the chronicler continues, "because poverty befuddled some and greed others, and delusion almost all, so that they did not know what they were doing and whom they were following." More than 600 men finally set sail across the Atlantic under the command of the Cuban.

A nobleman named Alvar Nunez Cabeza de Vaca accompanied the expedition on royal commission. He held the title of treasurer and had the task of securing a fifth of the captured treasures due to the crown and establishing an orderly tax administration in the new provinces. Nunez was a man in his late thirties. He bore the peculiar name "Cowhead" with pride in his ancestor, a simple shepherd who had once been awarded this noble title in the early

13th century for having shown the Spanish army the way to the rear of the Moorish enemies and to a decisive victory with a cow skull. Nunez himself had distinguished himself in the Italian campaigns and in the suppression of the Communero uprising. In other ways, too, he must have attracted the attention of the government because of his ability and reliability. For it was a high honor and a great mark of confidence to be placed in the post of treasurer.

Narváez spent the winter with his men in Cuban ports. In the spring of 1328, however, he hoisted sail and soon landed with 400 men at Tampa Bay, Florida. It is true that the pilot said that this was not the port on the way to Pánuco that he had wanted to head for; he probably meant Mobile or Galveston Bay. Yet what did it matter to the Spaniards at the moment when they had found a golden clasp between fish nets in an Indian hut, where the natives had given them signs to understand that further north, in Apalache, there was gold in abundance! They had no idea that the primitive-smart Redskins were telling them a fairy tale, as they did everywhere when they wanted to get rid of the white intruders and set them upon their own enemies. The gold rush seized Narváez and robbed him of all reason: he sent the ships ahead with the rest of the soldiers to the "nearby port"; there they were to wait until he himself had followed by land with the main army. Cabeza de Vaca argued in vain that they did not know where they were, that the horses were in bad shape, the provisions more than scarce, the country and its inhabitants unknown. He was outvoted in the war council. Everyone had only one desire: to get to Apalache, the land of gold, as quickly as possible.

And so began the arduous march through swamps and

thickets, across rivers and broken tree trunks, from one miserable Indian village to the next, in which one could only now and then acquire some food to satisfy one's hunger, accompanied by dense swaths of biting mosquitoes and biting flies, to whose perpetual torment one was defenselessly exposed. Still, people have always accepted hardship and deprivation when the yellow metal was beckoning them from afar. Slowly the men worked their way forward under the scorching heat of the sun, the knights armored on horseback, the lansquenets armored on foot. At Apalache, a bitter disappointment awaited them. When Cabeza de Vaca occupied the village with a squad of soldiers, he encountered only reed huts and cornfields. Not a scrap of gold was discovered in the nearly four weeks that the Spaniards stayed there.

Were they really in Apalache? Yes, they were indeed there! The Indians assured us that this was the largest place within a wide radius and that all around were wide lagoons, dense scrub, vast wastelands and deserted areas. The next Indian village was only nine days away, close to the sea. Where the sea was, there had to be the harbor, the ships! Narváez gave the order to leave. Away from this wretched wilderness! Swarmed by hostile Redskins who shot at them in an ambush with arrows against whose penetrating power not even the chain mail offered protection, the exhausted men made their way through jungle and swamp. Hardly anyone was spared from malaria and the number of the seriously ill who had to be laboriously dragged along increased daily.

With the last of its strength, the troop arrived at its destination. But when Cabeza de Vaca explored the seashore, he saw only a shallow bay that stretched for miles into the land. There was nothing to be seen of the ships! What was to be done now? To march on was an impossibility. The only means seemed to be to build boats in which to reach Mexico. No one had any idea of the actual distance—it was over two thousand kilometers. But where to get material and tools to make the boats? There was a lack of everything! Necessity is the mother of invention. Stirrups, spurs, crossbows and whatever else contained an ounce of iron were reworked, as best they could, into nails, saws, axes and other things. Ropes were twisted from palm fiber and horsehair, and shirts were stitched together to make sails. After seven weeks of hard work, five clumsy, raft-like barques of questionable seaworthiness were finally ready to sail. Aboard them, the 247 Spaniards who had escaped malaria fever, hunger and Indian arrows crammed themselves together and, entrusting their souls to God, ventured out to sea.

The boats steered a westerly course, in the direction of Mexico! Carefully, the men sailed close to the protective shore. Again and again they kept a lookout for food and fresh water. "For five days we had drunk nothing," Cabeza de Vaca writes at one point, "and we suffered such terrible thirst that we gulped down salt water. Some did this quite intemperately and because of this five people suddenly perished." The journey continued westward. One day they noticed that the sea water tasted sweet; they were at the Rio del Espfritu Santo. But in the strong current, the boats were driven far out to sea and lost sight of each other during the night. Later, the barge, led by Cabeza de Vacas, reunited with that of Narváez. In vain, the treasurer's ailing crew struggled to keep up with the other boat. "Seeing this, I asked the governor to throw me a rope so that I could stay with him. But he replied that as it was, it was no easy task to land in the night without incident... Everyone should determine how best to save his own life. In any case, he intended to do just that. After these words he rowed away in his boat." What curses may have been shouted at the expedition leader, who by his incompetence and imprudence had brought about the disaster and now dishonorably and inhumanly abandoned his followers!

Cabeza de Vaca continued his journey. He was only able to distribute a meager handful of raw corn to each occupant of the boat each day. Soaked, freezing, feverish, the people, completely out of strength, close to death, lay randomly on top of each other on board. Almost no one was able to take the wheel. A storm drove the barque to the shore, and seized by a surge, the ship was hurled onto the bank. This happened on November 6, 1528, on an island on the Texas coast near Galveston Bay.

The Indians who rushed over were helpful and brought plenty of food and drink. Soon the Spaniards thought they could continue their journey. However, just as they were undressing and pulling the craft into the water, a strong wave capsized the boat and threw the men back onto the beach."We escaped naked as we were born, losing all our possessions and, though they were worth little in themselves, they were worth much to us at the time... for it was November, and a severe cold prevailed, and our bodies were so emaciated that one could easily have counted our ribs and we looked like skeletons." The natives, the Karankawa, who were later so feared and so infamous as cannibals, compassionately took care of the shipwrecked people. They carried wood to warm them and they opened their huts for them to live in. In the same way, they welcomed the crew of the boat of Captains Andres Dorantes and Alonso del Castillo, who were also stranded on the island. Such hospitality is unparalleled! For the Indians were wanting and starving themselves. Now in winter, the fish traps were empty and only sparsely found were the water roots that had to be laboriously dug up in the reeds.

Most of the eighty Spaniards were no longer able to cope with the new privations and in a short time all but fifteen died of debilitation. Even of this group, three more became so seriously ill that they were abandoned and left behind when the survivors decided to set out in April 1529 to migrate on foot to Mexico. Cabeza de Vaca was among these terminally ill who remained on Isla de Mal Hado, the "unlucky island." But the Andalusian nobleman had a tough constitution. As a result, he recovered. And so began the evil time when the imperial treasurer, who had crossed the ocean to subdue the Indians, had to serve as a slave to the primitive savages of the Texas coast. It often happened that he could not find a morsel to eat for three days in succession and it was a small consolation that his brown masters fared no better. Naked, he stood in the bank reeds, where the broken canes tore his flesh as he searched for roots in the salt water. "From this work my fingers became so sore that they began to bleed just by touching a straw."

For a year Cabeza de Vaca endured this life, then he escaped to friendly Indians on the mainland. Here he was a free man who, as a racial stranger, was allowed to move freely among the feuding tribes and — warmly received by all, well treated and plentifully fed — traded escargots, mussels, skins, flints and similar goods.

He finally set out in the late summer of 1532 to venture into Mexico. He wandered along the Gulf Coast until he came to a tribe beyond Matagorda Bay that he had not yet met in his travels as a trader. How great was his astonishment when he heard that further inland there were three men living as slaves with another tribe who had the same white skin as he did, and that these Indians would also arrive in a few days for the nut harvest at the river that is now called Guadalupe. And indeed, soon Cabeza de Vaca found himself face to face with Captains Dorantes and Castillo and a Moroccan Negro named Estevanico, whom some one of the noble participants in the Narváez expedition had brought with him to America as his man servant. "We thanked God fervently," Cabeza de Vaca relates, "for reuniting us; it was one of the greatest days of joy we had yet experienced."

Dorantes had much to report. Three and a half years ago, he and his comrades had gone far west from Isla de Mal Hado, probably to the area where Corpus Christi now lies. There he learned the fate of two other boats: distressingly the end of Narváez, who—wounded in the fight against the Indians—had retreated nightly aboard his ship and had been driven by the waves into the open sea; more shattering still the sinking of the crews, who, mad with hunger, dried and ate the corpses of their companions until one remained, whom the Indians dragged away and later slew. And Dorantes went on to tell how the savages at Corpus Christi Bay had murdered his comrades out of wantonness, how he had fled with Castillo and Estevanico back to the tribe to which they now rendered slave service.

Was there any salvation left for the four Spaniards who, by God's providence, met again at Guadalupe? Cabeza de Vaca encouraged the three men to try their utmost to escape inhospitable Texas and return to the civilized world. It was agreed that all four would remain with the Indians as slaves and that they would then escape together in six months, at the time when the prickly pears were ripe, when the savages were moving farther west. The three

Spanish noblemen gave their word of honor to be unbreakable to each other, and for the Negro Estevanico, the slave of slaves, it was an order. And so they endured the manifold tribulations: the maltreatment they received daily; the disgusting food, spiders, worms, newts, snakes, which they had to eat; the hard work; the tormenting mosquitoes. They even endured that their waiting time was prolonged by a whole year, because the Indians got into quarrels and left the fig area prematurely. As if they were not to be spared any mental ordeal, they then heard that the crew of the fifth boat had also been completely slaughtered by the coastal Indians. What fate was destined for them, the last survivors of the Narváez enterprise?

They managed to escape in mid-September 1534. They came to a tribe that did not know that they had been slaves, but received them kindly. Yes, these savages were so astonished by their strange appearance that they were believed to be gifted with magical powers and brought the sick to them for healing. The Spaniards could not refuse such a request without putting themselves in danger. However, since they had no medical knowledge, they imitated the shamans whom they had often seen working among the Indians during the many years of their lives. But they were not of the opinion that they were performing mere hocus-pocus. They were devout Christians and believed in devilish demons that could be cast out with the sign of the cross. They prayed the Lord's Prayer and the Hail Mary to the sick; they begged God to have mercy on them and to heal the savages. And was it not obvious that God and the Mother Mary were helping them? No Indian went from there who did not affirm to be completely cured. Even a sick man, lying there half dead with his eyes twisted and without a palpable pulse, rose after they had crossed him and blown on him. This was as much a miracle for Cabeza de Vaca and his comrades as it was for the natives, and later even theologians in Spain argued about whether such laymen and "nefarious warriors" as the four castaways could have performed genuine miracles at all or whether it was not rather to be assumed that they had been in league with Satan.

The tribe diligently made sure that the four medicine men, who had such great healing successes, did not run away, and so they had to travel with them through the sand belt of Texas and spend the winter in an area a short distance north of the mouth of the Rio Grande. They stayed there for eight months, suffering unspeakable hunger. They finally managed to escape their hosts in May 1535. Probably the bad experiences in the coastal areas kept the four from following the hem of the sea. In bold determination they moved up the Rio Grande, wandered along the edge of the mountains that accompany the stream on the right bank, then crossed over to the other side and into the western tip of Texas, and from there across the Sierra Madre into the valley of the Sonora to the Gulf of California.

As arduous as this march was, it was in fact almost like a triumphal procession. Their reputation for miracles preceded them. Everywhere they were regarded by the natives as messengers from heaven, whose coming caused trembling fear and clamorous joy. Everywhere the Indians crowded to see the three majestically taciturn white-skinned medicine men and their merrily chattering black servant. Everywhere they brought them the sick for healing, hoped for a blessing touch for their children that would protect them for life against the violence of evil spirits. Each tribe was reluctant to see the godsent strangers leave. But the Redskins knew how to compensate themselves in their own way for the loss: they plundered the neighbors to whom they escorted the miracle workers down to the last arrowhead. Once this custom of collecting the "doctor's fees" became entrenched, the Spaniards made rapid and sure progress. Still, the role into which they had been thrust was not easy. "Frequently we were accompanied by three or four thousand people, and you can judge how much we were inconvenienced by the fact that we had to blow on and bless each one's food and drink, and were asked permission for every little thing they wanted to do."

Cabeza de Vaca, Dorantes, Castillo and the Negro Estevanico were the first westerners to roam this part of North America. The number of landscapes they traversed was endless, the number of tribes they encountered was infinite. They saw cultureless savages who ran around naked and lived from hand to mouth, they met nomadic hunters who stalked a black-brown, long-haired, hunchbacked steer, the buffalo, they stayed with primitive farmers who dressed in cotton cloth. But wherever they went, they discovered nothing that could have attracted a Spanish conqueror. Only once did they notice something. That was in a village near the Pacific Ocean, which had been christened Pueblo de los Corazones, because there the Indians had worshipfully given Dorantes six hundred open deer hearts. Here a resident brought cotton cloths, coral beads, and turquoises that came from the north, and Cabeza de Vaca saw emeralds as arrowheads that the natives to the north had traded for parrot feathers. "Beyond the high mountains to the north are populous cities with high houses," it was said. No doubt the Spaniards had missed these lands. Was it worth seeking it out?

This question, however, became meaningless when the four travelers, on their way south, met an Indian who was wearing the buckle of a sword belt and a horseshoe nail on his necklace. Excitedly they inquired of the man as to where he had got these things. They had come from heaven, was the answer. Bearded demigods had brought them, who—armed with swords and lances—sat on monstrous dragons and then moved to the sea, dived under water and hurried away on its surface. As fantastic as this tale sounded, the objects that adorned the Indian proved unmistakably that soldiers of a Spanish expedition had stayed here. The joy of Cabeza de Vacas and his comrades to find traces of their compatriots for the first time in eight years was inexpressible.

They then continued their march at a faster pace. The further they went, the more they saw signs of the proximity of their Christian co-religionists. What they first heard from the mouths of the Indians and then saw with their own eyes frightened them deeply. Over wide stretches the land lay devastated, the villages burned, and part of the population had been carried away. Frightened and starving, the rest sat in the mountains, subsisting on tree bark and roots. Spanish slave hunters had infested the area. Cabeza de Vaca already feared that the natives would make him and his companions pay for the outrages of his countrymen. However, even the Indians who had been most affected by the raids, looked up to the white medicine men with faith and admiration. When Cabeza de Vaca promised them that he would go to the Christians to make sure that they would not be harmed again, many hundreds crawled out of their hiding places and joined the escort of honor that the inhabitants of the "Village of the Heart" still gave to the Sons of the Sun.

One day, the scouts that were sent out reported that they had seen Spanish soldiers, hidden behind trees, carrying away many shackled Indians. Together with Estevanico, Cabeza de Vaca pursued the slave catchers. And then—it was early March 1536 at the Sinaloa River—the morning dawned where he faced four European horsemen. The riders could not believe their eyes when a man emerged from the wilderness in front of them, unmistakably of their own race despite his sun-tanned skin and tangled hair hanging down to his belt, without shoes, a palm weave around his loins and an animal skin thrown over his shoulders. Moreover, when next to him a Negro burst out of the bushes as they both called to them in Spanish! "They were in great consternation when they saw me dressed so strangely and in the company of the Indians. For a long time they looked at me in such astonishment that they neither addressed me nor came to the decision to ask me about anything." Cabeza de Vaca allowed himself to be led to the captain of the detachment and told him his story. Survivors of the Narváez expedition that had perished in Florida in 1528, now here on the Gulf of California? What a miracle of God Almighty! The captain could hardly believe it.

The three Spanish noblemen and Estevanico, who was now once again nothing but a slave, arrived in Mexico in July 1536. Antonio de Mendoza, whom history calls the "good" viceroy of New Spain, held a bullfight and tournament in their honor. Only gradually did the rescued find their way back to life as civilized Europeans and it was a long time before they could tolerate clothes on their bodies and sleep in beds again. For many weeks they were busy writing a detailed report of their experiences for the central authority of the Spanish colonies, the Audiencia of Espanola. Andres Dorantes and Alonso del Castillo remained in Mexico and were married off to wealthy widows by the Viceroy. Estevanico became the property of Mendoza, who had his special plans for him. Cabeza de Vaca, however, went to Spain to ask his king to appoint him governor of Florida.

When the treasurer arrived in Madrid at the end of 1537, Charles V had already conferred the North American territories on another man, Hernán de Soto. A different task awaited Cabeza de Vaca: in 1540, the emperor sent him to the La Plata River as governor to venture into the interior of South America and search for a silver country that the Indians told him about. Cabeza de Vaca penetrated as far as the tropical wilderness of Bolivia but failed to find this silver country. The unsuccessful venture had sad consequences for him when his officers rebelled, imprisoned him, and sent him back to Spain in 1545 amidst vicious indictments. For years the trial dragged on, for years Cabeza de Vaca sat in custody. Judgment was passed in 1551, forbidding him to ever again enter the territories of La Plata. The last document that mentions his name is an imperial order from 1556 to pay him twelve thousand maravedis—about a thousand marks—so that he could seek healing from his ailments.

Hunting for Fairy Tale Kingdoms

At the time when Cabeza de Vaca was staying with the Texas Indians as a slave, the gold country of Peru had also fallen into the hands of the Spaniards after the silver country of Mexico. In 1532, Pizarro had conquered the Inca Empire and snatched a new secret from the New World. But the North American continent was still terra incognita, and it is only too understandable that the Spaniards, especially in these years when Central and South America had gifted them with unheard-of riches, expected the exploration of the vast territories in the north to lead to the discovery of further wonderlands. With extreme excitement, therefore, they turned to the report of a man who, on a long trek, had come to know lands that lay even farther north than those regions to which Guzman, the Indian flayer, had penetrated in his slave hunts. However, their hope to find insightful information about the country and its people in the "Relaciones" of Cabeza de Vaca, valuable hints for new conquistador expeditions, proved to be deceptive. The Castilian knights, greedy for booty, had little use for the description of a sorrowful odyssey and a miraculous salvation. Was that really all, they asked, that the four castaways had seen and heard? Or had Cabeza de Vaca selfishly concealed the best and kept it to himself? Why had he been in such a hurry to get to Spain and apply for the governorship of Florida?

Strange things were happening in Spain and Mexico. When Cabeza de Vaca had finished his lecture to His Imperial Majesty in Madrid, uncontrollable rumors were circulating at the court, causing numerous noblemen to sell their possessions and join the company of Hernan de Soto, who was about to leave for Florida. In New Spain, the Viceroy Mendoza made preparations of a very unusual kind. He began to equip an expedition at state expense, something that had never been done before, and this could only mean that he had news that seemed to be very reliable. Undoubtedly, Cabeza de Vaca embellished his truthful, if sober, report in conversations and discussions, telling the emperor and viceroy things they wanted to hear. However much he may have let his imagination run wild, the fantasies of his compatriots ran even more rampant. They created the dream image of a fairytale kingdom of the "Seven Cities" from an old legend and a questionable Indian statement that were associated with the rumors about Cabeza de Vaca.

In the 8th century, so the legend went, seven Portuguese bishops had fled with many people from the victorious Moors and had founded seven flourishing communities on the gold- and pearl-rich island of "Antilia". From time to time, sailors who returned from tempestuous voyages and knew how to spin a yarn of many kinds assured that they had seen the Seven Cities with their own eyes. Strangely enough, they had never managed to set sail for them again. Nevertheless, what an Indian in Mexico had to say was in good agreement with these stories. As a boy he had often accompanied his father on trading trips, and in the process he had once come to a country in which there were seven rich cities. Each of these cities was as large as the city of Mexico, and in each of them there were many rows of streets inhabited only by gold and silver smiths. To reach this land, he said, one would have to travel far north and end up crossing a grassy wasteland for forty days. The more they thought about the Indian's story, the less the Spaniards doubted that it was about the Seven Cities of the Portuguese bishops and that up there at the "island" of Antilia was probably also the famous "Strait of Anian".

The responsibility that rested upon him in the planned use of state resources now made Viceroy Mendoza a little suspicious of all the unconfirmed claims. He did not like to set an army in motion without first having scouted the north. Soldiers were of little use for this purpose. The appearance of armed Europeans would have provoked the natives to resist prematurely. It was different when monks were sent out. They went to the Indians as messengers of peace under the sign of the cross, combining selfless missionary zeal with servile devotion to the crown. And the Franciscan Order eagerly took up the suggestion of sending one of its friars, at its own expense, to investigate whether there were Indian settlements in northern Mexico where it would be worthwhile to establish mission stations and monasteries. In Father Marcos, they believed they had found a suitable man to carry out such a difficult mission.

Marcos was a Savoyard from Nice. He had already been in America for many years and, to his horror, he had witnessed the atrocities of the conquistadors in Peru and Guatemala. He had then been active for a long time on the northern border of Mexico, where it was necessary to convert wild Indians. His piety and talents were praised, especially his experience in dealing with savages, but also his theological, geographical and nautical knowledge. The viceroy inculcated him to exercise the utmost caution. He did not go to the northern wildernesses as a missionary who was willing to risk his life for the sake of preaching the Gospel, but as a scout who was to bring reports back home. Marcos was joined by Cabeza de Vacas, Estevanico, a black fellow sufferer, as a guide, and some of the Indians who had followed the four survivors of the Narváez expedition to Sinaloa were to go along as interpreters. "And if God, our Lord, should be so gracious. let you find some great cities," concludes Mendoza's written instruction, then, "although the Emperor, our master, owns the whole world, take possession of them in my name for His Majesty with the signs and formalities that seem fitting to you."

Marcos and his company left Culiacán, then the northernmost border town in Mexico, in early March 1539. After they arrived at Easter in what is now Matape, the padre sent the Negro to advance about two hundred kilometers in a northerly direction and then to wait until he himself would follow. If something special was noticed on the march, Estevanico was to give news through Indians in the form of a white cross, the size of which was to depend on the importance of the discovery. Already four days after the Negro had departed, a native delivered a man-sized cros to Brother Marcos. The Indians, Estevanico reported, had told him "of the greatest thing in the world. Thirty days' journey to the north was a province of seven towns called Cibola. There were houses two to four stories high, built of mud and stone. The entrances of the houses were decorated with turquoise, which could be found in abundance. And behind this first land stretched many others, which should be even larger and richer. Then Marcos did not tarry any longer and hurried after Estevanico. He wandered up the valley of the Sonora and then down the San Pedro to the Gila River. The farther he advanced, the more the news about Cibola increased. Only the negro was nowhere to be found. He had made himself independent, went on ahead on his own contrary to the explicit order and only occasionally sending back Indian messengers with special messages.

Estevanico had his good reasons for avoiding the supervision of the pious monk. The memory of the times when he wandered through the wildernesses as a medicine man together with Cabeza de Vaca and the two other Spaniards had come alive in him again, and he had not been able to resist the temptation to surround himself once more with the glory of the miracle worker. Adorned with colorful feathers and tinkling bells, a mighty, rattling calabash hung around him as a sign of his shaman dignity, constantly circled by two Spanish bloodhounds, he had the

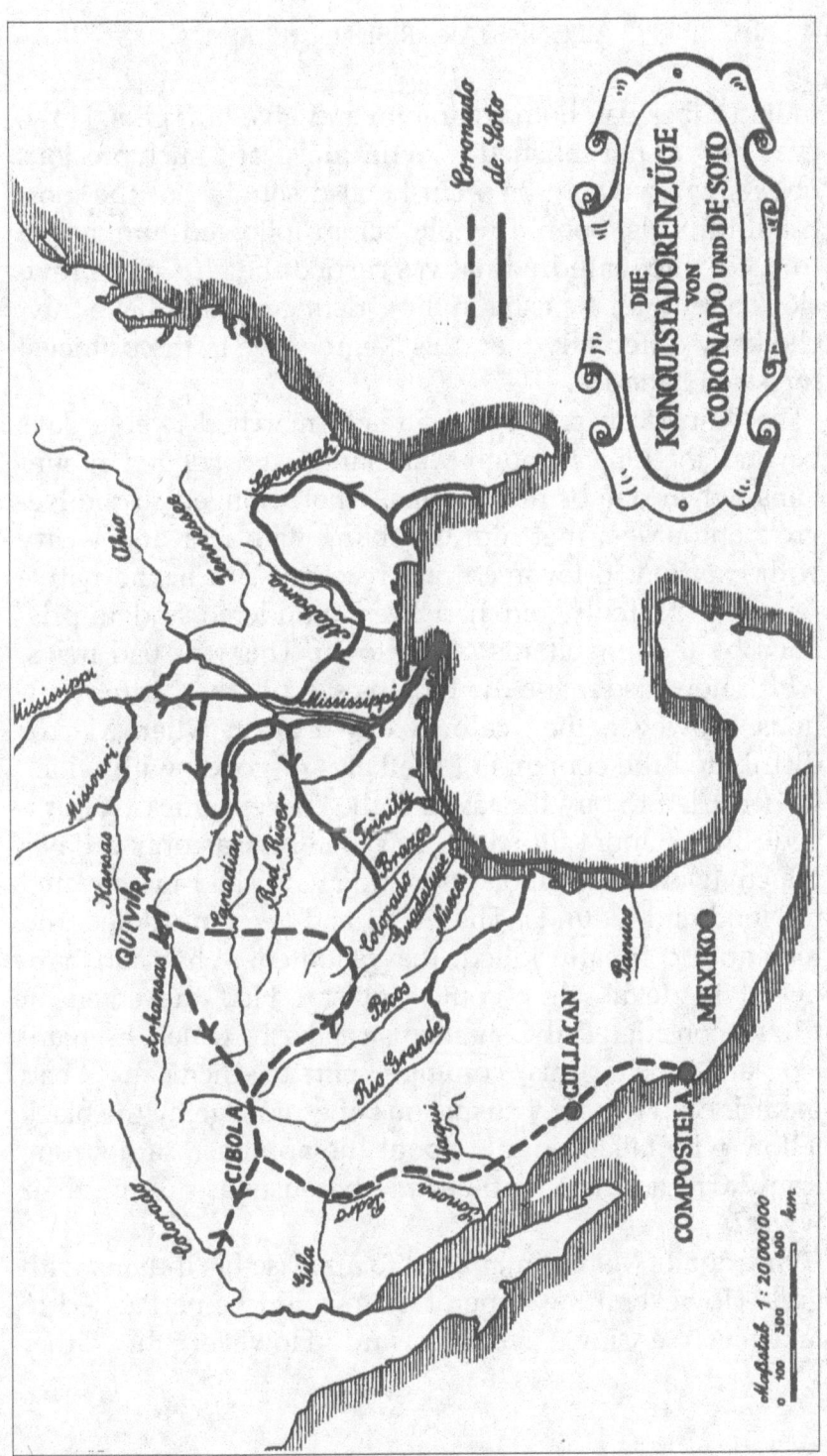

Indian tribes pay homage to him and give him gifts. However, he was not satisfied with turquoise and such precious objects, everywhere he went he also sought out the most beautiful girls. Soon a whole harem followed him, and a troop of three hundred natives carried the gifts and provisions after him. A pasha in the Orient could not have travelled any differently than this Negro slave in the primeval forests of America!

The Franciscan priest had already marched twelve days beyond the Gila through wastelands and rugged mountains, when one of the Indians, who belonged to the Negro's entourage, met him trembling with fear and weary with exertion. Estevanico had reached Cĭbola, the native reported excitedly, but had been plundered and imprisoned by the inhabitants of the town. This was bad news, which now also made the Indian escort of the padre rebellious. However, they calmed down again when Marcos distributed the contents of the bales of goods with which he had tried to buy the favor of the "Seven Cities". Courageously, the monk hurried on. When he was only a day's march away from Cibola, two Indians rushed up, covered in blood and wounds. The negro had been murdered and his entire company killed, they shouted. What had happened in detail, they could not say. Had the chiefs of Cĭbola considered the shaman's calabash, which Estevanico, announcing his coming, sent to them, as "bad medicine"? Were they suspicious of espionage by the black fellow who talked loudly about the approach of a strong army? Or had the Negro been lecherously assaulting their wives?

Once again, Marcos managed to appease his Indians with gifts. However, now none of them could be persuaded to take even a single step forward. However, the father wanted to at least have a look at Cibola from a distance. So he climbed a mountain from which he could get a clear view. There he saw a white city shimmering in the sunlight with high, flat-roofed houses, just as it had been described to him by the Indians. It appeared to him larger than Mexico, which was perhaps not exaggerated, because the new Spanish settlement that had been built on the rubble of the Aztec city housed no more than 1500 families at that time. With his own hands, Marcos erected a low cross on the mountaintop. It was meant to indicate that the land of Cibola had now passed into the possession of Charles V. Then he hurried back the way he had come, always afraid of being attacked by the natives who had now become unfriendly. Frankly he confessed, "I returned home with more fear than food."

The news of the discovery of the land of the "Seven Cities" spread like wildfire in the capital of New Spain. Marcos himself had casually told his barber all sorts of interesting things about his journey—soon the whole city knew about it. The Franciscan friars, proud of the great success of their friar, preached from the pulpits about the new proof of divine grace, which in turn would bring immense riches to the Spaniards. The more one spoke and preached about Cibola, the more vividly the descriptions were embellished. Marcos had not reported anything about gold and silver finds, but it was enough that he had claimed that it seemed to him as if he had been in an earthly paradise—the Spanish knights could not imagine a paradise without precious stones and metals.

Soon after Marcos' return, the Viceroy issued a call for participation in the conquest of Cibola. It met with a strong response. For some time, young noblemen had been coming over from Spain in increasing numbers, idly loitering and causing many a scandal with their love affairs. Now, at last, the eagerly awaited opportunity presented itself for these high-spirited knights to go out into the field and distinguish themselves, to risk their lives and gain riches. Early in 1540 they arrived in Compostela, about three hundred in number, well armed and well mounted. The New World had not yet seen a more brilliant array than that which paraded before the emperor's governor in that provincial Mexican town on a Sunday in February. In addition to the knights, the expedition included seventy Spanish archers and arquebusiers and more than a thousand Indian auxiliaries, not to mention the four monks under Father Marcos, who had been promoted to the rank of provost. Half a dozen guns, a thousand horses, endless lines of mules, large herds of cattle and sheep made up the supply train. Mendoza had spared no expense to equip the company in the best possible way. The certain booty that beckoned at Cibola seemed to justify departing from the principle of frugality for once.

Francisco Vazquez de Coronado led the army in gilded armor. This nobleman belonged to the viceroy's immediate entourage and was obviously in high favor with the Spanish court. A few years before, he had married the daughter of the former Chancellor of the Exchequer of New Spain, an illegitimate relative of Charles V, and with imperial permission he had been allowed to acquire two extensive latifundia. No one who saw him ride out of Compostela at the head of the expeditionary force doubted that Coronado was at the beginning of a brilliant career.

The young knights who followed him were just as cheerful and hopeful as their leader. They, too, believed they could easily force the hand of the goddess Fortuna. None of them considered what a move into the American wilderness would mean. They had dressed up as if they were going on an outing to a nearby showground. However, all too soon the worries began for both leader and followers. The army made very slow progress with the lumbering cavalry. The first difficulties with food supplies arose when a large part of the grain supplies spoiled during the crossing of the rivers. The proud knights had no choice but to get off their horses and march on foot alongside the exhausted nags. Many a Sunday outfit that had been taken along for who knows what reason, many a magnificent weapon that had been flaunted, lay discarded by the wayside.

The five hundred kilometer journey from Compostela to Culiacán took the army two whole months. Fortunately, a sufficient amount of food had been provided at the border town to replenish the provisions that were running low. Coronado allowed himself fourteen days of rest, but then he could no longer contain his impatience. While the bulk of the troops rested longer and slowly moved forward, he hurried ahead with an advance guard of eighty horsemen and thirty foot soldiers. Of course, Father Marcos did not miss the opportunity to be one of the first to enter the promised land that he had seen from the mountain. After a tremendously exhausting march, the Spaniards stood before Cibola at the beginning of July. The Indians hostilely denied them entrance. Coronado gave the order to attack, and in bold storm the jaded and famished Spaniards scaled the walls while a hail of arrows and stones pelted on them. After a fierce melee, the natives fled, and greedily the victors pounced on the stockpiled supplies. "We needed them," wrote one of the participants, "much more urgently than gold and silver."

When the Spanish warriors were satiated and looked

around, they experienced boundless disappointment. So this was Cibola, the much-vaunted miracle city? They were standing in a poor, dirty Indian village of admittedly strange construction. As Marcos had described it, the houses were two stories high and more, with flat roofs, to which one had to climb up on swaying ladders. There were also some turquoises embedded in the frames of the entrance openings. The supplies of grain and beans were considerable—there was no need to suffer shortages here. Where, however, were the treasures for the sake of which the hardships and dangers of the long march had been taken upon themselves? They were neither in Hawaikuh— the name of the conquered place in the native language— nor in any other village of the Pueblo Indians of New Mexico. For it was into this territory that the Spaniards had come. Cibola was the landscape where the Zuñi Indians lived. The Redskins themselves called it Shi-uo-na and that had sounded like Cibola to Father Marcos' ears. After all, the monk had only been able to report on the wealth of this region from hearsay, and to the primitive savages from whom he learned it, their sedentary and relatively cultivated neighbors seemed "rich." But this was not wealth as the Spaniards wanted it.

Coronado and his people turned in fierce indignation against the Franciscan priest who, they believed, had mendaciously deceived them. "Such curses were uttered against Brother Marcos," one report says, "that I begged God to protect him from them." What did it help that Marcos affirmed that everything had looked quite different in the deceptive distant view than it did now when seen up close? He was no longer sure of his life and had to be grateful to be sent away by Coronado with a letter to the Viceroy describing the sobering facts. Heartbroken, physically ill, the father returned to Mexico from his dreamland. He was never able to get over this blow to his reputation, and it was behind the walls of the monastery that he slowly wasted away.

Coronado had his subordinates search the territories of New Mexico and Arizona in all directions. Pueblo upon pueblo was discovered. Overwhelmed, one day a detachment stood before the natural wonder of Colorado Canyon. But no matter how much one crisscrossed the country, the miracle of gold and silver treasures was nowhere to be found. Nevertheless, in one village an Indian slave was picked up, whose tribe was located far away. The Spaniards called him the "Turk" because of his appearance. This man had things to say that made Coronado and his knights sit up and take notice. In his homeland of Quivira, a ten-kilometer-wide stream flowed, the "Turk" told the astonished Spaniards. Fish as big as horses swam in it, and the chiefs let themselves be taken for a ride in long canoes, whose prow was adorned with a huge golden eagle, under a canopy of twenty oarsmen. The chief takes his midday nap under a broad tree, which is adorned all over with small golden bells, whose soft tinkling in the gentle zephyr lulls him to slumber. Everyone ate from silver-forged plates, and bowls and jugs were made of pure gold. "Everything was believed, because he told it so naturally," wrote one of the Spanish soldiers. For the winter months in the quarters taken up in the pueblos along the Rio Grande, Quivira provided the conversational means by which the hidalgos helped themselves get over the Cibola disappointment and the grim cold. When in April 1540 the ice floes on the Rio Grande disappeared, they all agreed to entrust themselves to the leadership of the "Turk" and to march through the grassy seas in the east to Quivira.

A LONE STAR ARISES IN TEXAS

While Cabeza de Vaca had become acquainted with the inhospitable coastlines of Texas during his stay as a slave and trader, Coronado's eyes now wandered over the monotonous prairies of this country. His march took him through the "Panhandle," into western Texas to the headwaters of the Brazos. Not a tree, not a shrub, not a hill, not an Indian cabin was to be seen, only grass and sky. "The country is like a bowl," wrote one participant on the expedition, "when you sit down, the surrounding horizon seems only a musket shot away." He summarized his impressions as "Dead earth". Since the army left no tracks in the short, rapidly rebounding tumbleweed, it was necessary to use bones and cow dung to mark the way so that stragglers would not get lost. Soon Coronado also came across the herds of buffalo, numbering in the thousands and thousands, which Cabeza de Vaca had been the first European to see and describe. And with the buffalo he met the Indians whose lives depended entirely on hunting the brown, shaggy beasts. These Redskins were nimble, sinewy creatures who followed the movements of the bison on foot for hundreds of miles, while dogs dragged tents and household goods after them. Skillfully they knew how to sneak up on the grazing game to kill it with unerring arrows. Fearlessly, the Indians crawled out of their buffalo-hide tents, stared curiously at the strangers, and readily gave information about the lands in the distance. Even then the Spaniards saw that these nomads were braver and more warlike than the pueblo inhabitants. But they could not have foreseen that the Plains Indian would become one of their most feared opponents; they could not have known that they were bringing to the Apaches, Comanches, and whatever the tribes were all called, the very thing that made them the invincible masters of the Plains for centuries: the horse. It is not possible to prove with certainty that the herds of wild horses that later populated the North American prairies are descended from the steeds that ran away from Coronado on his Quivira march, but it is not impossible.

Neither the Apaches nor the Tejás we met could tell us anything about Quivira. All around there was only prairie and nothing but prairie, and the nearest Indian settlements were far to the north. Already the Spaniards had walked eight hundred and fifty kilometers through the grassy steppes of Texas for a month. Coronado, however, still did not want to give up faith in Quivira. True, he ordered the main body of his army back to the Rio Grande. He himself, however, moved from Texas with a small band strictly following the compass needle northward. After another six weeks had passed and another seven hundred kilometers had been covered, they finally arrived at the home of the "Turk". Quivira, located in the area west of present-day Wichita between the Arkansas and Kansas rivers, was an even more deplorable find than Cibola. Certainly, the countryside was fertile and lovely, dotted with wooded hills and refreshing streams. But the villages consisted only of small, round shrub huts with grass roofs, the inhabitants walked around naked, and except for a few copper clasps that served as jewelry for a chief, not a single piece of metal came to the Spaniards' attention. Under interrogation, the "Turk" confessed that his stories about Quivira had been tall tales. The Pueblo Indians, he said, had instigated him to do this in order to lure the whites to the prairies, where they would lose their way and perish. Coronado now no longer hesitated to have the "Turk" hanged from the nearest tree.

Although it was now certain that Quivira had been a mirage, Coronado carefully scouted the entire area. A patrol even reached the Nebraska border. But all searches were fruitless: there was no gold or silver to be found in this part of North America either. After three weeks in Kansas, Coronado returned to the pueblos of New Mexico, where the main army had long since returned to quarters. Many of the Hidalgos, who had not seen the land on the Arkansas with their own eyes, did not believe his report. It would not and did not enter their heads that Quivira was only an Indian tale.... They attributed it exclusively to the incompetence of their leader that the gold country had not been found, and they were already planning a new march into the prairies for the coming spring. Then Coronado fell from his horse during a tournament game and got under the hooves of the steeds. His severe skull injury left him completely despondent, and despite the grumbling of his knights, he decided to return to Mexico as soon as possible. In April 1542, the Spaniards left the pueblos on the Rio Grande. When the Indians, who had become rebellious, fired on the train from an ambush and they had run out of provisions, the army slipped from the hands of the commander; open mutiny broke out, and with barely a hundred men, Coronado reported back at Mendoza in the spring of 1543. "The viceroy did not receive him very graciously," the chronicler ends his account, "but nevertheless confirmed to him that he had done his duty; but Coronado lost his prestige and soon after his governorship of Nueva Galicia."

The trek to Cibola and Quivira was not the only failure the Spaniards experienced during this period. In the fall of that same year, thirteen miserable, emaciated figures in completely tattered clothing knelt on the beach at Pánuco and fervently thanked God for their salvation. They were the remnant of those six hundred warriors that Hernán de Soto had led to Florida in the summer of 1539. For three years this conquistador, a man of indomitable will, had passed through the vast lands of Florida, Georgia, Carolina, Tennessee, Alabama, Mississippi, Arkansas, Oklahoma, and Louisiana in constant battles with the savages. Inspired by the fanatical belief that he could once again force success as he had done in Peru, where he had accompanied Pizarro, chasing one Indian tale after another. The gold treasures he sought were always to be found somewhere far away, where he had not yet been, and he set out again and again to reach this unreachable goal. In 1541, the Indians of Oklahoma and Kansas were startled by the report, spread with lightning speed, that two armies of armored white men were approaching from the east and west. Only a few hundred miles separated Coronado and de Soto at that time. Yes, the dark rumors brought to him by the natives made Coronado think that to the east lay an empire over which a survivor of the Narváez expedition had arrogated himself lord. However, the letter he wrote to the "governor" remained unanswered. De Soto had already moved back down the Arkansas to the Mississippi and had finally been taught that there was no gold country to conquer in North America. In May 1542, a malaria fever threw him onto his deathbed, and in the floods of the "Father of Streams" he found his final resting place.

De Soto's men set out to march into Mexico on foot. They pushed southwest across the Red River into Texas and came as far as the middle reaches of the Brazos. But winter being at hand, and the country seeming too wild and barren to afford sufficient shelter and food during the cold season, they trekked the long way back to the Mississippi. And there they did the same thing that the lost participants of the Narváez march had done fifteen years before: they built boats and sailed in them along the Texas coast

A LONE STAR ARISES IN TEXAS

until, happier than their predecessors had once been, they reached their destination after two long months of travel.

After all this misfortune, the Spaniards considered it a foregone conclusion that there was no second Mexico or Peru to be found north of the Gulf. Discouraged, they turned away from lands that did not satisfy their hunger for gold. Certainly, the legend of Quivira continued to haunt people's minds for a long time. At the end of the 16th century, Juan de Onate, who conquered New Mexico for the second time, was tempted to make a new foray across the plains in search of the fabled gold country. But the time of the great conquistadores' northward marches was over with the year of 1543. For almost a century and a half, the territories behind the Gulf Coast from Florida to Texas dawned in their primitive state. And when the Spanish finally took notice of them again, it was not because they were expected to bring riches. In the meantime, the battle for the New World that Spain had to fight had shifted from the West Indies to North America, and there was now a frontier to defend in the Texas wildernesses.

SECOND CHAPTER

FRONTIER PROTECTION

If Spain had hoped that the rest of Europe would tacitly recognize the papal arbitration of 1492, which divided the earth between the two Iberian states, it was mistaken. Everywhere the treasures of Asia and America were looked at too covetously, too strong was the urge for recognition of the nations that had awakened from their medieval sleep to their first self-confidence, too fragile in the age of the Reformation was the spiritual authority of Vatican bulls. "The sun shines for me as it does for others; I would like to see the clause in Adam's will according to which I am excluded from the division of the world," Francis I replied in Paris to the envoys of Charles V, who asked him to renounce overseas activity once and for all. Later, after the accession of Queen Elizabeth, when the Island Kingdom under the first Tudors had recovered from the horrors of the Wars of the Roses, England also made its claims known.

At first, the French and the British were no more interested in the wildernesses of the New World than the Spanish; Jacques Cartier's attempt in 1541/42 to found a colony on the St. Lawrence River remained an episode. What aroused envy and what the dispute was about were the riches of Mexico and Peru. However, as long as the Spanish Empire was still at the height of its power, one did not even dare to think of snatching from it its American possessions. The question was raised all the more insistently whether the Caribbean Sea, as Madrid wanted it, was a "Mare Clausum" or whether it was also open to the navigation and trade of foreign nations.

They resorted to self-help in the face of Spain's intransigence. Early on, the sailors of Normandy and Brittany appeared in West Indian waters to take their share of the colonial spoils by force. These corsairs, as they were called, combined a Viking-like audacity with the deep hatred of the Calvinist against everything Catholic, and many of the Castilian sailors who—loaded with the yield of the Mexican and Peruvian mines—were heading for the motherland fell victim to their predatory grasp. Only when Madrid began to allow its merchant vessels to cross the Atlantic only when organized into fleets under the protection of strong war squadrons, could the silver ships go their way unmolested. The corsairs, however, saw themselves amply compensated for the loss of privateer booty by the profits to be made in the smuggling business with the Spanish colonists, and no threat of gallows and galleys was able to keep them from venturing time and again into the Caribbean restricted area. Even bolder were the Huguenots, who in 1562, with the evident intention of laying hands on the lifeline of the Indies, the Bahama Canal, built a fort on the east coast of Florida. As nonchalantly as the Spaniards fought the battle against the corsairs' smuggling operations, they now struck hard and fast where their colonial possessions were threatened with serious danger. They ruthlessly let the inmates of the Carlsburg fall to the sword, and by building the two forts San Agustin on Florida and Habana on Cuba they sought to secure themselves against such unpleasant surprises in the future. Nevertheless, they felt relieved when a few years later the Bartholomew's Night[2] broke the back of the Huguenots' power.

The battle against Spanish Catholic world domination, which French Protestantism could no longer continue, was taken up by English Protestantism. Alongside the corsairs, the "seadogs" appeared in the lanes of the Caribbean Sea —like them, they were prepared for every act of piracy and every smuggling exploit. The rich London merchants gladly put their money into such forays into the Indies, and none of them felt any compunction about the fact that the dividends which rewarded this speculative zeal were due to a considerable extent to common sea robbery. People had their own views about piracy in England in those days. "Oh, did you ever hear of a pirate bringing home millions? Only people who are content with small booty are pirates!" was the succinct declaration of Sir Walter Raleigh, one of the British naval heroes of the Elizabethan period. As for Hawkins, Frobisher, Drake and all the others, they were not content with small booty: they captured and plundered, robbed and pillaged on a grand scale!

Ultimately, it was the Seadogs' incursions that prompted Philip II to equip the famous Armada to chastise the island kingdom and put it in its place. But the "invincible" fleet perished miserably in 1588, and from that point on Spanish naval supremacy was a thing of the past. Never again was Spain able to build up such a strong navy as would

---

2 The St. Bartholomew's Day massacre (French: Massacre de la Saint-Barthélemy) in 1572 was a targeted group of assassinations and a wave of Catholic mob violence, directed against the Huguenots (French Calvinist Protestants) during the French Wars of Religion. (Wikipedia).

have been necessary to chase away all the smugglers and pirates from the Caribbean Sea, who were now wreaking havoc there in ever larger swarms. No matter how hard Madrid tried to keep control of the West Indies, in the end it had to watch as English and French colonists settled in the Lesser Antilles, and how even on Espanola, from which most of its own population had migrated to the mainland, the murderous rabble of filibusters and buccaneers, blatantly supported by the governments in London and Paris, formed a real pirate state. Worse still, even the silver fleets no longer sailed safely because there was no alternative for the obsolete convoy ships!

Given this state of affairs, it is only too understandable that the events in the West Indies worried the Spaniards far more than the landing of English and French colonists on the northeast coast of North America. Arguably, the founding of Jamestown in 1607 and of Quebec in 1608 represented a new violation of the old Spanish claim to possession of the entire New World. Yet, since they no longer had the power to assert it, they consoled themselves with the fact that it was ultimately irrelevant whether foreign peoples settled in those remote areas or not. So confident was Spain that the primeval forests of the north would keep any enemy at bay that it did not make the slightest effort to occupy parts of North America. Security precautions were not even taken on the Gulf Coast. No pirate had ever been able to find shelter on the surf-strewn Texas shore, which was barricaded by sandbanks. It had not yet occurred to anyone that the lands in the north of the Gulf might one day gain strategic importance. They only saw the danger that threatened them from the Caribbean Sea.

Life in the interior of Mexico went on undisturbed during all the enemy attacks in the West Indian waters. The viceroys even found the strength and the means to extend the borders of New Spain to the north. Hernán Cortes, after all, had not conquered Mexico, but only the Aztec Empire, the "Mesa Central," where sedentary Indians of fairly high culture lived, easily directed and exploited. There it was possible to cultivate the soil without artificial irrigation; there were also productive silver mines. In contrast, the neighboring lands to the north, with their aridity and savage natives, were uninviting. The constant disturbances of the peace, however, forced the Spaniards to subdue the neighboring barbarian tribes in sacrificial battles, and during these feuds it was discovered that the treasures which Coronado and Soto had sought in the distance lay very near the capital. In 1548 the exploitation of the mines of Zacatecas began, and in the fifties the development of the mines of San Luís Potosí. In search of further silver ore deposits, the Spanish outposts advanced northward like two greedy tentacles along the edges of the Mexican plateau.

To the west, on the Pacific coast, where the land was more fertile and precious metals more plentiful, the advance was more rapid than in the east. Even in the eastern Sierra Madre, however, the advance had reached Saltillo by 1575, and in 1583 Cerralvo was established in the new province of Nuevo Leon as the northernmost frontier and mining town. This rapid expansion of the Spanish domain, however, did not mean dense settlement. Only here and there, where mining was profitable, sparse settlements sprang up, which were no more than camps of prospectors, usually joined by a few cattle ranchers. Between these scattered frontier settlements were the "presidios", the fortified garrisons from which troops of soldiers kept the Indian tribes, always prone to rebellion, in check. Above all, there were the missions in which Franciscan friars or

Jesuit priests sought to introduce the savages to the rudiments of the Christian religion and European civilization, often enough finding martyrdom in the process.

The Spanish took the first step toward a permanent occupation of North American soil from Central America at the turn of the 16th century. At that time, New Mexico was conquered once again with the intention of exploiting the silver and gold deposits in the territory of the Pueblo Indians. But the miners soon left, because it turned out that the mining of the precious metal ores was not profitable due to the long transport routes and the correspondingly high shipping costs. The Franciscan friars, however, stayed. They were indifferent to the economic failure of the enterprise. They did not come for the gold of the heathen, but for the soul of the heathen, and a more comfortable mission field could not be dreamed of. Here the Indians lived in villages and did not need to be laboriously settled. The monks resided in the native communities more as parish priests than as missionaries, and the Redskins, probably more intimidated by the weapons of the Spanish soldiery than by the sermons of the Spanish priests, rushed en masse to be baptized. As early as 1630, the fifty fathers who worked in New Mexico could proudly report to their religious superiors that they cared for some 60,000 Christianized Indians. This was, of course, only an illusory success. The monks were constantly complaining about evil relapses into pagan idolatry. One day the Pueblo Indians had had enough of the strict regiment of the Franciscans, the constant encroachments of the governors, and the insolence of the two thousand or so Creoles and mestizos who had settled as farmers. In 1680, under the leadership of a former medicine man, they rose up to expel all the palefaces within a very short time and return to their ancient faith. The Spaniards, as far as they had escaped with their lives, fled to Texan soil. In the far western tip of Texas, El Paso was established as the first settlement at that time. From there, in the years from 1692 to 1698, the Pueblo Indians were subjugated once again and this time for ever.

At the same time as these events, the Spanish were making advances from both Nuevo Leon and New Mexico into the lands that are now part of the territory of Texas. There were many reasons for this. On the one hand, there were strategic considerations. They wanted to finally establish contact with the outposts in Florida, and with their persistent underestimation of the distance involved, they imagined that this would be easier than it actually was. Nevertheless, the Spaniards began to realize that it was impossible to leave the entire Gulf Coast unoccupied when the Antilles and the north of the continent were teeming with enemies. What attracted people even more strongly to the lands beyond the Rio Grande, however, were the old mirages of treasure and riches, which, in spite of all the disappointments they had already caused, still did not fail to have their effect. The Quivira fairy tale always found new believers. Other rumors were added. There was talk of the Seven Golden Hills of the Aixaos, of the Cerro de la Plata, a mighty silver mountain somewhere in the north, but above all of a "Kingdom of the Tejás" that would lie close to Quivira and would not be inferior to it in size and glory. When the Spanish soldiers crossed the Rio Grande from Nueva León to punish predatory tribes or to organize slave hunts, they also looked towards these wondrous things. As it happened, however, they were stopped by the sandy desert of southern Texas and never penetrated deep into the unknown territory.

The expeditions undertaken from New Mexico were

more successful. Never satisfied with a mission field alone, obsessed with the idea of not resting until the light of the Gospel had been brought to the last savage, the Franciscan friars had extended their activity further and further east into the wildernesses and prairies. When in 1629 emissaries of the Jumanos, a tribe then seated on the upper reaches of the Colorado River in Texas, appeared before Father Juan de Salas with a request to come and work among them, this pious man naturally set out at once to answer the call. Excited at the new prospects of saving poor heathen souls, he returned to Santa Fe from his visit to West Texas. The superiors of the order, however, could not see their way to establishing missions in that area. Since about 1650, however, the Spaniards had maintained lively trade relations with the Jumanos from New Mexico, in which not only furs and buffalo hides, but also beads played a role. On one of the expeditions, a Spanish troop even reached the border of the "Kingdom of the Tejás", which until then was still the subject of legend.

The Spaniards learned more and more about this tribe that would later give its name to the entire country. In 1676, the Bishop of Guadalajara, who had inspected the missions of the province of Coahuila, wrote down the first account of the Tejás that history has handed down: "Adjacent to Coahuila, in the northeast, lives a nation rich in people, which extends so far that even those who give an exact account of it do not know where it ends. In Coahuila there are many natives who have visited this people, whom they call the Tejás. The Tejás, it is claimed, comprise of an orderly state, the individual villages of which are administered by caciques appointed by that overlord who governs them all and resides in the interior of the country. Their houses are made of wood, they cultivate the soil, plant corn and other crops, wear clothes, and punish crimes, especially theft. The natives of Coahuila, however, know nothing more to report, because, as they declare, they are only ever allowed to visit the frontier places of the Tejás; for the overlord has forbidden any stranger to enter his kingdom." Although even in this report poetry and truth are still mixed, it sounds much more sober than the fantastic tales that circulated before about the "kingdom of the Tejás". Even if the bishop was in favor of occupying the land, it was not for the sake of fabulous treasures, but solely for the sake of missionary work.

It is doubtful whether the colonial authorities would have heeded the bishop's request and the pleas of fathers eager to convert if reasons of state policy had not made it advisable. In 1684, in fact, an Indian reported that in the east "Spaniards had arrived from the water in wooden houses and were trading with the Tejás." Mexico immediately knew what this news meant, as they had already been warned by Madrid. Those white men whom the native called Spaniards were in reality—Frenchmen! It was now clear that the Spanish colonial empire was also threatened by a danger from the mainland and that a border in North America had to be protected.

However, how the French got to Texas and what they wanted there—that is a story in itself.

Fort Saint Louis

After two years of investigation, in February 1668 the Supreme Court of the Inquisition in Mexico delivered its verdict against the former governor of New Mexico, who had been accused by the Franciscan friars of his province of serious offenses against the Church and religion. The fact that Diego Dionisio de Penalosa, as the man was called, was sentenced to be led through the streets of the capital as a repentant sinner with a candle in his hand was the least of it. At the same time, he was deprived of the right to ever again become a civil servant or officer, and was banished forever from New Spain and the West Indies.

This severe punishment was well deserved, according to the trial records. The character of the man was revealed by the following accusations: that he had acted as an agent of the Inquisition towards the widow of his predecessor and forced her to hand over her property to him; that he had violated the sacred right of asylum of the Church and arrested a criminal seeking refuge in front of the altar; that he had entered a place of worship without uncovering his head, and that he had attended mass standing next to the tabernacle with his spurs clanking. Since this was an ecclesiastical criminal case, the verdict of the Holy Office was mainly based on such religious outrages. But in fact, the official abuses that had come to light weighed far more heavily.

Like many of his predecessors, Penalosa had shamelessly tried to enrich himself during the time he was governor of New Mexico, and had treated those small Spanish settlers who were too poor to bribe him as badly as he had the defenseless natives. This had incensed the priests against him, who felt their prestige and revenues threatened by his arbitrary extortions. Since he betrayed his contempt for the Church all too freely, even going so far as to imprison the head of the Franciscans, it was not surprising that a vehement complaint was lodged with the Sanctum Officium, which then succeeded in bringing him down.

In his native Peru, Penalosa had already made himself

untenable, and now that he had also been expelled from Mexico, he would have had no choice but to go to Spain in search of an existence somewhere and somehow. These were bleak prospects for a man who had just played a significant role. Penalosa did not want to live a miserable life in obscurity. Feelings of hatred filled his heart, his brain was bent on revenge, and, devoid of all moral inhibitions, he did not shrink from committing the most shameful treason against the fatherland.

He appeared in London in early 1670, adorned with the most fantastic titles, and so confident was his manner that he gained admittance to the English court. Indeed, the British monarch took a liking to the "Count of Santa Fe", who could not do enough to develop plans on how best to conquer Habana, San Domingo, Panama, Chile and whatever else appealed to the English. True, Charles II had no use for such advice at that moment, since Parliament was averse to war with Spain. Nevertheless, he secured the defector's willingness to serve by generous donations of money, and when the Spanish envoy tried to put Penalosa in debtors' prison in order to get hold of him and carry him off to the Netherlands, the king summarily settled all the impostor's unpaid bills. In the end, however, the Spanish representatives succeeded in discrediting the "Adelantado of Chile" in London to such an extent that he had to vacate the scene.

Penalosa appeared in Paris in the middle of 1673. It was not difficult for him to establish relations with influential circles of the French aristocracy. As in London, high patrons were found to support him, and he soon became a well-known figure in the political salons and literary circles. People in Paris listened with great attention to his stories, which were a skilful mixture of poetry and truth. At that time, people in France were very interested in all American affairs. Since the gifted Colbert had taken charge of French financial and economic policy, the long-neglected colony in Canada had flourished, and while in the north of the New World the fur hunters and rangers, together with the Jesuit missionaries, were penetrating deeper and deeper into the virgin forests, settlers in the Lesser Antilles were planting the colonial products so much in demand. The outlines of a great French colonial empire began to emerge, and the time seemed not far off when it would be possible to wrest the empire from the humiliated Spanish, who had hardly been able to resist the attacks of the Sun King in Europe. It was extremely important, however, to hear from a man who claimed to be an expert on Spanish America—and to a large extent actually was—something reliable and tangible about the conditions in the Indies. So far, one had only been able to obtain scanty and meager news about it. For the Spaniards knew how to keep their overseas possessions, as extensive as they were, strictly closed to the prying eyes of other nations.

It was well known that Spain was powerless to stop the pirates in the West Indies because it no longer had a powerful navy. But the general opinion was still that the viceroys of Mexico and Peru had great reserves of power and that it was dangerous to advance into the interior of the colonies beyond the obviously weakly defended outlying areas. Now, however, Penalosa revealed that the Spanish Empire was nothing more than a colossus on feet of clay. He told of the financial hardships, of the deep discontent not only of the Indians but also of the Creoles with Spanish rule, of the pitiful military equipment. All this was exaggerated in these and those details, but not fundamentally wrong. For those French imperialists who were most eagerly in favor of colonial expansion, such expositions meant the most beautiful confirmation of their thoughts, and they did not fail to introduce the ex-governor of New Mexico to Colbert, the minister in charge of colonial policy.

Penalosa was quick to put himself in the right light for Colbert and to present him with a tempting goal of colonial conquest policy. He brought out the old Indian tale of the gold country of Quivira, lied boldly and impudently that he himself had undertaken an expedition there from Santa Fe, and described the miraculous kingdom in the most glowing colors. For the time being, however, Colbert had other concerns than taking care of the conquest of Quivira, nor did the European entanglements make it advisable to split the French forces by large undertakings in the New World. Penalosa had to wait for his hour, but he could be sure that his plans were only postponed, not cancelled.

Penalosa's suggestion to conquer "Quivira", that is, to attack the Spanish colonial empire on land from North America, found support and competition at the same time from an unexpected side. In 1678, the Canadian fur trader Robert Cavelier, son of a wealthy burgher from Rouen, who held the title of Sieur de la Salle based on a family estate, asked the French government for permission to explore and develop the Mississippi basin. Already willing to support the exploration of new fur regions, which always meant an extension of the colonial borders, Colbert approved this request all the more willingly, as he was very interested in an advance to the south, especially in connection with Penalosa's proposals. What was expected in Paris from such a pioneering act is revealed by the passage in the royal patent granted to La Salle, where it is stated that it would probably be possible to discover in these regions "a path on which one could advance as far as Mexico". Was not La Salle the man to solve this task? Whatever else one might say about his character, it could not be denied that he was a personality of stature that was not easily equaled in daring and willpower.

Actually, La Salle was supposed to have become a Jesuit. But he was much too independent and self-confident to be able to learn blind obedience and unconditional submission, and he had left the order even before the end of his novitiate. Since he had had to renounce his paternal inheritance when entering the Societas Jesu, it meant that he now had to look around for a livelihood. In 1666 the twenty-three-year-old decided to emigrate to Canada, where his brother, the Abbe Jean Cavelier, was already staying as a Sulpician monk. The Sulpicians, who were happy to receive anyone who wanted to help them develop their vast lands, welcomed the younger Cavelier with open arms and gave him a seigneury near Montreal, that is, a wide piece of wilderness on which he could build his own estate and lease the rest to small farmers. However, such a restless spirit as La Salle was not made for a settled life.

His head was full of ideas and plans and he was attracted by the endlessness of the virgin forests with their thousand dangers. With the instinct of a born entrepreneur, he sensed opportunities for economic activity that no one had yet recognized. In short, one day he returned his land to the Sulpician Order, had his cultivation work remunerated, and became a fur trader with the small capital he had thus acquired.

Until now, the traders had moved westward in canoes along the shores of the Great Lakes. La Salle left these well-trodden paths and endeavored to penetrate the areas south of Lake Ontario. What prompted him to do this, in addition to the economic success he expected from opening up new hunting grounds, was the suspicion that the Ohio was flowing further and further west and would eventually flow into the Gulf of California, thus forming something like a "Straits of Anian." What La Salle did in detail in the years after 1669 is unknown. It even remains doubtful whether he even reached the Ohio Valley at that time. Certainly, however, he heard at that time that the Indians named the stream after the sun with a word that sounded like "Lo-u-is." La Salle later took up this name, and christened the land through which the Ohio flows "Louisiana." And since for him the Ohio and the Mississippi were one and the same stream, he transferred this name to the whole middle part of North America. This was then to be interpreted as a double homage to the "Sun" King Louis XIV.

The fame of being the first Frenchman to have seen and navigated the "Father of Streams" was not taken by La Salle, but by another Canadian fur trader, Louis Jolliet, who in 1673 explored the Mississippi to the mouth of the Arkansas, thus clearly establishing that the stream pours into the Gulf of Mexico. La Salle heard of this discovery at Fort Frontenac at the entrance to Lake Ontario, which had been built on his advice to receive the trade that the Indian tribes of northern Canada were doing with the English colonies by way of the Iroquois and divert it into the French channels. With the profits (up to 25000 livres annually) he made on this business, La Salle could well be satisfied. And he did everything he could to further expand his business. Already he had a flotilla of fast canoes and small barges on Lake Ontario to help the traders transport their fur loads on this side of Niagara Falls. He was already entertaining the idea of having large freighters ply the interconnected lakes from Lake Erie to Lake Superior. But at the moment when he heard about Jolliet's Mississippi trip, an even grander idea came to him. The misfortune of Canada was that it had no ice-free waterway. Every winter the St. Lawrence River froze over, and for long months all commercial traffic came to a standstill. The most natural connection to the Atlantic Ocean, the Hudson, was blocked by the English. However, what if one tried to push through southward? La Salle made up his mind to accomplish this deed. In his daydreams he already saw the Mississippi as the main artery of New France, freeing Canadian trade from climatic fetters, he saw himself as the head of an enterprise that would economically exploit the newly opened land areas.

La Salle was in Paris in 1678 to obtain from the king a monopoly for the exploration and exploitation of the Mississippi basin, and he also managed to win over some financiers who advanced him considerable sums. The money was intended primarily for the construction of two ships, one of which was to cruise the Great Lakes as soon as possible, the other to be launched on the banks of the Mississippi. And indeed, a few months later, to the amazement of the Redskins, La Salle sailed the 45-ton "Griffin" from Niagara to Illinois. Loaded with valuable fur cargo, the ship set sail for home in the fall of 1679. It was never seen again! And since misfortune seldom comes alone, the sailer that was to bring the building materials for the second vessel to Canada also sank in the Atlantic. To this end, the financiers, inflamed by the numerous envious and hostile parties, began to seize La Salle's property. All his lofty plans seemed to evaporate into nothingness.

FRONTIER PROTECTION

In the maelstrom of such misfortune, others might have given up the race. For La Salle, however, there was no surrender. His will was unbroken, his belief in his star unshakable, and the self-assurance with which he was convinced of the correctness of his plan bordered on stubbornness. Once again he managed to raise funds, satisfy his creditors and equip another expedition. In January 1682, with a band of 23 Frenchmen and 21 Indians, he made his way through icy Illinois to the open waters of the Mississippi, and with a fleet of canoes descended the vast stream to its delta. There, on April 9, he solemnly erected a cross and the arms of France and took possession of "Louisiana" in the name of the Sun King. This meant offering the French sovereign—without regard to the rights that the Spaniards had possessed to these territories from time immemorial—a colonial empire that stretched from the Alleghany Mountains to the Rocky Mountains and from the Gulf Coast to the Canadian Lake District. This claim was certainly not modest. For the time being, however, only the jungle thickets and ripples at the mouth of the Mississippi had heard it, and everything else depended on whether Paris could decide to follow the words with action, the proclamation with occupation.

La Salle hurried to France as quickly as he could. He explained to the Parisian statesmen the importance of his discovery for the future of the Canadian colony and for the power of the French Empire in the New World. After all, the great economic advantages that he expected for himself from the development of Louisiana depended entirely on the Fleur de Lis banner flying at the mouth of the Mississippi. To bait the politicians, he did not hesitate to claim that the Mississippi delta was only 180 kilometers from the Rio Grande, and that it would be an easy matter to break

A LONE STAR ARISES IN TEXAS

into Mexico by conquest from there. The measurements were not so faulty even in those times that La Salle could underestimate a distance of 1500 kilometers in such a way. While in the older Spanish atlases the position of the Mississippi is indicated quite correctly, on the map sketch, which La Salle presented, its outflow into the gulf shifts by twelve degrees of longitude westward. A gigantic Ohio takes its course through half the continent up to the border of New Mexico and turns only then to the south. In Paris, at any rate, these geographic blatherings were taken at face value.

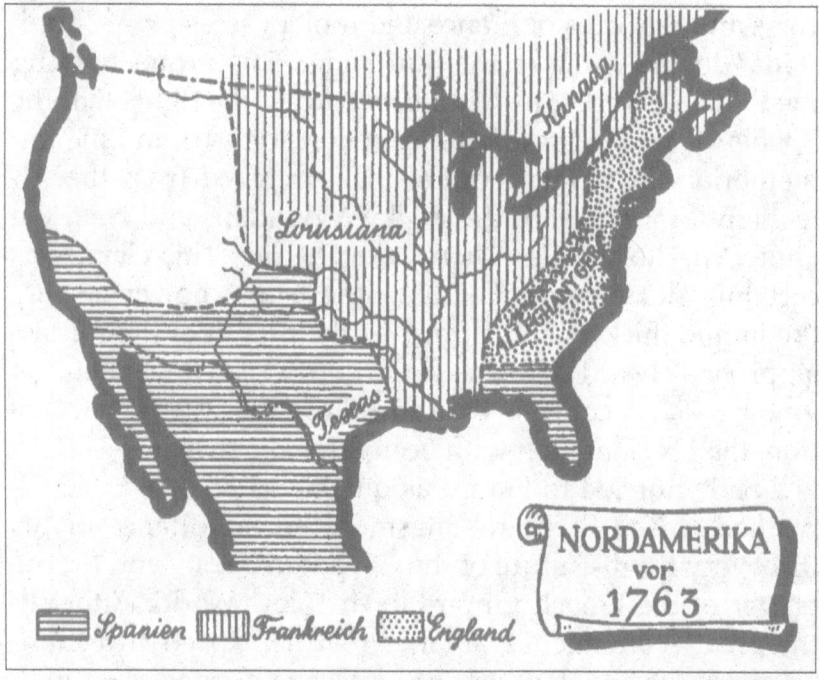

To his chagrin, La Salle found that in his effort to galvanize the French government into action in America, he had a rival who was about to outrank him. Penalosa had not been idle during all this time. Even recently, when war once again prevailed between Spain and France, he had submitted to the Colonial Ministry a carefully worked out plan for attacking the Spanish possessions, and although some people were repelled by his pushy, loudmouthed manner, he was still considered in Paris to be the most reliable expert on American conditions who could be found. Penalosa had long since stopped talking about such nebulous things as Quivira. What he was now advising seemed to have hand and foot. French troops should establish themselves at the mouth of the Rio Grande or raid Pánuco, and from there conquer the silver-rich province of Nueva Vizcaya. In that province, he assured, only about 500 pathetically armed soldiers were available to the Spaniards. It would be difficult for the viceroy to send help, since he was not allowed to denude the central areas around Mexico City of military forces for fear of Indian uprisings. The inhabitants of those lands, however, regardless of whether they were Creoles, Indians or mestizos, would joyfully welcome liberation from the Spanish yoke.

La Salle did not consider being pushed to one side by the Spanish adventurer. In a new report he claimed that Nueva Vizcaya could be conquered much better from the mouth of the Mississippi than from Pánuco. And since he no longer cared about one lie more or less, made plans to raise an army of 4000, even 15000 Indians in Illinois. He achieved with his fantasies what he wanted to achieve — the government agencies worked out a project that combined Penalosa's and La Salle's proposals. La Salle was to hurry to the mouth of the Mississippi with a band of French soldiers and colonists, build a fort there, and call upon the Indian tribes of "Louisiana" to fight against Mexico, while Penalosa was to follow some time later and recruit an army among the buccaneers on San Domingo.

Then, in the spring of 1685, the joint attack on Nueva Vizcaya was to take place from both the Gulf and the Mississippi.

At least the first part of this program was put into practice. In July 1684, four ships with about 350 sailors, soldiers and colonists on board sailed from La Rochelle under the leadership of La Salle. Penalosa, on the other hand, never left France because shortly after the departure of the Mississippi expedition, peace was concluded between the negotiators of the French and Spanish kings at Regensburg, and the Parisian government did not revert to its plans for the Americas even when war broke out again later. It was precisely the sad fate of La Salle's enterprise that had taught them that the risk of an attack on the Spanish Empire was still much greater than Penalosa had made it out to be. Since then, the role of this characterless fellow was played out, no one had any interest in him anymore, and in 1687 he died in abject poverty in the French capital.

On the long sea voyage, La Salle had enough time to reflect on the difficult situation he had maneuvered himself into. How he thought to unite the warlike tasks he was to perform on the Mississippi with his own economic goals remained his secret. He was probably never serious about attacking Mexico. However, he did not talk to anyone about his true intentions, his orders were unclear and contradictory, and he gruffly rejected any advice. Some of his subordinates believed that he was mentally disturbed, and certainly the severe attacks of malaria from which he suffered from time to time had affected his mental powers, making him even more irritable, inaccessible, and dogged than he already was. Much, on the other hand, speaks for the fact that he nevertheless knew exactly what he wanted. For example, as far as space permitted, the ships were loaded with merchant goods. What else could it serve but to be exchanged for furs in Louisiana or smuggled into the Spanish colonies?

In mid-January 1685, the soldiers and colonists went ashore on the Texas coast, and a few weeks later, in order to get rid of an annoying overseer, La Salle gave strict orders to the captain of the frigate that had been attached to the expedition for protection during the crossing to weigh anchor and sail away. This was all the more reckless since it was not yet clear where they were, and one of the two remaining ships had already run onto a sandbank and sunk. La Salle had wanted to head for Espíritu Santo Bay, today's Galveston Bay, which since the days of Pineda had been praised as the best natural harbor on the Gulf Coast and seemed far more suitable for the construction of a fort and a trading post than the swampy lowlands of the Mississippi Delta, with which, at least according to the old Spanish maps teeming with errors, it was supposed to be connected by a tributary. Unfortunately, La Salle overestimated the drift of the Gulf Stream and missed not only the mouth of the Mississippi River, but also the entrance to Galveston Bay. Continuing steadfastly westward, he finally reached Matagorda Bay. Here he thought he was in the right place and landed, unaware that he was already some seven hundred kilometers from the "Father of Rivers".

Some distance inland, in the middle of the coastal prairie and in view of the wide bay, La Salle built Fort Saint Louis to house the 180 people under his command (including women and children). Soon the worst enemies were diseases and Indians. Before the summer was over, about thirty dead had to be buried. This mortality continued to grow and grow. The brackish water they drank caused dysentery and, as long as they did not know how to hunt the buffalo, the lack of fresh food produced scurvy. Regardless of the health of his people, however, La Salle demanded the heaviest labor. Miles of lumber had to be hauled across the grassy steppes in the blazing heat of the sun. In the process, the rations that could be distributed became ever scarcer, the men's resistance ever weaker, and a good portion of them perished miserably from malnutrition and exhaustion. Added to this were the sacrifices demanded by the constant battles with the natives. At any moment, the inmates of the fort had to be prepared for an attack by the Indians, and no Frenchman was allowed to show himself outside the protective palisades if he did not want to run the risk of being attacked.

La Salle spent his time up until the spring of 1686 searching the shores of Matagorda Bay and the surrounding area for the branch of the Mississippi River that he believed flowed into the bay. Yet reconnaissance expedition after reconnaissance expedition proved fruitless, and the mood of the people at Fort St. Louis grew more and more desperate. It sank into hopelessness when the last ship on which it might have been possible to escape to San Domingo failed on one of its trips into the bay. Individual soldiers escaped to the prairie thinking that it was better to live as savages with the savages than to wait in the fort for certain doom. La Salle was also overcome by gloomy thoughts. Nevertheless, he picked himself up again, determined to march northeast through the wildernesses to Illinois to bring help. In April 1686, he set out with twenty men. By August he had returned to Matagorda Bay, accompanied by only eight soldiers—the others had perished or deserted. Although he had advanced hundreds of miles, he had not discovered the Mississippi. Nevertheless, it was of no avail, for the attempt to reach Canada had to be made all over again. Among the forty men who were still holding out at Fort St. Louis at that time, he chose the seventeen strongest, and in January 1687, dragging with him all the goods that still had some value, he departed with this band, leaving the remaining men, women, and children to an uncertain fate.

The seventeen ragged figures, who laboriously made their way north through the wilds of Texas, marched to save their lives. There was no longer any sense of subordination, discipline, or comradeship between them and each of them thought only of himself and his own and had become the mortal enemy of his neighbor. La Salle had lost all authority. In adversity and distress, the proud man had only become more withdrawn, harder and agitated. His orders met with revolt and aroused a hatred that raised thoughts of murder. On March 18, 1687, the ambush shot that ended his life was fired on the Trinity River. Carelessly, the conspirators dragged the body into a thicket and abandoned it to the wolves and vultures. However, one act of blood always gives birth to new acts of bloodshed. The murderers quarreled with each other over the distribution of La Salle's belongings, killing each other in the process. Texas was witness to much gruesomeness in the wilderness at that time. Only five men, led by Abbe Cavelier, who had accompanied his brother on the expedition to the Gulf Coast, made their way to Illinois. But instead of immediately reporting the death of La Salle and the dismal situation of those unfortunates who had stayed behind at Matagorda Bay, the Sulpician monk described the state of the enterprise in rosy colors. God only knows how he could reconcile this with his Christian conscience! Only in Paris did the Abbe come out with the truth—after he had previously monetized all his brother's possessions and saved them from the seizure of creditors! One shudders before so much heartless greed.

Monks as Frontier Guards

When Penalosa presented the plan to conquer Quivira to the French king in 1678, the Spanish government was immediately informed of this incident through its intelligence service. However, in Madrid, the councilors looked at each other in amazement. Quivira? What kind of country was that? In what part of America was it located? Even the officials who had served overseas and knew the colonies well were unable to answer this question. The archives were diligently searched, and sure enough, among the files kept as "papeles curiosos", a report from 1631 appeared, in which the Franciscan priest Alonso de Benavides, who had long been the head of the missions in New Mexico, fabricated all sorts of things about the kingdoms of Quivira and Aixaos, which were brimming with precious metals. Yet, just as his information had not been taken seriously before, so now it made no impression on the responsible statesmen. The Indian Council concluded that the Quivira project of the treacherous ex-governor was a fantasy and did not require any countermeasures.

However, this quiet dismissal of the Quivira rumor did not mean that the Spaniards were not thinking about the possibility of a French attack on their American colonial empire. On the contrary, they were full of apprehension, and Penalosa's doings were watched with special attention. The Sun King's addiction to conquest was something Spain had seen enough of in Europe. There were signs that he was on the verge of reaching out to the treasuries of the

FRONTIER PROTECTION

New World. In a presumptuous tone, he had already demanded free trade in the Indies for his subjects. French squadrons had appeared in the Caribbean Sea, apparently to scout coastal waters and port sites. Moreover, what was the meaning of the bustling activity that could be observed in the shipyards and naval ports of Brittany? Rumors also leaked out about voyages of discovery and the plans of a Canadian fur trader, but this man was described as such a scatterbrain that no weight was attached to any of them. Thus it happened that the Spanish spies completely missed the outfitting and departure of the expedition of 1684.

It was not until the fall of 1685 that the Spanish learned of the French Mississippi venture entirely by accident. At that time, one of their frigates had captured a corsair ship in the Caribbean Sea, and among the captured pirates was a young Frenchman who, during interrogation, revealed that he had sailed with the expedition from La Rochelle the previous summer, but had abandoned it during the stay at San Domingo and joined the pirates out of necessity. He said that, as far as he knew, La Salle was intending to establish a colony at a place called "Micipipi". The accuracy of this statement was all the less doubtful since it was also confirmed by the other pirates. The news caused the greatest consternation in Mexico and Madrid. So what had been feared all this time had come true after all. It was perfectly clear what danger a French fort on the Mississippi delta meant for the Mexican northern provinces, indeed for all of New Spain. Now action had to be taken and now there could be no rest until, as the Spanish War Council put it, the thorn which France had thrust into the heart of America had been torn out. With an energy remarkably different from the dispirited, feeble procrastination that had become common among the Spaniards, they began to search for the French colony on the Gulf Coast. Expeditions were sent out by land and sea, from Vera Cruz and Habana, from the Mexican northern provinces, and even from Florida, but all without success.

They were about to abandon this futile search and rely on the news from London, which reported the demise of La Salle's settlement, when in May 1688 the governor of Coahuila, Alonso de Leon, on a punitive raid against the Toboso Indians, captured a Frenchman who ruled as chief over a native tribe beyond the Rio Grande. Jean Gery was undoubtedly one of the soldiers who had deserted from Fort Saint Louis and sought their salvation by fleeing to the savages. He was subjected to harsh interrogation in Mexico, but his answers were so contradictory, incoherent, and nonsensical, his manner so strange, that the Spanish colonial officials concluded that they were dealing with a mental patient.

The governor of Nueva Vizcaya sent some strange documents almost at the same time that had been given to him by a Jumano chief in Parral. They were the remains of a logbook written in French and a parchment with a drawing of a ship and some scribbled lines. They were supposed to have come, as the Indian indicated, from the French fort at Matagorda Bay destroyed by the savages of the coast. Upon closer inspection, it became clear that the sentences on the parchment were the distress call of a Frenchman who lived among the Redskins and, even at the risk of falling into the hands of the Spaniards, longed to return to the world of civilized people and Christians. The signature was: Jean de l'Archeveque de Bayonne and it caused the Spaniards many a headache. Was it to be assumed that the Archbishop of Bayonne had personally accompanied the French expedition to the Gulf Coast? But the knowledgeable clerics assured that the Pyrenean city was not the seat of an archbishop at all. A puzzling matter that had to be put aside for the time being!

These new discoveries provided the impetus for another move to Texas to gain definitive clarity on the location of the enemy fort and the fate of its occupants. With a hundred soldiers, Governor Alonso de Leon and the Franciscan priest Damian Massenet set out in the spring of 1689. Guided by Indians familiar with the area, they reached Guadalupe in April. A few days later, Leon was standing in the deserted fort that the unfortunate crew of La Salles had built on Matagorda Bay. The six small huts they found were already half-ruined. Still the crossbeam over the entrance of the largest blockhouse showed the notched inscription, "1684 usque ad 168-". The incomplete last year of the date pointed to a tragedy. One could see in the settlement how terribly the savages had been ravaging as they attacked and massacred the defenseless inhabitants. There, in a corner, were still three skeletons bleaching in the sun. One of the Spaniards sat down and wrote a poem lamenting these poor victims, but at the same time expressing his undisguised satisfaction that God's wrath had punished the criminals who had been so bold as to invade the sacred precincts of the King of Castile.

Alonso de Leon did not want to return home without having paid a short visit to the land of the Tejás. Indeed, on this excursion to East Texas, he made two interesting discoveries. In the camp of a Tejás chief he came across two Frenchmen, one of whom was the "Archbishop," whose name was just L'Archeveque and who was otherwise nothing but a simple soldier. From him the Spaniards heard the details of La Salle's enterprise. L'Archeveque also told of the murder of the Sieur, but he wisely concealed the fact that he himself had been involved in the conspiracy. Now, while the governor was interrogating the two Frenchmen, Father Massenet had been conversing with the Tejás chief, if one may call wrangling with the aid of an imperfect interpreter a "conversation", and inevitably the "conversation" had touched on religious questions. Curiously, the savage had pointed to the sky when the word "Dios" was pronounced! Yes, he carried a small shrine with him, decorated with a cross and four images of saints, with a light burning in front of it day and night! How was this possible, when Christian missionaries had never worked in this region?

Then Father Massenet remembered the sensational little book published many years before by the Franciscan friar Benavides, whose report on the Quivira had been registered in the archives of the Council of the Indies in Seville under the heading "Curiosities". When Benavides was in Spain in 1630, he had visited the young abbess of the Concepción nunnery in Agreda, whose miracles were then talked about far and wide. The pious Mother Maria de Jesus told her guest how she often fell into a state of rapture and ecstasy and was then carried across the ocean by angels, sometimes several times a day. Over there, however, she would preach the Gospel to the savages in unexplored areas of New Spain and had already suffered martyrdom there. For many years she had been working in Quivira, among the Jumanos and numerous other tribes. In particular, however, she had devoted herself to the conversion of the Titlas, whose chief had been baptized by her. Benavides had been so enraptured by these wonderful stories that he had carefully written them down, and for the Fathers in New Mexico this booklet by their former superior became a special incentive in their missionary work.

And suddenly Father Massenet had the revelation that the Titlas, who had once been converted by Mother María de Jesús, could be no other Indians than the Tejás. When he asked the chief if his tribe had ever been visited by a nun, the Indian told him that he had heard from his parents that many, many years ago a beautiful strange woman had often appeared here in the country. Massenet might have rejoiced at this affirmation, and he was not sparing with gifts, whereupon the chief could not do enough with assurances of friendship and urgently asked the good father to come to him again soon. This invitation would not have been necessary: the Franciscan was already determined to leave no stone unturned to return to the Tejás and continue the work of St. Mary.

Both Leon and Massenet, in their reports, warmly urged the Viceroy to no longer hesitate in permanently occupying the land beyond the Rio Grande. The priest pointed out what a rich harvest of souls there was to be brought into the folds of the one and only sanctifying Church. The governor emphasized the fertility of the soil, the abundance of buffalo and game, the astonishing level of culture of the Tejás. All this, and the consideration of having to secure at all costs these lands from enemy incursion, determined the colonial authorities in Mexico to extend the frontier of the Spanish Empire to Texas. However, they did not want to listen to Leon's proposal to establish a chain of military bases, so-called presidios, in the new province. They balked at the great expense inevitably involved in the military occupation of such a remote country, and besides, they believed that the Tejás, once won over to the Spanish cause by missionaries, would be strong enough on their own to repel another French incursion. Therefore, as in other provinces of the Spanish colonial empire, the frontier guards in Texas were not soldiers, but monks.

In March 1690, Father Massenet and three of his friars, accompanied by a force of one hundred and ten men under the command of Governor Leon, set out from Monclova for Texas. Passing the remains of La Salle's fort, Massenet set fire to it with his own hand to exterminate the last vestiges of the French incursion. Early in May, the convoy, well received by the Indians, reached the settlement areas of the Tejás. As their chief told the governor, four Frenchmen had recently appeared in a village of his tribe, but when they heard of the approach of the Spaniards, they had turned back home to their settlements, which lay far, far away on a great river. From the fact that the Indian chief described the leader of the French as having one arm, it is clear that he was not spinning a yarn. For this man could have been none other than the upright and brave Henri de Tonty, the commander of the base which La Salle had established in Illinois. When this Goetz von Berlichingen of the Canadian wilderness, to whom, like the German knight, an iron fist had to be substituted for his lost arm, finally learned in the winter of 1689 the truth about the fate of La Salle and his colony on the Gulf Coast, which the Abbe Cavelier had insidiously concealed from him, he set out at once to rescue the men and women who had remained behind at Fort Saint Louis. In February 1690, according to his diary, he had advanced as far as the Red River. In April he came to a Tejás village, but had to turn back there because the Indians refused to provide him with guides who knew the way. Of course, Governor Leon could have had no idea of these connections. Probably he did not take the chief's story quite seriously either. Moreover, even if a French settlement existed somewhere in the endless distance to the east, how was he to find it when every clue was missing! All he discovered of Frenchmen in Texas were a few boys and a girl whom the savages had spared in their attack on Saint Louis and raised along with their own brood.

In the meantime, several miles west of the Neches River, a small church and a house for the priests were built, crudely constructed from wood by the hands of soldiers. With procession, mass, gun salute and flag parade, the Mission San Francisco de los Tejás was solemnly inaugurated and the work of the monks could begin. Leon wanted to leave a force of fifty men to protect the Fathers. But the chief urgently asked that all the soldiers leave, and he assured them that no harm would come to the priests. Father Massenet fully understood this wish. The Spanish soldiers, all unmarried people, had indeed behaved very badly, and not even the wife of the chief had been safe from their physical declarations of love. The immorality of the military could only disturb the work of conversion, and so it was decided that only three soldiers would remain with the three monks.

Massenet himself, the fourth, had in fact decided to return with Leon to promote the establishment of further missions in Mexico. His urging was completely successful. Since the beginning of 1690, war was again raging between Spain and France, and the rumors that Frenchmen had landed anew on the Gulf Coast refused to disappear. The viceroy therefore thought it advisable to consolidate Spanish influence in the Tejás as soon as possible, even appointing a special governor for Texas, Domingo Terán de los Rios, an old fighter who had already completed thirty years of military service in Peru and Sinaloa. At the beginning of 1691, Terán, along with Father Massenet, moved to

Texas to establish new missions, explore the land geographically, and investigate reports of a French presence.

What Massenet heard from his friars in San Francisco de los Tejás did not sound too pleasant. True, they had established a subsidiary station with the beautiful name Santissimo Nombte de Maria. But in spite of all their efforts, they had not yet succeeded in converting a single Indian. Only when an epidemic raged among the tribe, eighty natives had been baptized on their deathbeds. Terán also felt that the attitude of the Redskins had changed. Their behavior was unfriendly and insubordinate. A large number of horses and mules were stolen, and when the chief went on the warpath against an enemy tribe, he let the governor know that he did not wish to see him in camp on his return. In this situation, Terán refrained from launching further missions, as the whole expedition was a failure due to his lack of interest and energy.

Not even the proud name La Nueva Montana de Santander y Santillana, which he gave to the province, became established. In itself, he had been right in declaring that the name "Texas" was wrong. The Indians among whom the Spanish missionaries were to work did not call themselves Tejás, but Hasinai. "Teja" was only a greeting called to each other by the natives of the land, and meant something like "friend." It was used, as the ethnological research believes to be able to determine, by fifty different Texan tribes, all of which lived in enmity with the feared, warlike prairie people of the Apaches, thus was, so to speak, a watchword to distinguish friend from foe. But the name Texas became so entrenched in Spanish minds that it could not be eradicated, even when the Viceroy later officially named the country Nuevas Filipinas.

If it had been up to the monks, who had now been

preaching among the Tejás for a year without results, the two missions at Neches would have been abandoned immediately. Father Massenet, however, did not want to know anything about that. He was still convinced that he would be granted to germinate the seed that the pious Abbess of Agreda had scattered on her ecstatic journeys. With two companions and a guard of nine soldiers, he took on the work of conversion himself. It soon turned out that the brothers, who had warned against continuing the Texas mission, had not been too pessimistic. The outbreak of disease, the death of a priest, the destruction of the branch mission by floods, the destruction of crops by floods and drought, the bitter hunger and hardships that the monks would have gladly endured if only their work had had the slightest success. But the Indians were stubbornly hostile to their pious zeal. Even Father Massenet finally realized that the Hasinais had never been concerned with the Word of God, as he had believed, but only with gifts and European goods.

Gradually the attitude of the Hasinais became decidedly hostile. In August 1693, the monks heard that the Indians intended to attack the mission and murder its occupants at the next opportunity. From then on, one of the fathers or soldiers stood constant guard next to the loaded cannon, the burning fuse in his hand. A few weeks later, the situation became so untenable that the monks buried all their belongings along with the cannon, set fire to the mission and stole away at night. For several days the Indians pursued the fugitives, but did not dare to attack them. After four months of wandering in the Texas wilderness, Father Massenet and his companions reached Monclova, exhausted and starving. Three of the Spanish soldiers, however, had absconded along the way and returned to the

Tejás. Heaven knows what made life in the wilderness seem so dear and tempting to them! They had probably gazed too deeply into the eyes of some Indian girl. A fourth soldier, Joseph de Urrutia, fell ill on the run and had to be left behind on the Trinity River. He long played a great part among the East Texas tribes as a chief and war hero, until later he returned to the Spaniards and rendered them valuable service in Texas.

Juchereau de Saint Dénis

How was it that after the escape of Father Massenet not the slightest attempt was made to reoccupy the Hasinais' land? Well, in the meantime one had come to the conviction in Mexico and Madrid that La Salle had only landed by mistake at Matagorda Bay and that not the western but the eastern part of the Gulf Coast was the real target of France's attack. Much more important than taking care of Texas, therefore, seemed to be to establish an outpost on the route between Florida and the mouth of the Mississippi River to prevent the French from attempting to land and to counteract the influence that the English trappers were beginning to gain on the Indian tribes of Alabama from Carolina. As early as 1693, a plan to militarily occupy Pensacola Bay was floated. But a number of years passed before it was realized. It was not until November 1698 that Spanish troops were landed at the bay.

And so it came to pass! After the Peace of Ryswyk in 1697, which brought the heavy fighting in Europe to an end, Louis XIV had a free hand again to turn to the American questions, and he did not hesitate to finally become serious about the occupation of Louisiana when he heard that preparations were being made in London to found a colony on the Gulf Coast. It was then that the race for the Spanish inheritance began between France and England. On the Mississippi, the French were faster than the British. After finding Pensacola Bay occupied by the Spanish, Sieur d'Iberville, the leader of the French expedition, had sailed through the delta of the great river, unloading soldiers and settlers a few miles above the estuary and building Fort Biloxi. Shortly thereafter, an English ship sailed up the Mississippi, also with troops and colonists on board and also with the intention of establishing a settlement there. But Iberville spoke so emphatically that the British commander was bluffed and turned back on the spot. Even today, the bend in the river below New Orleans, where the British who came too late gave in, is called the "Detour Anglais".

The Spanish did not learn of the founding of Biloxi until quite a while later. An attempt to expel the invaders failed miserably, and further attempts were not made because in the meantime the grandson of Louis XIV had ascended the orphaned Spanish throne as Philip V, and the weak Iberian state found itself dependent on the protection of France when the War of Succession broke out. Unmolested, France was able to fortify and expand its position in Louisiana in the years that followed, and the Spaniards had to resign themselves to the Fleur de Lis banner on the Mississippi even later, after 1713, when Madrid no longer needed to swim in the wake of Parisian policy.

At first, France did not like Louisiana very much. Actually, they had only established themselves there to prevent the country from falling into the hands of the English. The political significance of the new acquisition was initially minor, and economically it did not meet expectations. There were no mineral resources, fur hunting was mediocre, and a little bartering with the natives did not bring in much. Also, since the Minister of Finance was not in the mood for constant subsidies, Louisiana was leased to a merchant for fifteen years in 1712. The latter, Antoine Crozat, had agreed to the deal because he reckoned that with the friendly Spanish-French relations that existed at the time, Mexico would no longer take the old prohibitions, which excluded all foreign trade, so seriously. In Vera Cruz, however, Spanish customs officials summarily turned away a ship he had sent there from Mobile Bay with goods. Thus, by sea, traffic with Mexico was obviously still impossible. But how about trying to open a trade route overland, through Texas? This, however, was a risky enterprise. It was not until the Rio Grande, where the Presidio and Mission Juan Bautista had been founded in 1703, that the first Spanish settlement was encountered after a march of over a thousand kilometers through virgin forests and prairies. Was it not to be feared that the Spaniards would still apply the old laws here, capture the traders and confiscate the goods?

While the prospects of a foray into Texas were still being debated in Louisiana, Governor Cadillac was handed a strange letter that had been written on the Rio Grande, passed from Indian tribe to Indian tribe, and after a year and a day had been delivered to the Mississippi. The letter came from the Spanish Franciscan priest Hidalgo and contained the urgent request that the French monks take care of the salvation of the Tejás. This letter had the following meaning. From Juan Bautista, where he was stationed, Hidalgo had made repeated missionary journeys to Texas, and in his zeal for the faith he could not understand why so little was being done for the conversion of the savages of that country. Since then, he had incessantly besieged the authorities in Mexico to grant him permission to resume the missionary work among the Hasinais, which had been interrupted in 1693. But the New Spanish government, shrewdly aware of the bad experiences of the past, flatly rejected his requests. The salvation of pagan souls with all due honor! But the founding and maintenance of missions cost money, and such expenditures could only be justified if the work of the monks also served politics. Texas was of no political interest at the moment; there was no sign of French intentions to advance westward. Yes, if Texas was threatened — then the situation would be different, then the establishment of missions would be a state-political necessity! Well, Father Hidalgo provided the Viceroy with proof that Texas was threatened by the French. He summoned the Frenchmen, who would not come of their own accord, by invitation.

The letter he drafted was very cleverly worded. He addressed the friars on the Mississippi, spoke at length of the blessings of the Indian mission, but also mentioned in passing that some opportunity or other for trade with the Spaniards would surely arise in Texas. As he had calculated, the French lapped it up. Had he spoken only of conversion, Governor Cadillac would probably have put the letter aside, bored. But establishing trade relations! That was exactly what was so desperately wanted in Louisiana! And immediately they set about equipping an expedition to explore the possibilities that the Spanish priest had hinted at.

The delicate task of establishing the first link with the Spaniards was entrusted to Louis Juchereau de Saint Dénis. A more intelligent fellow could hardly have been found! Saint Dénis, then a man in his mid-thirties, was a native of Canada, had thus breathed the air of North

America since his first cry of life, and possessed that special instinct for all things colonial which only a colonialist can possess. From early youth he had roamed the wilds as a coureur des bois, and had acquired an unsurpassable dexterity in dealing with the Redskins. He was fluent in a number of Indian dialects and had a perfect command of Spanish, which made him particularly suitable for the Rio Grande. His travels had often taken him to the Red River and into Texas, and he was a welcome guest among the tribes of that region, thanks to the coveted goods he brought in exchange for furs, horses, and cattle. However, the contents of the bales he lugged with him when he showed up at Red River in early 1714 were not destined for the Indians. A large part of these treasures—they came from Crozat's supplies and had a total value of 100,000 livres—was stowed away on an island of the river. Natchitotches was the name given to this stronghold after the savages who lived in the area; it was the origin of the French base that later marked the border between Louisiana and Texas. It was very convenient for Saint Dénis that the Hasinais told him how they wished for the return of the good Spanish monks who had once given them so many beautiful things. It is true that he carried an official letter from Governor Cadillac stating that the purpose of his journey was quite harmless. But no doubt the Spaniards would be even more persuaded of his friendly intentions if he could act as interpreter of the Tejás' wishes. In the middle of 1714, accompanied by fourteen Frenchmen and a numerous Hasinai detachment, he set out for the Rio Grande.

Captain Diego Ramón, the commander of the Presidio Juan Bautista, must have been astonished when, one day, at the gates of his fort, there stood a troop of Frenchmen asking for admittance, the leader of which politely inquired about Father Hidalgo. Unfortunately, the reverend was absent. However, this Saint Dénis referred to letters he had received from the Franciscan. The captain therefore believed that he had done the right thing by first receiving the strangers in a friendly manner and then obtaining instructions from Mexico on how to proceed with them. The distance from the Rio Grande to the capital was long, about 1600 kilometers, and it took quite some time until a courier had hurried the distance there and back. So they had to wait patiently in the small border town! But Captain Ramón had a granddaughter living under his care in Juan Bautista. Manuela Sanchez did her part to entertain the handsome, brash Frenchman Juchereau de Saint Dénis, and the end of the story was that a real engagement was celebrated in the fort on the edge of the cultural world. The wedding took place shortly before the order arrived from Mexico to bring the Frenchmen before the Viceroy for interrogation.

Saint Dénis was questioned in Mexico by every trick in the book. The cunning Indian trader was not at a loss for answers—a man like him was able to confound the chancery officials who questioned him any time. Wisely, he did not mention a word about trading intentions. The only reason he had entered Spanish territory was to talk to Father Hidalgo, to support the requests of the Tejás, and to say how much the governor of Louisiana wanted the Franciscan order to continue its work of conversion in Texas. And since he had become the son-in-law of a distinguished Spanish officer and had even agreed to enter Spanish service himself, in the end even the Viceroy felt that he should be believed.

Despite all this, the appearance of a French expedition on

the Rio Grande had raised concerns. Apparently, France was beginning to take an interest in Texas again, and it was therefore thought advisable to fall back on the suggestions of Father Hidalgo. What a grin the clever Franciscan may have had on his face when he read the instruction from his religious superior to get ready to take up missionary work among the Hasinais! Even if the paths he had taken were crooked—the end sometimes justifies the means! The order to lead the band of twelve monks, three lay brothers and some settlers to the Neches and to take over their protection with 22 men was given to Captain Domingo Ramón, an uncle of Mrs. Saint Dénis. Lieutenant Diego Ramón, the father-in-law, and Juchereau de Saint Dénis, the son-in-law, now a guide and quartermaster in Spanish service, were attached to him for support, so that it was almost a Ramón family enterprise that left Mexico for Texas in early 1716.

Saint Dénis in Spanish service was quite another matter! Certainly, he had high and holy sworn his allegiance to the Viceroy. He had also advised him to push the Spanish frontier to the Red River in order to keep the western half of the Gulf Coast firmly in his hands. But while still in Mexico, he had mysteriously managed to send a letter to Governor Cadillac in Louisiana, announcing the coming of the Spanish and urging him to occupy all of Texas as far as the Rio Grande as quickly as possible. Cadillac, however, did not have time to do so. Nevertheless, when the Spaniards arrived in Hasinai country, they found Natchitotches guarded by French troops. The monks didn't mind, they just wanted to get to the Tejás, and they had their hands full trying to get between the Red River and the Neches. The six missions with the sonorous names: San Francisco de los Neches, Nuestra Senora de la Guadelupe,

FRONTIER PROTECTION

La Purlsima Concepcion, San Joseph, San Miguel de Linares and Nuestra Senora de los Dolores. Saint Dénis, on the other hand, hurried to Louisiana with his father-in-law, established a trading company there, and then returned to the Rio Grande with a mule caravan loaded with English linen, Flanders flannels, woolens, and other woven goods. Manuela accompanied him on the trip, as it was such a wonderful opportunity to visit her grandfather once again.

The old Ramon in Juan Bautista, however, now had misgivings about getting involved in smuggling and endangering his position. Pro forma, he confiscated part of his son-in-law's goods—the other part was inconspicuously turned into money—and Saint Dénis, pro forma indignant, hurried to Mexico to negotiate with the colonial authorities. There, however, they were in no way inclined to allow him to open a Franco-Spanish intermediary trade, and even threw him into remand prison on suspicion of smuggling. Saint Dénis extricated himself from this situation with a fistful of lies. The fabrics he had brought to Texas, he told the Spanish officials, were not merchandise at all; they had been given to him in Louisiana as compensation for his wage demands. After all, he had resigned from French service and had come to Mexico to fulfill his obligations to the Spanish king. And he talked so credulously that they dismissed him and released his goods for sale. But when the linen and lace were sold at an unheard-of profit, Saint Dénis preferred to leave Mexico as quickly as possible.

When he was heard of again, he was the commander of the French fort Natchitotches. He remained so until the end of his life. He was, depending on how one looked at the matter, either a pleasant or a troublesome neighbor. The Spanish monks, for example, unanimously held that he was a pleasant neighbor, and indeed their relations with the "enemy" fort commander were excellent. When the priest of San Miguel of a Sunday walked the ten kilometers to the French site on the Red River to say Mass for the garrison, he knew full well that he could trade with Saint Dénis for whatever his monk's heart desired. Moreover, he was not the only one who knew this! There was not a Spaniard in East Texas who did not participate in Saint Dénis' well-organized smuggling business with the clearest conscience in the world. The pious fathers and noble dons cannot be blamed for straying a little from the path prescribed by law and virtue. If it had not been for the French contraband, they would have depended exclusively on the caravans that supplied them with food, clothing, and implements from Mexico or Saltillo. But these caravans came very irregularly, the supplies were meager, and the goods expensive and poor. The frontier had its own unwritten laws of neighborly friendship and help.

It was certainly not the fault of Saint Dénis if these laws were sometimes disregarded and infringed upon. He had been very displeased when an ugly "incident" occurred right at the beginning, in 1719. At that time, Spain had maneuvered itself into a conflict with the "Quadruple Alliance" by its attempt to overturn the results of the Peace of Utrecht. Warlike events in Europe, however briefly they lasted, were also having an effect in the colonies. The possession of Pensacola Bay was fought for in earnest that year. In Texas, a young French officer, who was commanding at Natchitotches, marched to Mission San Miguel, arrested the two inmates there, a lay brother and a soldier, and, taking with him everything that could be moved, returned "victoriously" to Red River. Now, when the Fathers and Captain Domingo Ramón heard of this "attack," they believed a general advance by the French was imminent. And being far too weak to resist, also fearing Indian unrest, they decided to abandon Presidio and the missions and retreat to West Texas, where the staging post of San Antonio had been founded in 1718. Saint Dénis was furious when he found the Spaniards no longer in Hasinailand. To spoil his business like that! What was such a greenhorn like this lieutenant, who thought he had to take the governor's orders literally, doing on the frontier anyway! And to make up for the damage done, Saint Dénis sat down and wrote a letter of apology to the Spaniards. The whole thing was only a mistake, he said, and there was not the slightest danger of reoccupying the Tejás missions.

The Viceroy, however, had in the meantime already set in motion an army of five hundred men to "drive" the French from East Texas. To his amazement, the leader of the Spanish corps, the energetic Marques de Aguayo, found everything in perfect order. However, he saw to it that Texas became a firm Spanish possession. He led the Franciscan fathers back to their old missions among the Tejás. He strengthened the presidio at Dolores, which had hitherto provided protection for the friars. He established a new presidio at San Miguel, Adaes, which was designated the seat of the provincial governor. At San Antonio he founded two new missions, and at Matagorda Bay, on the very spot where La Salles' Fort had once stood, he established a presidio and a mission. When Aguayo left Texas, ten missions were in operation, and close to three hundred soldiers kept frontier watch.

Saint Dénis was not sad about this: the greater the number of Spaniards in Texas, the more the turnover of his "trading companies" increased. Now, if he had limited himself to doing smuggling business with the presidios and missions, the governors of Texas would have hardly become angry with him. However, he also traded with the Indians! Even to the Tejás he supplied rifles and ammunition, which the Spaniards had strictly forbidden, and the tribes living north of the Camino real, the main road from Juan Bautista via San Antonio to Adaes, the Caddos, Tonkawan and Witchita, came in the course of time completely under French influence, thanks to his skill. This caused concern to the Spaniards. Their policy was also to win friends and allies among the Indians. Only in this way, with the small number of soldiers that could be stationed in the Texan wilderness, could Spanish rule over the land really be secured.

Serious friction arose between the Spanish governors and Saint Dénis over the Indian trade. Admittedly, the disputes were not always as badly intended as they sounded; sometimes more noise had to be made on both sides than was necessary in order to feign "faithful fulfillment of duty" to the superior authorities. Nevertheless, it also happened that Saint Dénis was honestly indignant with the Spaniards who tried to get in his way. He was not to be trifled with when he announced warlike countermeasures. In such cases the Spaniards gave in. Saint Dénis and his agents were so much superior to the Spanish monks in their treatment of the Redskins that it would have been easy for them to stir up the Indians and make life a misery for the Spaniards. Once the point of contention had been settled, however, the old friendly neighborly tone again prevailed on the Texas-Louisiana frontier and the governor of Texas and the commander of Natchitotches again made their official and unofficial visits to each other. In 1731, during the uprising of the Natchez Indians, Spanish soldiers even rendered aid in arms to their French comrades on the Red River. And the governor did not fail to be present at Saint Dénis' funeral in 1744 in a highly official manner, even though he wrote to the viceroy after his return from Natchitotches, "Thank God, now we can breathe a sigh of relief!"

Redskins under the Fleur de Lis

The danger of a French raid on the Texas front did not last too long. For the last time, a French detachment tried to establish itself at Matagorda Bay in 1721, but it was driven off again by the warlike Karánkawan without any action on the part of the Spanish. And then came the time when France found itself embroiled in increasingly fierce battles with the English in the north of the New World, where, since its forces were insufficient for a two-front war, it was glad to see something like a truce emerging on the frontiers it shared with Spain that gave it a free hand. Yes, over the decades, the same antagonism against the British island empire brought the two Romanesque states closer and closer together. The family treaty that the Bourbon houses in Paris and Madrid concluded with each other in 1733 was the first milestone on a path that finally brought them to alliance and brotherhood in arms in 1761 — on the eve of the day when France, succumbing to English superiority, withdrew from the struggle for North America.

Yet it would be wrong to believe that Texas was no longer threatened by Louisiana and that peace and friendship prevailed in the North American Southwest. Things were not that simple! Life in the American wilderness largely followed its own laws and could not be so easily aligned with the twists and turns taken by European politics. The

Franco-Spanish rapprochement was too slow to forget yesterday's enmity over tomorrow's friendship. The Spanish feared that the pressure on Texas would immediately increase again as soon as the French forces were no longer tied up on the other fronts of the New World, and the French, as long as they could hope for a victory over the English, secretly held on to their plans of conquest against Mexico. As before, the two neighbors observed each other with watchful suspicion, doing everything they could to secure their colonial possessions from each other and to outstrip each other in advancing into the hitherto unoccupied land areas.

The question of who owned what in North America had not yet been decided. Even if the French laid claim to a Louisiana that stretched westward to the Rocky Mountains, the Spanish still felt that they were the rightful masters of the entire continent. Between French and Spanish colonial possessions in North America, there were few places where boundary lines could have been drawn on maps with geographic accuracy. Under these circumstances, wherever there were no military posts and the ground was still Indian land, property rights remained open and disputed. However, since neither France nor Spain possessed the men and the means to actually occupy the vast virgin forests and prairies, they sent emissaries out into the wildernesses to enlist the Indian tribes as friends and confederates and to use them as pieces in the political chess game. But the disposition of the Redskins was changeable, and a slackening in the effort to win their friendship was tantamount to a decline or even a loss of the hard-won influence. The "frontier" knew no status quo! Everything was in motion, incessantly the Spanish monks and the French rangers wrestled with each other for the soul of the savages, incessantly also the Indians themselves with their feuds and enmities among each other and with their raids against the European settlements posed new challenges.

Thus, the history of Texas in the first half of the eighteenth century is filled with the attempts of the Spaniards to counteract the influence exerted by the French agents upon the Indians of the outlying areas. Indeed, not even in East Texas had it been possible to keep out the Coureurs des Bois. Completely unhindered, however, the French traded their wares for furs and bear fat with the Attacapan tribes on the Sabine River and Galveston Bay. With the Caddos on Red River the Rangers were of one heart and soul, and from there they penetrated as far as the Witchita and Tonkawan, who had their residences north of the trail from San Antonio to Adaes. Far worse, however, was that the Coureurs des Bois also won the friendship of the Plains Indians, supplied them with firearms, incited them to attack the Spanish settlements, and even moved from the Missouri and Red Rivers across their hunting grounds to Santa Fe to trade with the Spanish colonists. To be sure, strict orders from the viceroy very soon put an end to French smuggling in New Mexico. Yet the task remained to counteract the "encirclement" of Texas and to put a stop to its constant threat of Indian raids. The solution to this problem was energetically tackled only after 1745, when various reforms in the mother country as well as in the colonies began to infuse the Spanish empire with new vitality and a new will to live. The missions at Matagorda Bay among the Karánkawan were then reorganized, while new stations were established at all vulnerable points, at Galveston Bay, among the Tonkawan, in Apache territory. None of these missions were successful, and despite the devoted work of the Franciscan fathers, they had to be abandoned after a few years.

Most of all, the Spanish regretted the failure of the Apache mission. From the very beginning, the Apaches had been a serious problem not only in Texas, but also in New Mexico, and had increasingly turned out to be a serious threat to the settlements in these northern provinces, which were quite weak. They were one of the tribes that nomadically populated the endless grasslands of the North American Southwest, always following the movements of the buffalo herds. Daring horsemen, masterful with bow and spear, they knocked down the bison, their horse close to the body of the brown monster in a stretched gallop. These wild devils were hated and feared by the neighboring tribes, who appeared as if from nowhere during their raids on nimble nags, only to disappear again into thin air. Unruly in their self-confidence and unruly in their sense of strength, the Apaches were extremely warlike and quarrelsome, at the same time deceitful and faithless, vengeful and cruel, and these traits of character seem to have been especially possessed by the Lipan, that branch of the tribe which for nearly two centuries, relatively small as it was, became the scourge of western Texas.

As early as 1691, Father Massenet had encountered the Lipan on his journey to the Tejás, although at that time they still had their homes high in the north, on the headwaters of the Colorado, Brazos, and Red Rivers, and only occasionally ventured as far as central Texas on their buffalo hunts. The Spaniards had gambled with the Lipan from the beginning, for they were the "friends" of their enemies, the Hasinais, and as soon as the first Spanish settlement was established at San Antonio in 1718, which was not behind a protective wall of Indian tribes like the missions in East Texas, the tiresome Apache raids began. They were the subject of incessant complaints in the reports of missionaries, officers and settlers to the colonial authorities. Kidnapping, martyring, murder, plundering, cattle rustling, horse stealing—it was always the same thing that the Spaniards in San Antonio had to suffer from sometimes more, sometimes less. Alternating between peace negotiations and punitive expeditions, the colonists in Texas sought to control the Apache evil, but neither remedy had resounding success. The Spaniards could not shake off the suspicion that the Indians were continuing their raids not only on their own initiative but also at the instigation of others. As early as 1723, a captured Lipan squaw, when asked why her tribe was constantly on the warpath with the Spaniards and stealing their horses, replied that the Apaches were trading with "other Spaniards" in the north, to whom they sold the horses. This had been an unmistakable reference to French machinations; for the "other Spaniards" could only be French.

As time went on, the Apache raids on San Antonio got worse. No road was safe anymore. Mission Indians working in the fields were slain, their bodies horribly mutilated. In the immediate vicinity of the presidio, herds of cattle were driven away in full view of the guards. There were moments when the inhabitants all feared that they would not escape with their lives. The reason for this growing threat was that the Lipan had moved their residences further south, to the San Sabá River area. This had not been done voluntarily. A powerful enemy had appeared in their rear, the Comanches, prairie Indians who were not inferior to the Apaches in ferocity and belligerence. Under constant fighting, the Apaches found themselves pushed out of their old hunting grounds and ever further southward. Throughout the 18th century, the Indian world here in West Texas was in turmoil: the Apaches, who in the 30's were still sitting on the San Sabá, were already dwelling on the banks of the Rio Grande shortly after the middle of the century. The Spanish settlements felt the consequences of this "migration of peoples".

The Spanish authorities could do little to help the missionaries and settlers in San Antonio, but the Apache danger threatened the entire northern frontier as far as Coahuila and New Mexico, and distress calls rang out from all sides. In 1733, the garrison of San Antonio was increased from 45 to 38 men—so small was the force that had to defend against the attacks of hundreds of Indians! To reassure the inhabitants, they appointed as commander of the presidio that Joseph de Urrutia, who once, when Father Massenet fled from the murder plans of the Tejás, had stayed behind on the Trinity River and had lived for years among the East Texas tribes as an Indian among Indians. Urrutia was rightly considered the best Apache expert and Apache skirmisher there was in the province at that time. The sixty-year-old combatant and his son Toribio, who succeeded him in command after his death, did their utmost to keep the Lipan in check and to chastise them. Finally, in 1749, according to the Spaniards, who did not yet suspect that they owed this success to the Comanches, a punitive expedition by Toribio prepared the Apaches for peace. Yes, to the amazement of the soldiers and the joy of the monks, the Lipan even asked for missionaries to be sent. Soon after, the leaders of the tribe appeared at San Antonio to solemnly seal the pact of peace and friendship, and around the pit where the hatchet and a live horse had been buried, the officers danced festively with the chiefs and the monks with the "indios bravos." The settlers of San Antonio breathed a sigh of relief!

Many more years passed before the Franciscan fathers could begin missionary work among the Apaches. As always, the viceroy lacked the money to finance such an undertaking, and perhaps the friars would have had to wait even longer if a wealthy mine owner had not offered to pay for the Apache missions out of his own pocket. This generosity was not a sign of special piety, but rather a well-balanced business interest: Rumors of silver ore deposits on the San Sabá had been circulating for a long time, and in order to investigate these rumors, the governor of Texas had sent an officer, Bernardo de Miranda, to Los Almagres, the "Red Earth" areas on the Llano and San Sabá, in early 1756. By March, Miranda was back from his exploratory trip and gave such an auspicious report of all that he had seen and found that the Spaniards' eyes glazed over. "In the Almagres district," he wrote, "the silver mines are so numerous that I undertake to give a mine to every inhabitant of Texas, without anyone having to complain of having come off worse than the others." In proof of his assertions, Miranda produced an abundance of ore pieces which, indeed, when melted down in the capital by the great mine owner Don Pedro de Terreros, showed the unusually high silver content of seventy percent. In short, Terreros finally undertook to maintain any number of missions in the Apache territory for three years in return for the exploitation of the silver mines.

There were strong political reasons for accepting this offer. The peaceableness of the Lipan gave rise to hopes of a rich harvest of converts, and it also seemed good to counteract French attempts to influence them in good time. Above all, however, it was necessary to close the wide gulf that gaped between the settlements in Texas and New Mexico and which was not without danger, especially in view of the activities of the French agents. Thus, in 1757, at Pedro de Terreros' expense, Spanish missionaries and soldiers marched to the Apache hunting grounds on the San Sabá, while at the same time, farther south on Honey Creek, a tributary of the Llano, the Los Almagres silver mine was opened. Colonel Parrilla led a force of well over a hundred soldiers, most of whom had taken their wives and children with them, so that the whole expedition numbered about four hundred people, and at the head of the six monks was Father Alonso Giraldo de Terreros, a cousin of the donor. Construction of the presidio began immediately on the spot, with the mission erected a few miles away so that the soldiers would not disturb the godly work of the Franciscans. Only the Indians, for whose sake the Spaniards had come to this wilderness, were nowhere to be seen.

After several weeks of waiting in vain, one of the Fathers set out to search, but no matter how far he wandered, he encountered no Apache. Finally, after months, about three thousand Lipan gathered at San Sabá near the mission, coming from a foray to the Rio Grande and carrying a large number of horses and mules that they had obviously stolen from Spanish settlers. The monks nevertheless greeted the Indians warmly with pious speeches and fine gifts, reminding them of their promise to settle in the mission, urging them to convert and be baptized. But the Lipan chiefs made excuses. They had first to go to the buffalo hunt and fight a dispute with the Comanches and then later they would become Christians. Already they were up and away, and the Franciscan fathers, who had already looked forward to snatching thousands of souls from the prince of hell, watched them go in disappointment. The Apaches did not come again. Only now and then did a single band appear at the San Sabá. Each time the Indians were in a strange hurry to leave again and ride off in a southerly direction. It seemed as if they were on the run from an invisible enemy.

The question was what was going to happen. In the presidio and in the mission, the days passed monotonously with the usual chores of frontier life — tilling the fields, herding cattle, a little handicraft, a little hunting. Three monks grew tired of the idleness and left. They no longer wanted to be fooled by the Lipan. In their opinion, the whole enterprise in Apache territory was hopeless. Colonel Parrilla shared this opinion and advised his superiors to recall the soldiers and monks as soon as possible and to deploy them in a more suitable place. However, the Viceroy, especially Don Pedro de Terreros, would not hear of this. Mexico was still hoping for a rich yield from the newly discovered silver mines. So the outpost at San Sabá had to hold out and wait for the events that were to come. The winter passed without anything worth mentioning happening. Spring came...

Then, in the first days of March 1758, the wilderness around the Spanish settlement suddenly came alive. Brown figures were seen everywhere. A few dozen horses were stolen from the corral, a band of hunters was attacked and wounded by Indians. These were the enemies of the Apaches, the Comanches! Colonel Parrilla requested the three monks, who lived in the outlying mission with a few assistants and a five-man guard, once, twice, three times, to seek refuge behind the palisades of the presidio. He feared evil.

But Father Terreros refused to go to safety. He was convinced that the Redskins would not harm him if he received them kindly. Parrilla shook his head at so much pious unreasonableness. However, it was of no avail, he had to let the priest have his way!

Shortly thereafter, the savages appeared in brilliant masses in front of the mission. There might have been a thousand, perhaps even two thousand horsemen, their faces painted red and black, their bodies decorated with pictures of terrible monsters. A Comanche chief, hulking, with a blunt, brutal look, in French uniform, commanded the horde. Demanding entrance, the Redskins rattled the gate of the mission fence, shouting in hard-to-understand Spanish that they came as friends. The mission inmates had already prepared to sell their lives as dearly as possible, the firearms were loaded, next to the two cannons the fuse was burning. Then the sergeant of the mission guard saw among the Comanches numerous Tejás. He had served long in East Texas and knew the friendly disposition of that tribe. There was nothing to fear, he explained to Father Terreros. The gate was unbarred, the Indians poured into the mission courtyard, and the monks began to distribute gifts of tobacco, food, and the like among the noisy crowd. Did the savages really have only peaceable intentions? An oppressive tension was in the air. Already some Indians began to go into the supply rooms themselves and take out "presents." Horses were being herded away from the corral. Why were there so few animals here, they asked. Over at the presidio there were more, Father Terreros replied. The Comanche chief said that they dared not go there; they would be received unfriendly if the priest did not issue them a letter of safe conduct. Terreros complied with this request. Some Indians dashed off in the direction of the presidio. With uncanny swiftness they were back again. They had been threatened at the gates of the presidio. Father Terreros saw through the ruse, but nevertheless offered to escort the savages personally to the presidio. Perhaps in this way he hoped to draw the Indians away from the mission and save his companions. As he rode high on horseback out of the mission gate, a shot rang out and he sank over the back of the horse, dead. That was the signal for murder and plunder. The whole mission went up in flames, and only by a miracle did one of the priests escape with three other Spaniards and take refuge in the fort.

The Comanches lacked the courage to attack the presidio. After destroying the crops, stealing the horses, and slaughtering most of the livestock, they left the scene of their atrocities. But the news of this raid created a mood of panic throughout the northern front. In their minds, the Spaniards already saw the Comanches flooding across the weakly defended frontiers and wreaking untold havoc on their frontier settlements. Now they realized how dearly they had to pay for the Apaches' "friendship"! So great was the hatred for the Lipan among the Texas tribes that the same Tejás who had been good friends with the Spanish in East Texas joined the Comanches in driving the Spanish out of Apache country. Again, the Spanish suspected that it was the French to whom they ultimately owed the Comanche raid. The governor of Texas did not mince words and told the commander of Natchitotches plainly his opinion of the matter. Well, like all Indians, they had also supplied the Comanches with weapons but the French indignantly rejected the accusation that they had had a hand in it.

Colonel Parrilla proposed again to abandon the presidio and mission at San Sabá. That would be out of the question, was the reply from Mexico. Now, after the attack of the Comanches, it would look like cowardice. On the other hand, Parrilla's other suggestion, to equip a large expedition and to teach the Comanches a lesson that they would lose any further desire to raid Spanish settlements, was received with approval. Moreover, a new Comanche raid on the San Sabá, in which nineteen Spaniards were killed, showed how necessary it was to chastise the dangerous savages. In the fall of 1759, Parrilla set out in a northeasterly direction with an army of nearly six hundred men-in addition to 380 Spaniards, mission Indians and Apache bands marched with him. The colonel led his troops further and further into the wilderness. For without engaging in battle, the Comanches were fleeing northward. After seven weeks of marching, the Spanish vanguard was attacked by Indians close to the upper Red River, and when Parrilla followed with his main force, he suddenly found himself facing a field fortification with weir and ditch, over which the Fleur de Lis fluttered. However, behind the palisades stood not Frenchmen but Comanches, who received the Spaniards with a hail of bullets. Soon the Spanish soldiers were also threatened on the flanks by mounted Comanches, also armed with rifles. The battle lasted four hours, 52 Spaniards were killed, and as night fell and the situation became more threatening, Parrilla ordered his men to retreat. With Indians fighting in Indian fashion and with Indian weapons, he would probably have been able to cope. But Indians who wielded European weapons and seemed to have gone through a European war school—that was too much for him and his not too well trained and disciplined troops! Under the constant persecution of the Comanches, the retreat of the Spaniards turned in the end into a real flight. With difficulty, Parrilla and his soldiers reached the protective ramparts of the presidio at San Sabá. The French had thus defeated the Spaniards at the Red River by Indian hand!

The Spaniards tried for a number of years afterward to induce and convert the Apaches to a settled life in the missions. The wooden presidio building became a solid stone fort, the ruins of which can still be seen today. New missionaries took up the work, but even their efforts bore no fruit. The Lipan continued to prove completely unreliable, and the Comanches did not stop threatening the San Sabá garrison with their attacks. Finally, in 1768, Parrilla's successor had no choice but to abandon the position on his own responsibility and move the presidio to the Nueces. This earned him a severe reprimand from the Viceroy, but the colonial authorities were sensible enough not to order him back to the San Sabá. A year later, the presidio was moved even farther south to the Rio Grande. In the meantime, Spanish policy toward the Apaches had fundamentally changed, and later, in league with the Comanches, they took up the war of extermination against these raiders, who had long since once again become the terror of the northern provinces.

It is not known just how long the silver mines at Honey Creek were in operation. The place where the Spaniards had once dug for precious metal fell into oblivion, and what had been sober reality in the 18th century in the 19th century became the inexhaustible material of treasure digger stories, of which especially the legend world of Texas is so abundant. Even if today's Texas is just as modern-American as the other states of the Union in everything and anything else, a touch of romance wafts over this land from the past. The ancient Indian tales of Cerro de la Plata haunt the air and at the witching hour Spanish horsemen and monks parade through the streets as they did long, long ago. Moreover, during the nights, the cattle herders tell each other around the campfire about treasures that the Spaniards buried and hid in moments of danger. Oh, one knows exactly where that happened! One only does not know it so exactly to be able to go and lift the treasure! Yes, who would know the key word, would become rich all at once! Even the one who would find the silver mine at San Sabá! There are piles of silver ingots ready to be picked up. James Bowie, the hero of the Texas Revolution, is said to have seen them with his own eyes, or so the legend goes. Salvage companies have even been founded, spending tens of thousands of dollars on their explorations. Until this very day, however, Los Almagres have not revealed their secret...!

THIRD CHAPTER

INTERLUDE

The French were only interested in the possession of Louisiana, which was never economically profitable, in connection with Canada. When it became certain at the end of the Seven Years' War that Canada was lost to them, they did not hesitate to sell the useless colony and to force it on the Spanish confederate, so that it would not fall into the hands of the English. The Peace of Paris of 1763 corrected the secret Franco-Spanish treaty of donation and Spain was granted only the parts west of the Mississippi, renouncing at the same time Florida. The eastern half became British.

A completely new situation arose for Texas after the disappearance of the Fleur de Lis from Louisiana. For decades, it had served the Spanish poorly as a protective wall against French ambitions to attack Mexico. Now, however, with the frontier running 250 kilometers further east, the borderland had suddenly become landlocked. Some of the forces and costs that the viceroy had expended to maintain the province in a somewhat defensible condition could now at least be saved. To be sure, the number of soldiers who were in Texas at the time of the

A LONE STAR ARISES IN TEXAS

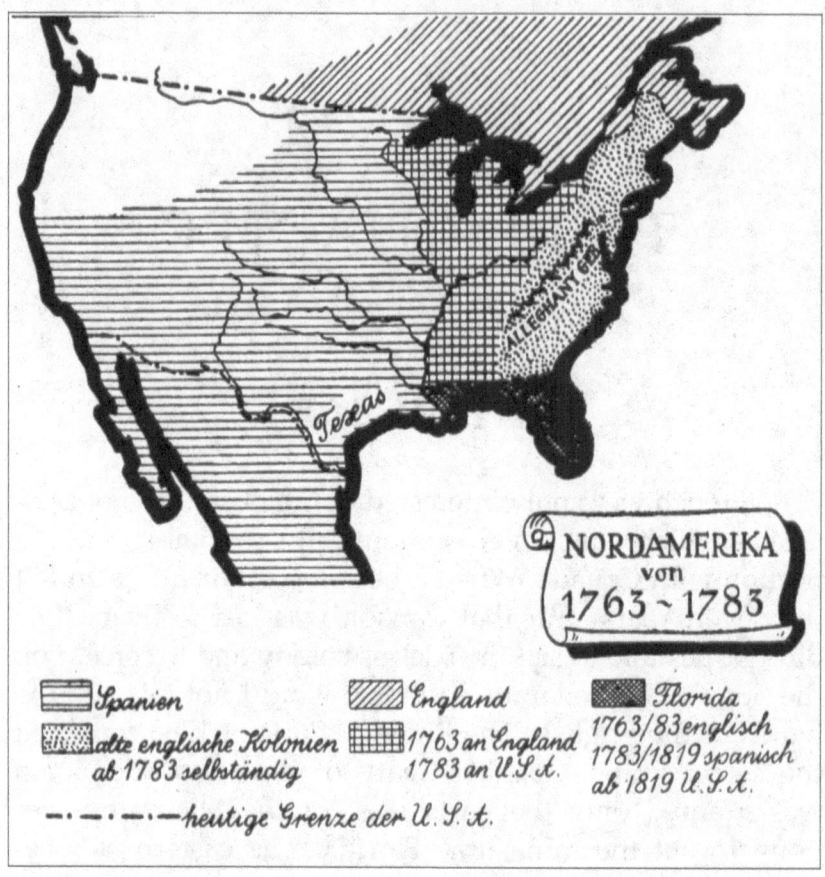

Louisiana Purchase was far from imposing. Eighty men lay garrisoned at the governor's seat of Adae, and the presidio of San Antonio, despite the constant Apache danger, had only a garrison of twenty-three! After all, the province's military strength had not always been so small. On the whole, Texas had already cost a pretty penny, with no prospect of ever recouping it through revenue from the land. As early as 1744, the sums spent up to that time were estimated at three million pesos, with current expenses at 63,000 pesos annually. These sums were all the more im-

INTERLUDE

portant for the colonial government because the transfer of the border to the Mississippi and the simultaneous occupation of California made considerable new demands on its treasury. Texas, however, was not an isolated case. The reorganization of the entire former Northern Front was under discussion, and the question of what should happen in Texas had to be resolved within this larger framework.

At that time, there was even more at stake. It was the reorganization of the Spanish Empire par excellence. Many reforms had been carried out since the Bourbons ascended to the throne but a thorough renewal of the outdated machinery of the state had not been attempted either out of a false respect for the "tried and tested" or out of a lack of insight into the needs of the moment. This changed when Charles III took the scepter in 1759. The new king was an open-minded man who had absorbed the ideas of the Enlightenment theory of state and economics and, in the light of these ideas, saw how much was medieval, overdue and backward in his empire.

Spanish trade policy, for example, was still governed by the principles that had been established in the 16th century. To ensure that the state did not miss out on any customs duties or taxes, traffic with the colonies was strictly regulated and registered. Only in Seville—and later, when the Guadalquivir silted up, only in Cadiz—were ocean-going ships allowed to depart and arrive. Only a few merchants in this port had the right to export and import. It was no wonder, then, if prices were excessively high and the quantity and quality of goods excessively low and if smuggling flourished in the colonies, depriving the Crown of a large part of its customs revenues! Charles III put an end to many of these abuses. In 1765, the monopoly of Cadiz was abolished and the prohibition that forbade the colonies to trade among themselves was lifted. Import duties were greatly reduced and overly oppressive trade restrictions were dropped. However, the principle that only Spaniards were allowed to trade with the Spanish colonies was not changed. The measures taken, however, were sufficient to counteract smuggling to a large extent and the considerable increase in customs revenues was the best proof of the validity of the new policy.

At the same time, a reform of the administrative service began. The entire colonial administrative structure was reorganized, the viceroy and the governors were given more power in the sense of tight centralism, outdated laws were repealed, tax collection was improved, and a close eye was kept on the civil servants. In a word, everything was done to make the rusty, decrepit, creaking administrative apparatus, which almost threatened to grind to a halt, workable and efficient again.

This radical work of renewal was mainly in the hands of some capable inspectors that Madrid had sent to the colonies. In the northern provinces, it was the Marques de Rubí who looked after things. What he saw on his tour of inspection along the previous frontier, however, was not very pleasant. Wherever he went, he found the settlers in distress, the presidios in a wretched state, and since the passage of Louisiana to Spain, there was no longer any need to fear the French, but the Indian danger had grown enormously. In Sonora, the natives had risen in bloody revolution, New Mexico suffered severely from the raids of the Comanches, Coahuila and Nuevo Leon and Texas were afflicted by the robberies and murders of the Apaches. Under these circumstances Rubí thought it most advisable to withdraw the outposts wherever they had been established in defense against the French and which

INTERLUDE

now had no longer any raison d'être. Instead, from the Gulf of California to Matagorda Bay, under the unified command of a general commander, a chain of strong, well-manned, and well-fortified forts was to be established, capable of providing the northern provinces with effective protection against the Redskins. For Texas this meant the abandonment of all presidios, missions, and settlements east of the line from San Antonio to La Bahia, that is, the abandonment of the positions in East Texas, on Galveston Bay, and on the San Sabá.

How did the Marques de Rubí come up with these proposals? What was Texas like around the middle of the 18th century? Well, the province was still completely a wilderness, with only a few oases of Spanish civilization. Fourteen missions, seven presidios, two settlements—sparse enough was the settlement of the land! Only the two oldest settlements, Adaes and San Antonio, were important. At Adaes lived about five hundred Spanish colonists, at San Antonio there may have been as many, the few monks and soldiers who manned the remaining posts were soon counted. All told, about twelve hundred people—that was the entire white population of Texas at that time! And at that, one must stretch the term "white" a great deal! For there were few pure-blooded Spaniards who moved into this country; most had mixed blood. What kind of racial mishmash this was, can be seen in a draft list drawn up for the hundred and ten soldiers who accompanied the Marques de Aguayo to Texas in 1721. One will certainly not err in generalizing the findings of this list. Only 44 of that band were Spaniards, the rest being composed of 31 mulattoes, 21 coyotes (one parent mixed between mulatto and mestizo, the other mestizo), 17 mestizos (mixed between Spaniard and Indian), 2 castizos (father mestizo, mother

Spaniard), one lobo (father mixed between Chinese and Negro, mother mulatto), one free Negro, one Indian. Moreover, of these one hundred and ten soldiers, one hundred had come directly from prison and only one had volunteered!

It was not surprising that the monks complained bitterly about the miserable behavior of the soldiers, who mistreated the Indians, abused the native women, and did not distinguish between my property and yours. That is why the fathers wanted the presidio as far away from their mission as possible, although they could not and did not want to do without it. When the Marques de Aguayo moved the presidio to the other bank of the San Antonio in 1721, he thought it might be even better if not only the width of the river but a Chinese wall separated the soldiers from the mission inmates. "In the presidios of Texas," reads a contemporary account, "are to be found only the most ill-disposed Spaniards and half-breeds, who seek a refuge here in order not to have to work, or for still worse reasons." This judgment from the mouth of a monk may have been biased and exaggerated, but it was certainly not taken completely out of the air.

The colonists also settled near the presidios. The garrisons, small as they were, always had a need for food and other agricultural products, and since the soldiers, with their pay, were the only people in the province with cash in their pockets, it was possible to do some business with them. The only problem was that it was not to everyone's taste to move with the military into the Texas wilderness, where the work was hard and life dangerous. This required a frontier spirit, and few Mexicans possessed it. For this reason, all efforts of the colonial authorities to further colonize the land from Mexico failed. The idea of bringing in colonists from outside the country was already being considered in the time of the Marques de Aguayo. They planned at that time to settle four hundred families from the Canary Islands. The result of this project was miserable enough, although the emigrants were promised the title of hidalgo, that is, elevation to nobility, as a reward for themselves and their descendants. Only ten years later, no more than fifteen families arrived in San Antonio, and even those had to be compelled to do so.

It took a long time for the immigrants from the Canary Islands to find their way in Texas. San Antonio, however, was also a dangerous place! After 1760, the Apache plague became so bad here that the settlers could only do their field work in squads, a loaded rifle within reach at their side. The farmers in East Texas had it much easier under the peaceful Hasinais. Moreover, they profited there from the surreptitious trade with Louisiana, which, since the old border barrier had remained in place, continued to flourish after 1763. Smuggling, however, was the only trade option available at all! Texas had no port, all traffic with the capital went overland: endless the journey and costly each transport!

Rubí's view that there would not be very much to give up if East Texas were vacated undoubtedly had some validity. There was something else in favor of this arrangement. The missionaries, who were working there with rather moderate success, were urgently needed for new work. In 1767, Charles III had expelled the Jesuit Order from the entire Spanish Empire, and the Franciscans now had to take over the work of conversion in North America that the Societas Jesu had so successfully begun in California.

It was therefore no sacrifice for the monks that they had to leave Hasinailand in 1773. Things were different for the settlers. The grain was ready to be harvested in the fields — it had to be left! It was impossible to herd all the cattle — they had to be turned out into the woods! And the familiar log houses, some of which were inhabited by the third generation, had to be left to decay! Some colonists fled into the wilderness to escape the governor's orders as they determined to stay in the old homeland, even if no Spanish soldier would offering "protection" from the friendly Tejás anymore. The rest moved to San Antonio under severe hardship. Nevertheless, when they were shown the land near the town which they were henceforth to cultivate, they unanimously declared that they would not enter into such an exchange. So adamantly did they insist that they be allowed to return to East Texas that the colonial government finally relented. However, they were not allowed to return to Adaes because the suspicion that it was more the smuggling profits than the old farms that had such a magnetic effect on the settlers could not be shaken. The Trinity River seemed far enough from the Louisianan border, however, and a new settlement was established there in 1774, named Nuestra Señora del Pilar de Bucareli in honor of the viceroy. The settlement soon developed into a thriving community. Yet it was a thorn in the side of the authorities as there were for there were signs enough that the inhabitants were finding ways and means to resume smuggling — in particular, moving arms and ammunition to the Red River Indians — in the old style.

Bucareli did not exist for long. In 1778 the Comanches attacked the village so severely that the colonists emigrated. Without first asking permission, they moved back to Hasinailand, where they felt safe from Comanche attacks. A new settlement, Nacogdoches, was established on the site where Mission Dolores had once stood, and the next few years proved how important it was to have an outpost in this Texas-Louisiana border district from which to gain influence over the "northern tribes".

This was because in all the time that Texas had been an "Interior Province", its relationship with the Plains Indians remained the country's greatest concern. Just establishing barrier forts, as Rubí had recommended, was not enough to solve the Indian question. The Viceroy was simply unable to raise as many soldiers along the frontier as would have been necessary to provide real security for the provinces. Furthermore, even if he had had the regiments and the money at his disposal, the sparse population of these lands would have made such an effort hardly worthwhile. The presidios could only ever be one means among others in Indian policy. This had also been the case in the past, where the mission had always been established alongside the presidio and both the threat of arms and the preaching of peace had had an effect on the Redskins. The only question was whether the mission system was appropriate in Texas or whether other methods should be used against the prairie tribes.

Missionary Work in Texas

It was once said that the Indian was a brother to the Spaniard, a friend to the Frenchman and a stranger to the Englishman. There is some truth in this statement, although one must be careful not to take such exaggerated formulations too literally. Nevertheless, it will probably surprise some people to hear that the relationship between the Spaniards and the natives of the New World was a brotherly one. The old historical legend that makes the Spaniards the most imperious and heartless European nation ever to come into contact with colored peoples has not yet been eradicated. This "colonial lie" has been circulating since the days when Bishop Las Casas publicly denounced the cruelties of the conquistadors in the mid-16th century. Certainly, the philanthropic Dominican was a thousand times right when he indignantly opposed the outrages committed against the Indians in the first decades after the discovery of America. Yet his writing was a political polemic, intended to sharpen the conscience of the Madrid government and induce it to intervene, and therefore, as always happens in such cases, painted the black even blacker than it actually was. However, while the Spanish kings took the charges of the Episcopalian Indian lawyer to heart, they did their best to make amends for the sins of the early days, and established a native protection legislation unparalleled for centuries. The enemies of the Iberian Empire used Las Casas' report to morally defame the Spaniards in the eyes of the world.

The nations, which so self-righteously condemned Spain, would have had every reason to beat their own breasts, since their conquerors had done just as much evil to the natives as the Spanish. It is an eternal custom in the life of nations, however, to pin something on the other when it is necessary to justify one's own interests and to cover up one's own crimes! In any case, the English and the French, in their struggle against Spain, knew very well how to use the material of Las Casas as solid anti-Spanish propaganda, even at a time when the horrors of the Conquista had long been forgotten in the Indies and the Indians enjoyed the best state care.

If the Spaniards saw in the Indian a fellow human being who, like themselves, possessed a soul in need of redemption, and did not, like the pious Pilgrim Fathers, count him as a "devilish people" who had to be exterminated, one must not conclude from this alone that they were more Christian, more humane, more idealistically minded than the Puritans. All Europeans who came to America were ultimately concerned in the same way with their own advantage, and if they treated the natives differently, it was because the method they used corresponded best to their interests. The Anglo-Saxons went to the New World as settlers, farmers, and planters, seeking soil to clear, plow, and cultivate. The red man, who felt himself master of the wilderness and did not want to voluntarily give up his hunting grounds, that is, his economic existence, stood in their way, and with the self-confident unconcern of the European, who always considers his own right to life to be superior, the English began to buy out the Indian with fraudulent contracts, to drive him out by force, and, if there was no other way, to destroy him mercilessly. The French were different! They were primarily concerned with furs, with which the Parisian furriers could trim the garments of the elegant courtiers and the rich citizens and with beaver skins, from whose hair the European hatters made their goods. The Indians provided them with invaluable services such as hunters, trappers, and middlemen. No wonder they sought to make good friends with them! The Spaniards, on the other hand, were bent on the extraction of precious metals and the establishment of large haciendas. Without the help of the natives they would never have succeeded in operating the mines and cultivating the plantations. Had they proceeded against the Indians in a manner similar to that of the English, their overseas possessions would have hardly yielded them a return. They also soon realized that the hen that lays the golden eggs must not be slaughtered, but everything must be done to care for her. The Spanish Indian Protection Act is the fruit of this realization. It saved the Redskins from exploitation that would have destroyed them. It did not, however, change the fact that they were and remained literally and figuratively subject to "tribute" to the white master.

Only those Indians who had already reached a certain level of culture could be used for the work that the Spaniards wanted done. In Mexico and Peru, this was the case. The natives there were sedentary and accustomed to state order and a regulated way of working, and thus fulfilled all the preconditions for forming the lowest supporting layer of a hierarchically structured colonial social system. Things were different in those areas where the Indians still lived in a state of complete savagery or even roamed nomadically through primeval forests and prairies. If these Native Americans were to be incorporated into the edifice of the Spanish colonial system, it was necessary to wrest them from their savagery and make them "useful members of human society". It remains the imperishable merit of the Spaniards to have dared to undertake this task. No other European nation made a similar attempt in those centuries, since no other possessed the will for such a work of civilization, nor the confidence in its success. Certainly, it was political and economic necessities that prompted the Spaniards to venture upon the accomplishment of such a difficult task, but behind this, the driving force was the belief in the ability to educate everything that has a human face, a belief that sprang from the deepest religious foundations. It was the belief, common to the whole of Christendom, but fully accessible only to the religious fervor of the Spanish people, that God's creative hand had created men equal in the last analysis, despite all differences of skin color and bodily form, and that devoted love was capable of leading even the simplest soul along the path of true human morality. Although it may at first seem surprising that the same Spaniards who at home wielded the terrible instrument of sectarian intolerance, the Inquisition, with fanatical implacability, should in America take care of the immature children of the wilderness with untiring sacrifice and forbearance—on closer inspection both prove to be expressions of that ardent, zealous piety which is the hallmark of Iberian Catholicism. Yet how could the monks who were entrusted with the work of civilization and sent out into the wildernesses have carried out the dangerous and thankless work if they had not been animated by genuine zeal for their faith!

The conversion of the Indians was a priority for the monks. Experience had shown, however, that missionary work, if one did not want to be content with a mere pseudo-Christianity, was impossible without civilization, that one could not make any savage understand the basic teachings of the Christian religion and morality if one had not first accustomed him, at least in the most rudimentary way, to a civilized way of life and to regular work. The wishes of the Catholic Church thus coincided with the wishes of the Spanish state, and so, with abundant financial aid from the Crown, "missiones" were established everywhere along the borders of the Indies, that is, smaller or larger settlements in the midst of fields and pastures, with a church and convent, farm buildings and stables, adjoined by a walled Indian pueblo. In these settlements the Fathers, assisted by lay brothers, lived together with those savages who had agreed to become Christians, in order to instruct them, with never-failing perseverance, not only in the mysteries of the Christian faith, but also in the secrets of proper agriculture and simple crafts. The one was as difficult as the other, and both could only succeed because love and care were combined with strict discipline and inescapable compulsion. For even if entry into the mission village was, at least in theory, voluntary, once the Indian had made the decision—perhaps driven by economic need, perhaps enticed by gifts and promises, in any case usually without being aware of the consequences of his step—then he was bound and had to endure the educational work. If necessary, the soldiers, who could be summoned from the nearby presidio, ensured that he stayed and obeyed, although the priests preferred to get by with amicable encouragement and lesser means of coercion.

The Spaniards generally expected that after ten years the missionary children would be ready to stand on their own feet, both religiously and economically. Then the mission fields were to be divided among the "indios reducidos", as the civilized Indians were called in contrast to the wild ones, the "indios bravos", the monks were to look for new mission areas and the land and people were to be placed under the colonial administration and the church clergy. It often turned out that this period was not sufficient for the conversion and education of the savage tribes, but had to be extended by many years, possibly even into infinity. But this failure of the actual civilization work, if it occurred in the areas immediately on the frontier, was not necessarily regarded by the Spanish government as a failure. In these frontier districts it was sufficient for it if the friars could report that the Indians were firmly in their hands, thus forming a wall of protection against all enemies, red or white, who threatened the Empire. If necessary, the Fathers were not only missionaries, but also political agents. Whether it

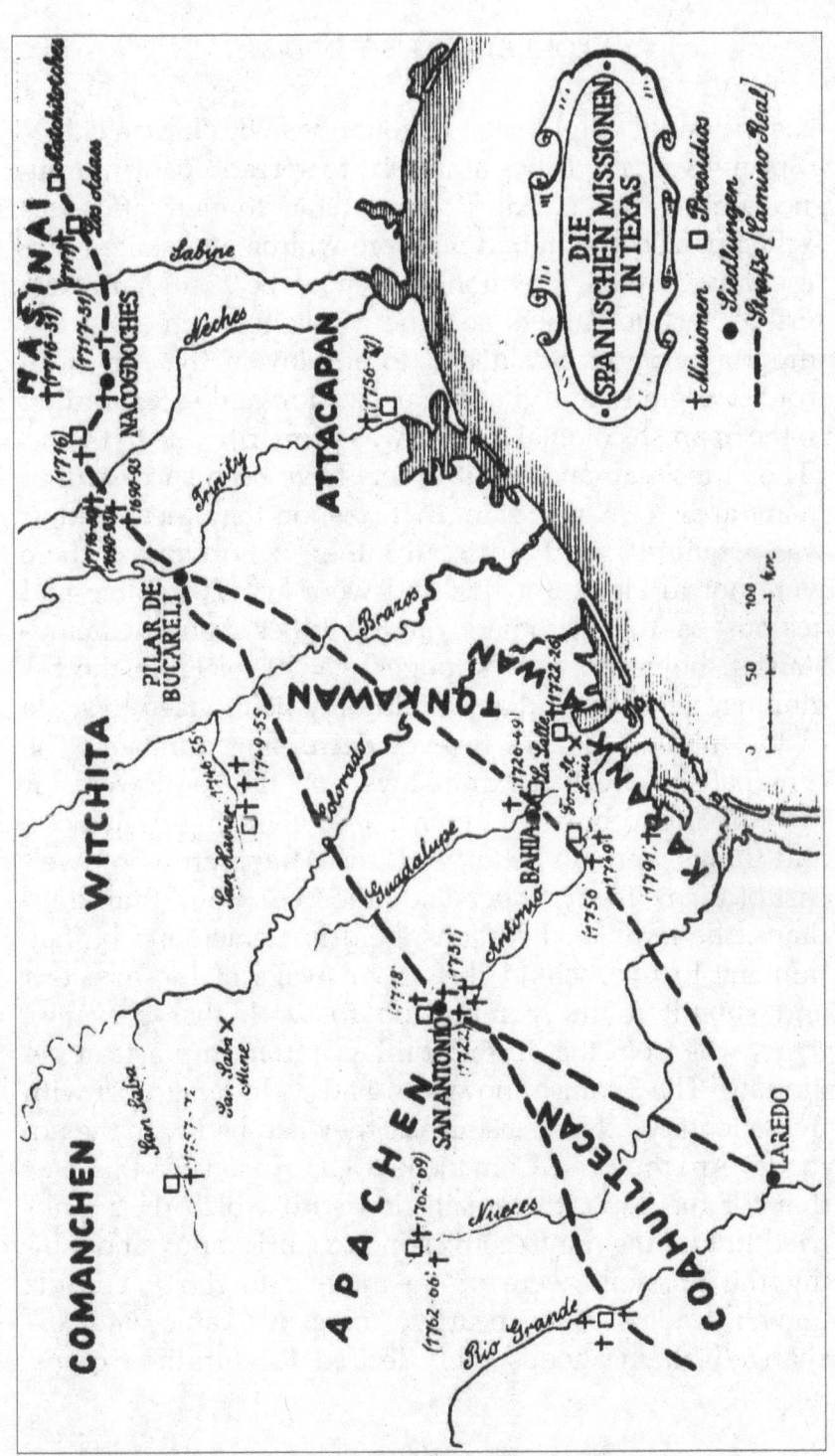

was to conduct diplomatic negotiations with Indian chiefs, to pacify warring tribes amicably, to spread Spanish influence among the Redskins, to counteract foreign influences — the Spanish crown had no more willing and skilled representatives than the monks. It may be confidently asserted that the Fathers and the Missiones were the most important factors Spain had to employ in the American frontier regions, and that the expansion and safeguarding of the Spanish colonial empire was primarily due to them.

The Franciscan and Jesuit orders have been successful in many areas of New Spain. In Texas, on the other hand, it was a failure. The Franciscan fathers who worked there were not to blame for this and were just as capable and zealous as their brothers on the other fronts. Circumstances, however, were stronger than they! From the beginning, the Texas Indians could only be induced to settle in the mission villages in ever decreasing numbers. The cannibalistic, warlike Karánkawan on the coast were far too barbaric to be at all amenable to civilizing influences, and things were no better with the Attapacan who dwelt east of them. To try to persuade the free, proud prairie Indians, the lords of the plains, bold horsemen and buffalo hunters, to live behind the prison walls of the missions and submit to the compulsion to work that prevailed there, was from the outset nothing but an impractical beginning. The Spanish, however, had as little success with the sedentary, arable Hasinais as they had had with the nomadic Apaches and Comanches. The reason for this was that for the Tejás, the small gifts with which the monks tried to lure them into converting to Christianity and joining the missions were of no interest to them. For the French traders from nearby Louisiana came and exchanged all the goods they desired for furs and crops.

INTERLUDE

Only the weak, lenient Coahuiltecan, who were native to the west of San Antonio, toward the Rio Grande, found themselves partly willing to answer the call of the Fathers. That is why San Antonio was the center of the Spanish missionary work in Texas. It was only here that the Franciscans managed to erect stone buildings in place of the wooden makeshift houses. These were churches in the characteristic Mexican colonial style, mostly of unpretentious simplicity, but sometimes also adorned with rich sculptural work, facilities whose remains still bear witness today to the passionate will to conquer the Texan wilderness and its indigenous people through the power of the Gospel of Christ. Elsewhere, the traces of the Spanish "missiones" have passed into oblivion. After all, most of the 27 religious establishments inaugurated in Texas during the hundred years from 1690 to 1791 lasted only a short time, and where, as in East Texas, they were maintained longer (of the six missions established there in 1716, three were transferred to San Antonio as early as 1731, and the other three were abandoned in 1773), it was such fruitless vegetating that one Father summed up the result of his life's work in the words: "The Son of God did not command us to convert, but only to preach. As the apostle says, the power to convert does not come from the one who plants, nor from the one who waters, but only from God who makes it flourish. And only for this reason have the hardships of these forty years been bearable at all. But the time is not entirely wasted, for we have seen many little children become blessed through holy baptism."

What life was like in a mission at San Antonio is vividly described in a report from 1762 by a friar from San Antonio de Valero, later to become the famous Álamo:

"Every day, in the morning before and in the evening after work, all the Indians recite together the creeds of the Christian religion, as set forth by Ripalda in his catechism. Three or four times a week the priests introduce the Indians, by means of the same catechism, to the mysteries of our holy faith and to the duties of Christian men, careful to choose only such examples and explanations as are adapted to the inexpressibly simple spirit of the natives.

"The pagans are taught separately with the help of interpreters until they understand the initial principles, which takes a great deal of time. If they have the inclination to remain in the Mission (and even the longest converts do not have it to the fullest extent), they receive Holy Baptism. The boys also receive special daily instruction from their overseer, and often, in order to ascertain their progress, from the priests themselves.

"The dying and sick, if they are still pagans, are immediately baptized, and if they are already Christians, they receive the sacraments of Penance, Holy Communion, and Extreme Unction....

"The missionaries are particularly concerned about the physical well-being of the Indians. This is also part of their duties and is so important because the distributed gifts form the main livelihood of the mission inmates. Through them the savages outside are attracted, who closely observe and consider the advantages enjoyed by their brothers of the race. Thus, then, in every mission, on every Sunday and on the high holidays, four or five cattle are slaughtered, according to the number of those under care, and each ward is given his share. Mutton is distributed to the sick. As much grain is given to the Indians as they need for their household. They are also given beans, pumpkins, water melons, sugar melons, pepper, salt and sugar. Sugar is obtained from sugar cane, the regular planting of which is given the utmost importance in every mission. This is because it is the best way to please the Indians, who are particularly fond of sugar.

"Cotton and wool are used to make scarves, shawls, clothing and blankets so that the natives can dress themselves and keep warm. If more has been made than is needed, and if people can be found who want the goods, they are sold against checks. The checks are sent to the treasurer of the order and from him to the order's custodian. He procures cloth, flannels, hats, knives, cooking pots, bowls, earthen pans, mortars, tobacco, glass beads, plowshares, axes, crowbars, picks, reins, thread, needles, saddles, and whatever else is needed, including such goods as are given to the Spanish wardens and servants in payment for their work in the fields and pastures of the mission....

"The horses are needed to tend the cattle, round up the herds, and for other work, but most of them run away or are stolen, either by the savages or by runaway mission Indians.

"When they are sick, the Indians are cured with the medicines available in the country or brought here for this purpose. The sick are cared for by the Fathers or others. In serious cases, the sick receive their food from the kitchen of the monks and are exempt from work. Therefore, it often happens that the Indians pretend to be sick, and the missionaries pretend not to notice, so that they do not run away from them.

"The work of the Indians consists in tilling the fields, herding the cattle, irrigating the fields, pulling the weeds, harvesting the grain and building their huts and other buildings of the missions. They work in community, but with such tardiness and nonchalance that it is always necessary for a Spaniard to supervise. Four of them do not accomplish as much as one could easily do. Even at the loom and the forge, as carpenters and masons, trades taught them for their own benefit by the monks with no small effort, they work with a complete lack of energy, as befits their innate laziness. Women and children are employed in spinning and combing cotton. This work is very moderate, adapted to their ignorance, clumsiness, and indolence, and does not hinder their spiritual welfare or the fulfillment of their family duties."

So much for the monk's report! The life of the Indians in the San Antonio missions was certainly not difficult, and one would think that the natives would have been glad to find a shelter where they were relieved of all existential hardship. A large portion of the Coahuiltecan were also quite content with their existence in the mission pueblo. But others felt so oppressed by the mental effort they were expected to make and by the pressure of regular work that they preferred to leave the mission and return to the wilderness. It even sometimes happened that all the mission inmates left at once. Then the fathers, usually accompanied by presidio soldiers, had to go out into the forests and steppes to find the lost sheep—every single soul was fought for!—and to bring them back to the mission by amicable coaxing or brute force. This could make life sour even for the most hardworking priest. "The missionary boys," Father Santa Ana wrote in 1740, "are tractable, but make infinite trouble, because they must be treated like a mother bringing up her child. Before five, six, or even seven years of age they cannot be brought to a proper understanding at all, and usually each one flees two or three times into the wilderness, sometimes a hundred leguas inland. However, we have the patience to look for them, and as soon as they see the Father, they come to meet him like lambs. This is the greatest plague that the missionaries have to endure, for they must then wander without way or direction, accompanied only by a missionary Indian, often a hundred or even two hundred leguas (one legua = about four and a fifth kilometers!), during which misfortune frequently befalls them and they are constantly threatened by an enemy who wants to strike them dead and eat them up." In one point, however, Santa Ana's description is too euphemistic. The runaways did not always behave peacefully like lambs and often defended themselves with weapons, and it also happened that they drowned themselves in a river or threw themselves off a cliff for fear of the beating they would receive for their escape.

The heyday of the San Antonio missions was in the decade before the middle of the 18th century. At that time, there were about 1700 "indios reducidos" in the "pueblos". A vast arable area was cultivated and large herds of cattle, sheep and horses were to be cared for. Then, however, the number of mission inmates began to decline, until by 1785 there were only five hundred Indians living in the five missions. The Apaches were to blame, occupying west Texas around this time and pushing the Coahuiltecan, already severely depleted by smallpox and measles, far into Mexico via the Rio Grande. This deprived the missionaries of the reservoir from which they replenished their institutional staff. Missionary work in Texas began to falter completely, and finally it was so outlived that in 1795 the missions at San Antonio were abolished and their property passed into secular hands. Only the missions at La Bahia continued to exist into the 1920s, but the Fathers had lost all authority, the Indians came and went as they pleased, and in the end they stayed away altogether. No one cared about the beautiful church buildings anymore and they had fallen into disrepair and were destroyed even before the Spaniards left Texas.

Athanase de Méziéres

As great a success as the Spanish mission system had been elsewhere, particularly in the second half of the eighteenth century in Upper California, it had failed in Texas, and the responsible statesmen in Madrid had to ask themselves, on the basis of the experience gained in Texas, what Indian policy they wanted to adopt in newly acquired Louisiana. Monastic methods were not to be used against the tribes of the North American Plains. These powerful, freedom-loving, equestrian peoples, who had no food worries and whose passion for hunting and war lay in their blood, could not be settled and civilized. Farsighted and agile, the reform-minded Charles III drew conclusions from this realization. While he allowed the traditional mission system to continue in the old possessions, he ordered the adoption of the agent system for Louisiana, which the French had developed so finely and handled so effectively. Spain did not need to be at a loss for men who understood the profession of Indian agents, since many of the French Rangers agreed to transfer to Spanish service after the change of flag.

The agent system had been one of the most essential means of French colonial rule during all the time that the Fleur de Lis had fluttered over Canada and Louisiana. France, too, had sent missionaries to the North American wildernesses—only the English did not care about the salvation of the Indians. From a political point of view, however, these monks were also nothing more than agents. In their conversion work, to put it bluntly, they confined themselves to the extensive use of baptismal and holy water. That ambitious goal of their Spanish brothers, to lead the savages on the path of a truly Christian way of life, and that meant to educate them to become cultural people, was alien to them. The French were never interested in the civilization of the Indians. Their friendship was enough for them, and the friendly relations usually arose of their own accord from the bartering that the Coureurs des Bois did. Sometimes it was only glass beads that the rangers offered, but it was also such valuable things as guns and ammunition. It was also, God be lamented, firewater! The savages, however, were eager for European goods and found it very painful when the traders failed to arrive. That is why they supplied the French not only with furs, buffalo hides and deerskins, which were abundant in their hunting grounds, not only with horses and mules, which they stole from the Spaniards, but they were also politically at their beck and call. Even if there were many Coureurs des Bois who went off on their own and had only their private business in mind — most Indian traders had a permit from the French government in their pocket, felt themselves to be their representatives and worked according to their instructions. And they did it gladly because they knew that the government's advantage was also their own advantage. What, for example, could make a more lasting impression on the Indian clientele than to occasionally present them with gifts in the name of the magnanimous French king? Oh yes, the French knew how to preserve the business as well as the political friendship of the Redskins through small gifts! In any case, they had achieved a great deal with the prairie tribes through their clever, skillful approach!

A LONE STAR ARISES IN TEXAS

From the point of view of traditional Spanish colonial policy, the adoption of this French agent system was a revolutionary innovation. Trade with the "indios bravos" had hardly existed in Spanish America before. It contradicted the mission system, for what could have tempted the savages to join the missions if they were freely supplied with European goods? All through the centuries the Spaniards had held to the principle that only to the Indian who had passed through the mission school and had become "Christian" in the religious as well as in the cultural sense was admission to the coveted glories open. However, the necessity of counteracting French influence among the peoples beyond the northern frontier compelled deviation from this principle here and there. Nevertheless, this trade with a political background was strictly supervised by the authorities. It had been completely out of the question, however, to entrust a private citizen, a person who was neither a civil servant nor a cleric, with political orders. In the sharp separation between the sphere of action of the citizen and that of the official had lain the strength, but also the weakness of the Spanish state. The colonial authorities, who had not learned to rethink, observed the activities of the Louisianan Indian traders with deep mistrust, and it took a long time before it was understood everywhere that private citizens, who were also of foreign nationality, were able to serve the cause of the state faithfully and honestly. At least the coexistence of the old and the new Indian system was facilitated by the fact that Charles III, wisely foreseeing the inevitable friction, did not annex Louisiana to Mexico, but subordinated it to the Audiencia of Habana. Yet it was precisely at this point of contact with Texas that a number of difficulties and incompatibilities arose.

INTERLUDE

The Spanish government was primarily concerned with two things in the deployment of the Louisianan Indian traders: winning the friendship of all the tribes that populated the vast land areas from the Gulf of Mexico up to Canada and that had hitherto been incited against the Spaniards by the French, and sealing off the Mississippi border against the English trappers who were beginning to invade western Louisiana and threaten to cause as much unrest among the natives as the French had once done. Counteracting the English danger was especially the task of the posts that were established along the Mississippi like St. Louis. On the former southwestern front, on the other hand, the main question was how to overcome the enmity of the Apaches, Comanches and the peoples along the Red River, the "northern tribes".

The most suitable means to make these Indians compliant seemed to be, for the time being, to deny them the supply with European goods, especially with weapons. Expressed in the language of the present: one imposed on the prairie tribes the means of pressure of economic sanctions. However, such sanctions can only be effective, if at all, if they are strictly and consistently applied. Therefore, the Spanish government ordered that only concessionary traders were allowed to move into Indian country and that all "vagabonds", that is, all those rangers who roamed among the Redskins without permission, were to be ruthlessly exterminated. At the same time, it forbade the purchase of horses and mules from the Indians, most of which were only stolen goods. This, too, seemed to be a means of getting the prairie tribes out of the habit of raiding the Spanish "interior provinces".

According to these general political guidelines, the agent system in Louisiana began to work for Spain, just as it had worked for France before. Only that the traders were inculcated—and this was characteristically Spanish—not to take advantage of the Redskins under any circumstances, not to sell them a drop of the devastating firewater, to see to it that the nomads settled down, and to see to it that no Indian died without first receiving holy baptism. The Coureurs des Bois fulfilled their duty to the King of Spain as faithfully as they had formerly done to the King of France. What could the Spaniards have done in Louisiana without the help of these men! There would be a goodly number of French-sounding names to mention who rendered great service to the Iberian colonial empire in the decades after 1763. But one of the first to be recorded on this page of the Spanish-American annals is the name of Athanase de Méziéres. It was not least due to him that the Spaniards secured their province of Texas, which was still seriously threatened by Indian raids.

Athanase Christophe Fortunant de Méziéres came from a noble Parisian family. One of his sisters was married to the Duke of Orleans, and other close relatives held high offices in the army and government. Like the sons of so many French noblemen, Athanase chose the military profession, and he arrived in Louisiana in 1733 as a very young ensign. It may be that he was very soon ordered to Natchitotches, which was to remain his headquarters for the rest of his life. However, there is no documentary evidence of his presence at the French fort on the Texas border until 1743. Yet, when one surveys his abilities and accomplishments, one would think that he must have been apprenticed to Saint Dénis, the very Saint Dénis who had founded this post on the Red River in 1713 and who had commanded it ever since as a cunning frontiersman, a cunning smuggler, and an excellent connoisseur of Indians. Perhaps the old frontier captain lived to see a tender affection budding between his daughter Marie and Athanase. He never came to welcome Méziéres as a son-in-law, however. When the two celebrated their wedding, two years had already passed since the Spanish governor had sighed with relief at Saint Dénis' death. Unfortunately, the marriage was short-lived: Marie died in 1748, leaving her husband a little daughter. Much later, in 1759, Méziéres married a second time, and this union was richly blessed with children, until it came to an abrupt end in 1777, when an epidemic took away the wife, a son and a daughter within a week.

Méziéres advanced over the years to lieutenant, to captain, and finally to second-in-command of the fort commander, who, like him, was a son-in-law of the old Saint Dénis. It seems that he enjoyed the officer's life at Natchitotches. Besides, why shouldn't he like it! After all, there was no question of boring uniformed barracks duty. Since the Frenchman and Spaniard had been facing each other on standby at the Texas frontier for quite some time, military duties played little part. Yes, he was an officer—but here in the Louisianan wilderness, that meant, first and foremost, pursuing Indian policy. There it was a matter of making "business trips" across the jungles to cultivate relations with the Redskins, to control and direct the agents and—unofficially, of course—to assist smuggling into the Spanish territories. Along the way, they themselves participated financially in the Indian trade, and also had their own farm to run. Old Saint Dénis had shown his sons-in-law how to combine state and private business! Méziéres must have been or have become quite a wealthy man. At the very least, he owned a sizable plantation. In a census, he stated that he owned 53 slaves and that ten thousand pounds of tobacco were stored in his storerooms.

Méziéres' life was certainly not monotonous or one-sided! And whatever task the French nobleman was confronted with on the frontier, he mastered it. Not like so many of the Coureurs des Bois, who were gifted with the nose of a bloodhound for the incidents of the wilderness! Méziéres was an educated man, rich in knowledge, with a taste for mathematics, a keen observer, brilliant in his use of words, not only in his native language but also in Spanish, which he mastered to perfection. His psychological intuition served him well in his dealings with the savages as well as later in his dealings with the Spanish authorities. He could hardly have been called a daredevil. What he did, he did with deliberation and caution. When it was necessary, however, he was able to act with lightning speed and to proceed with a courageous determination that ensured success. And whether he sought to intimidate in effective speech by brutal threats or to win by warm assurances of friendship in a conference with Indian chiefs, whether he behaved boastfully or modestly toward his superiors, he was always the sober politician who pursued his aim with calculating shrewdness and did not shrink from unscrupulousness if occasion demanded it. For example, setting betrayal against betrayal, he hatched a murder plan against the Tonkawan chief, and the only reason he did not have it carried out was because the Indian committed himself to a fight against the Apaches and thus again became a valuable tool in the service of Spanish frontier policy. This pragmatic political trait in Méziéres's nature, however, was by no means a sign of callousness. In many passages of his extensive correspondence he professes to be a devout Christian. The loyal devotion with which he, the French nobleman, made the cause of the Spanish state his own, the matter-of-factness with which he sacrificed his entire fortune in the service of this state, so that on his deathbed he had to ask the Spanish authorities to take care of his destitute children—this shows sufficiently how even this realistic frontiersman did not lack a spiritual depth and an idealistic mental foundation.

When O'Reilly took over the government of Louisiana as Spanish governor in 1769, he attached great importance to Méziéres continuing his service on the Texas frontier. As the governor of Texas, Baron de Ripperdá, explained, there was no one who knew Texas and Louisiana and the Indian tribes on the borders of the two provinces better than this Frenchman. With broad powers, Méziéres was appointed district governor of Natchitotches. This meant that he was entrusted with a wealth of administrative tasks and was expected to pacify the Indian tribes on the northern border of Texas. These tasks were so extensive and heavy with responsibility that Méziéres could no longer think of managing his plantation on the side and he did not hesitate to sell it! Then began for him a time of incessant travels crisscrossing Indian country, often taking him far up the upper Red River and Brazos and back to Natchitotches via San Antonio.

Méziéres, with great energy and prudence, set out to reorganize the agency system according to the directives of the Spanish government. As mentioned, the goal of these changes was the economic strangulation of the anti-Spanish tribes. Combined with Méziéres' diplomatic skills, this blockade policy had a surprisingly quick success. As early as 1771, he got the "Norteños," that is, the Caddo, Tonkawan, and Witchita peoples between the upper Red River and the Texas settlements, to move to San Antonio to make a solemn peace with the governor of Texas. There were enough Spanish officials and monks who distrusted the Frenchman's work of peace, who claimed that it was all a sham, who suspected that Méziéres was only trying to start the arms trade with these tribes again. The Louisianan agents generally had to put up with such suspicions for a long time. They were also unfounded. It is humanly understandable that after so many decades, even centuries of bitter enmity, many Spaniards had little confidence in the new subjects of French descent. How wrong the critics were, especially in the case of Méziére, was proven by the fact that the "Norteños" largely fulfilled their treaty obligations. The Spanish government itself judged the character and performance of its district governor more correctly than the petty minds of Texas and Mexico. Not only did it give him permission to travel to Paris to settle family matters, but it also promoted him to the rank of lieutenant colonel in recognition of his services. Almost at the same time, Méziéres was retroactively awarded the Order of St. Louis by the French king!

When Méziéres returned to his post at Natchitotches, he saw his next task as reinforcing and strengthening friendly relations with the Indian tribes on the upper Red River and bringing other peoples into the work of peace. Baron de Ripperdá would have been happy to help him in this work. It was, after all, a strange thing at all that the securing of the Texas frontiers by former Frenchmen should be carried on from Louisiana, while the Spaniards in Texas itself were not stirring. Ripperdá proposed, therefore, that the same policy of trade and gifts toward the northern tribes should be adopted in Texas as in Louisiana, in order to show Spanish friendship to the Indians directly, without the mediation of the French agents. However, he came off badly with this proposal to the Viceroy, who was an inveterate supporter of the mission system. As if the new course taken in Louisiana did not concern him, the Viceroy not only strictly forbade the establishment of trade relations with the savages from Texas, but he also strongly urged Ripperdá to prevent the Louisianan agents from entering Texas territory. People who supplied the natives with European goods and weapons, who supplied the Texan population with "contraband" from New Orleans, were not to be tolerated in New Spain! The Redskins belonged in the missions, and the Texans had to do their shopping in Mexico City! This unreasonableness made Méziéres' work extraordinarily difficult. It was just as well that at least his immediate superior, Bernardo de Gálvez, the twenty-one-year-old governor of Louisiana, was an understanding man. Baron de Ripperdá's sympathy for Louisianan methods eventually even cost him his position: he was punitively transferred to Honduras!

A new wind first began to blow in the "ProvinciasInternas" in 1776, when the general commander was placed under the direct control of the Spanish king and El Cavallero de Croix, an extraordinarily energetic man, took over as commander-in-chief. Croix's most pressing concern was to finally control the dreadful Apache plague that threatened to depopulate Texas and Coahuila. He took up the plan that Ripperdá had already submitted to the Viceroy on the basis of Méziéres' proposals. In alliance with the "Norteños", those tribes that have been the most ferocious enemies of the Apaches since time immemorial, a campaign of destruction was to be set in motion. When the general commander held war councils in various towns of his administrative area, he was unanimously told that such an enterprise could only be carried out with the advice and help of Méziéres. Immediately Croix sent for the experienced frontier officer to join him in San Antonio, and within a short time Méziéres had prepared a detailed memorandum for presentation to the Spanish king. With three hundred Spanish soldiers to be assembled from the interior provinces and Louisiana, and with a thousand Indians of the "northern tribes" that he himself planned to call together at the Red River, he planned to pincer the Apaches and wear them down. In order to avoid all unnecessary bloodshed, however, and to keep the Indian allies from martyring the captives, the Texas and Coahuila missions were to pay a premium for each Apache brought in. Méziéres immediately set out to stir up the "Norteños" to fight the Apaches. Again he rode hundreds and hundreds of miles through the Texas wildernesses, again he visited tribe after tribe, again he conferred and conspired in endless negotiations with the chiefs. When he returned to Natchitotches at the end of 1778, he could be satisfied with the results of his trip: preparations for the great blow against the Apaches were in full swing as far as the "northern tribes" were concerned. Unfortunately, Croix was ordered to postpone the battle against the Apaches. At the moment when Spain intervened in the fight against England in support of the revolutionary British colonies, it was impossible for the colonial government to send troops from Louisiana to Texas, and other soldiers were not available. This, after all, now meant a regrettable delay in the enterprise, but did not prevent it from being promoted as much as possible. For this purpose, it seemed advisable to call Méziéres to Texas, and in 1779 the commandant of Natchitotches was ordered to set up his base in San Antonio from then on.

Méziéres did not intend to ride directly to the Texas capital. He wanted to make one more visit to all the tribes he had visited the year before. Yet, as he set out on his new journey into Indian Territory, he fell from his horse, and his injuries were so severe that it took him three months to even begin to recover. His sense of duty drove him from the sickbed. Gathering all his strength, he set out anew but was no longer able to cope with the strain. The consequences of his fall were more disastrous than he could have imagined. He had to break off his tour prematurely. When he arrived in San Antonio, he felt that his life was coming to an end. Once again, in a long letter to Croix, he summed up his love and attachment, his fears and anxieties, his wishes and hopes that he cherished for Texas, and an excerpt from this letter may complete the picture of his character:

"In the official communication of May 19, Your Grace said that Texas is one of those provinces to which you pay the greatest attention, and indeed, of all the lands in the Indies which enjoy the wise rule of our Catholic Monarch, there is none more worthy of notice. Its fertility and beauty have often been described. Yet, what are the other conditions in the province?...

"There are only a few settlements in Texas: San Antonio, which calls itself a villa and yet does not even look like a simple village; La Bahia del Espiritu Santo, whose establishment was undoubtedly necessary to protect the coast, but which is much too far inland to serve this purpose; the defenseless Nacogdoches, which poverty and misfortune could choose as its throne. And why is it all like this? When one considers the possibilities offered by the land, with its abundance of water, its soil yields, salt flats and livestock, when one remembers the vast sums of money royal munificence has thrown out for the presidios for half a century, one ought to come across the greatest progress. Again, I ask, why is this not the case? Because the inhabitants are indolent! And where does that come from? Because any impetus is missing! And why? Because there is no trade! And that is a shame! Do we not have the sea very nearby? Does not there lie open and wide that bay where once the founder of Louisiana, Don Roberto de la Salle, anchored with three ships, whose colonists were slaughtered by those Karánkawan who are still in possession of the bay and can still commit their abominable misdeeds with impunity? All this, although our cattle have multiplied to such an extent that we have had difficulty in selling them, and have no longer taken the trouble to herd them, so that today we can catch the animals we need for breeding and consumption on the Guadelupe, on the Colorado, on the Brazos, where they run wild!

"In order, however, to tell the whole truth without hesitation! Don't you see that the inertia and dullness you deplore also come from the fact that the best land is occupied by the treacherous Tonkawan, by the faithless Apaches, by the rapacious Comanches, by the deceitful Karánkawan? Soon there will be another enemy, who is our neighbor and whose name I am disgusted to mention because of my hatred—I mean the English, who will make all these tribes their confederates by gifts, by lies and deceit, who will go wherever their restlessness and greed drives them... This enemy is already in sight. He is making his way through the Cadodachos and Natchitotches. Already in one and a half months he may have sneaked secretly and silently through the deserted wildernesses, which offer enough food, and face us. Granted, he will not come in battle dress immediately! Granted that he will at first confine himself to winning the friendship of the Indian tribes, to wresting the friendly ones away from us and to strengthening the hostile ones in their hatred against us! Then he will contrive terrible things!

INTERLUDE

"Take heed and believe it! In the midst of the deepest peace, the English settlers advanced from the distant shores of the Atlantic Ocean, no impassable mountains, no stormy lakes, no torrential streams, no immense forest thickets were able to stop them from inciting the well-meaning Indians of Louisiana to revolt without restraint and with baseness. And their meanness went so far as to make the lives of the French an object of trade with the Indians. The price of each scalp was fixed at five pounds sterling, which was paid out in the shape of guns, bullets, powder, daggers, and other weapons. Farms became desolate, the cultivation of the fields was unthinkable, many tragedies were caused by this shameful trade. Those who were attacked saw themselves forced to repay like with like! O shame on my countrymen, shame on myself! We were sent out for nothing else than to commit murder, and the soldiers' thoughts were only directed to that. And all praise and honor went to the one who knew best how to do it! From tribe to tribe the Indians passed on the cut off scalps. And when the reward was handed over to them, they thought about how they could best get new scalps, hurrying off to new acts of terror. If these were necessary reprisals, they were heinous ones that brought Louisiana to the brink of ruin and sullied its honor.

"You will undoubtedly ask why I am reporting all this in view of the fact that civil war is raging between the English, they are drawing swords against each other, inflicting deep wounds on themselves, avenging their misdeeds on themselves. They will say that now there is well-founded hope that such horrors will not be repeated. Oh, what a mistake! If the colonists remain our neighbors, how can we live in peace and harmony with people who have attacked their own king, their own motherland, with such fury! If the royalists become our neighbors, what efforts will they make to entrench themselves in that part of Louisiana which will then be theirs, what territories will they rob to indemnify themselves for their losses! Should both parties get along again and everything go back to the way it was before, their power will be even more to be feared. Already the English citizen has forgotten that he owns Sunday dress, the farmer that he owns a plow—they think only of their weapons! The liberal professions and the craftsmen now care only about war things. All of them are soldiers! What do I say? All are corsairs! They only think and want to think about war, and in order not to get into quarrels among themselves again, they will fall upon the foreigners.

"Oh, these worries of a subject would be only too justified if they were not frightened away by your Grace! From your kindness and wisdom he does not expect slow-acting remedies, but swift, thoroughgoing deeds. Be so gracious as to permit the exportation of meat, hides, lard, fat, wool, flour, grain, mules, salt, and all the other agricultural products in which this province is so abundant, without benefit! Be so gracious as to facilitate the importation of all that can be purchased in the markets of Tampico, Campeche, and Louisiana! Allow that a port be established at Espfritu Santo Bay! What a boost that will give! What development will agriculture and cattle raising take! What a lot of foreigners will be attracted by the trade! How many will stay in the country and forget their fatherland, rejoicing in the climate and the wealth of these lands, and in the care and protection of the man who governs here!... Command that the mines of Los Almagres give up their long-discovered treasures! Command that the friendly Indian tribes, not excluding the Comanches, be allowed to come and exchange

INTERLUDE

the spoils of their hunt for our goods! Order these Redskins to leave our settlers in peace, to drive out the Lipan, to show us other tracts of country where it is as delightful as here! Your Grace can plan and command as he pleases: we will carry it out! Then our King will be recompensed for the expenses he once made and is still incurring.

"Then the settlers will find the peace and prosperity they desire; each settlement the inhabitants it lacks and the whole province the happy dawn of a new era. Your Grace, however, will enjoy some of the many laurels that lie in store for you."

The campaign against the Apaches, which he had prepared, had to be abandoned now that it was defunct. It was finally in 1790 that action could again be taken against the Lipan. Near San Antonio, with the participation of the "Norteños" and the Comanches, the great battle took place. The Apaches were not completely destroyed at that time. They remained the terror of the North American Southwest, and it was not until the end of the 19th century that the Union Army dealt with this savage tribe of Indians after protracted battles.

FOURTH CHAPTER

AMERICAN NEIGHBORS

At the time when Athanase de Méziéres was warning against the unrestrained expansionism of the Anglo-Americans, the danger threatening the Spanish colonial possessions from the Mississippi was still relatively small. So far, the British authorities, worried that the American colonies might become too large and too independent, had tried to prevent immigration into the eastern river basin as far as possible, and for the time being only a small band of pioneers made inroads into Kentucky and Tennessee. But the Spaniards were in no doubt as to what was to be feared in the future. "A carbine and a bit of corn in a haversack," wrote the governor of Louisiana, "are enough for an Anglo-Saxon to wander the woods alone for a whole month. With his carbine he shoots buffalo and game, defends himself against the Indians. The steamed corn replaces his bread. From a few logs, laid in layers in a square, he builds himself a house, and if he builds another storey above it, he has a fort that is impregnable for the savages. Cold does not frighten him. When a family is tired of its settlement, it moves elsewhere and settles there with the same ease.... If such people succeed in reaching the banks of the Mississippi or the Missouri, and in navigating those rivers, nothing will be able to prevent them from crossing the streams and entering our provinces."

The Spanish government, in order to avert this danger, made every effort to avoid Louisiana's immediate neighborhood with the young Union of former British colonies. As the War of Independence neared its end, it was urging the conversion of the eastern Mississippi basin into an Indian territory, thus establishing a kind of buffer state. The United States, however, not wanting to have its route across the Alleghany Mountains blocked, reached an agreement with the English above the heads of its Spanish ally, and Madrid had to watch as beyond the "Father of Streams" the Star-Spangled Banner took the place of the Union Jack. Nevertheless, in gratitude for the aid in arms it had given to the rebellious English colonies, Spain regained Florida, and never has its possessions in North America been greater than in the years after 1783. Two-thirds of the space that now belongs to the Union was in its hands at that time.

The Spaniards' joy over the recovery of Florida did not last long. It soon became clear how wrong those had been who hoped that an independent "New England" would remain a weak entity, beset by internal and external existential needs, with which it would be possible to live together in harmony. No sooner had the North American Confederation overcome the critical early years and given itself a firmer constitution and a more efficient government in 1787 than it betrayed an expansive restlessness and uneasiness that exceeded all fears. Year after year tens of thousands of land-hungry settlers now passed over the Alleghanies, and slowly but inexorably the "frontier," like a lava flow, advanced westward. The trappers, who stalked the beaver and the buffalo and bartered with the Indians, formed the vanguard. They were followed by the squatters who cleared the wilderness with lead and hatchet. Then came the mass of farmers, who took possession of the land without quite settling down, because further west there was the lure of new arable land that seemed even better.

The Spaniards tried in vain to stop the Anglo-Saxon advance by inciting the Indian tribes in what was once eastern Louisiana to resist. The Redskins were overrun by the onslaught of white pioneers, and one day the first tidal waves of the "frontier" reached the Mississippi. They came to a halt here, contrary to expectations. The fur hunters and Indian traders crossed the river into Spanish territory. But the settlers themselves shied away from the waterless and timber-poor prairies with their dangerous red horsemen. The pressure of Anglo-American expansion was felt all the more strongly in the south, where West Florida, that narrow coastal strip stretching from the peninsula proper to New Orleans, barred their access to the sea. Unimpeded navigation to the Gulf was a necessity of life for the backwoodsman. After all, where would he go with his harvest blessings without a convenient and cheap route to markets? When the Yankees, who then still held the political reins, hesitated to vigorously represent the interests of the "frontier," a movement arose among the "backwoodsmen" in Kentucky and Tennessee to break away from the Union. Spain vigorously unleashed the peso to foment settler discontent, but the end of the story was that Washington recognized the danger of secession and forced Madrid to release the Mississippian shipping. The frontier accepted this as a down payment on their even broader demand to wrest control of the estuary from the Spanish altogether.

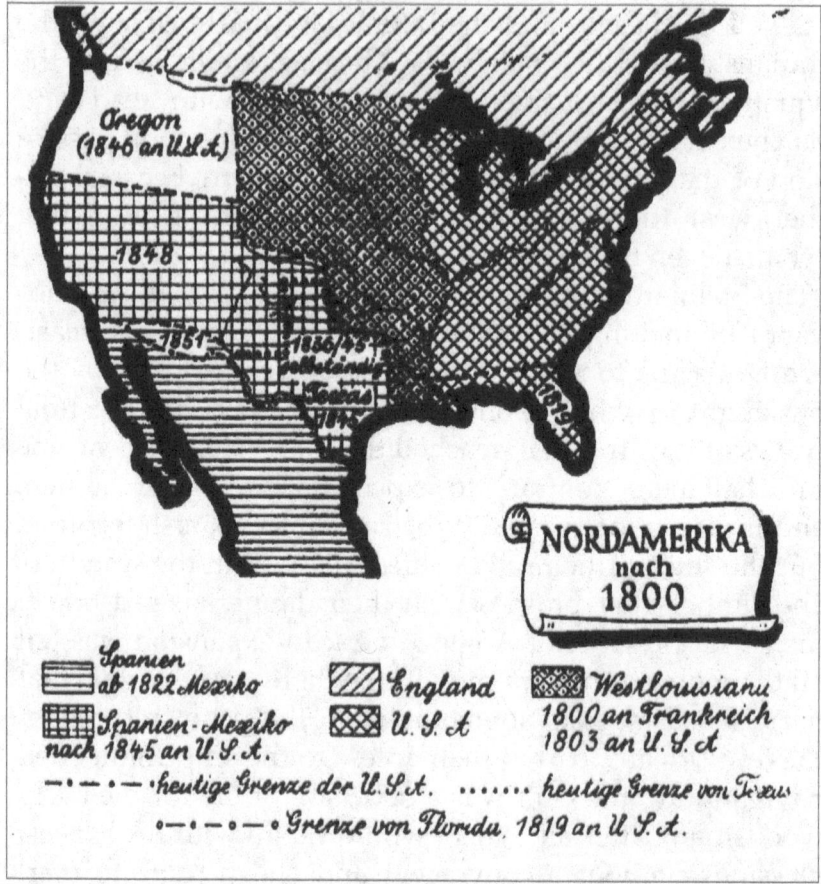

However, before the Americans found an opportunity to strike a blow against Florida, big politics intervened to change North American ownership. Under the leadership of Napoleon Bonaparte, France once again aspired to world domination, and the dreams of a great French colonial empire in the New World were also revived. Things got off to an easy start for the French. They demanded the Louisiana back from Spain, which they had once given to it as a gift. In Madrid, the bitter pill of restitution was thought to be sweetened by the advantage of knowing that the strong France was again involved in the struggle for North America. In the United States they thought differently! There, when the first rumors of the secret Franco-Spanish treaty of 1800 leaked out, a storm of indignation arose, and the Americans were so unwilling to accept a shift of political power on the North American continent that their president Jefferson informed Napoleon that a landing of French troops in Louisiana would be answered with a declaration of war. Faced with such a forceful stance, the Corsican now backed down in the end. A new war with England was imminent and he could not afford to spoil it with a second naval power as well. To avoid all difficulties, he sold the territory, which covered almost two and a half million square kilometers, to the United States for fifteen million dollars in 1803. The protest of the Spaniards, who had not even left Louisiana yet, went unheard.

Texas was now again frontier province, after an interim of forty years. Only this time a far more uncomfortable neighbor stood at its gates than the French had once been. Spain could not shake off the fear that the Union was about to extend its hand to Mexico. The Bishop of New Orleans knew how American immigrants would take their young sons in their arms, point westward, and say, "There lies Mexico! Just wait—someday you'll march there!" Disturbing rumors spoke of dark intentions that Aaron Burr was scheming, the Burr who had once been vice president of the United States and had later gunned down the great conservative statesman Hamilton in a duel. In the Mississippi valley, weapons were collected, volunteers recruited! Was it a matter of separating the West from the Confederacy? Was it to invade Florida? Was it to conquer Texas? No one knew, and no one knows to this day. For just as Burr was about to strike, the Washington government had him arrested, but in court the plotter swindled his way out of it.

As soon as the first reports of Burr's obscure machinations reached Mexico, the Viceroy took the necessary precautions. In 1806 he ordered an army of 1300 men to Texas. One had to be prepared for all kinds of surprises in this province. The Union had the nerve to claim that Louisiana, which Napoleon had sold to the Americans, extended to the Rio Grande. They invoked claims to ownership that La Salle had once made, and refused to accept that these claims had long since been invalidated by the Spanish occupation of Texas. However, in Mexico there was not the slightest thought of giving the Americans access to the Rio Grande. On the contrary, the colonial government ordered the general of the army that it had moved into Texas to re-occupy the old pre-1763 frontier. Yet when the Spanish commander set up his posts on the Arroyo Hondo, a small creek halfway between Natchitotches and Adaes, the American commander of Natchitotches passionately objected. The situation became critical. The commander-in-chief of the Union forces in Louisiana rushed over, the garrison of the American fort was reinforced, at any moment there was a threat of the rifle shot going off over here or over there that would have meant the beginning of a Spanish-American war. At the last minute the danger was averted. The two opposing generals, acting on their own responsibility, concluded an agreement according to which the Arroyo Hondo would form the American border and the Sabine River the Spanish border, and the land in between would be considered "neutral territory". This remained the case until 1819, when the border between Spain and the Union was basically settled and from then on Texas ended at the Sabine River!

AMERICAN NEIGHBORS

For thirteen years, the "Neutral Zone" across the Sabine River played a role in Texas history. Not a very laudable one, however! For this strip of land became the Dorado for all riffraff from Mexico or the Union who had reason not to show their faces in public. Petty thieves and thugs, criminals and murderers, adventurers of every kind and stamp met here. They lived from highway robbery and banditry, from slave smuggling and piracy. They spared no property and no life, they made East Texas more unsafe than the prairie Indians of West Texas, they brought the whole province into such disrepute that decades later it was still said in the Union states: "What, he wants to go to Texas? I suppose he too has murder on his conscience?" Both Spaniards and Americans sent soldiers into this no-man's land when the plague became too severe, in order to smoke out the robbers' nests. But even if they unearthed and burned down a few hiding places, and tortured the ones they caught miserably in order to scare off the others —it didn't help! Until the territory was granted to the Union and federal troops cleared the air of the riffraff, the "Neutral Zone" remained the domain of lawlessness.

What was even worse from the Spanish point of view than all the outrages and crimes committed by the band of robbers in No Man's Land was that whenever an attack was planned against Texas, the revolutionary leaders, pirate chiefs and buccaneer generals found here a recruiting ground that supplied them with the most daring troops, who could be used without hesitation for any purpose, as long as booty beckoned. There were many such attacks after Miguel Hidalgo unfurled the flag of revolt in Mexico and the Viceroy had to strip the province of troops in order to ward off the revolutionary movements in the central regions of New Spain.

A LONE STAR ARISES IN TEXAS

The Travails of Revolution

The Spanish colonial empire defied all the storms of world history for almost three and a half centuries. Certainly, the Spaniards were lucky that even in the times of their greatest national impotence none of their opponents found the courage or the elbow room to attack the Indies with full force. Yet their empire was spared even the gravest threat to its existence. The trials that it withstood were frequent and severe enough to prove how firm was its structure, in spite of all the cracks that appeared, and how little there could be in immediate danger of collapse. Even if one takes into account the mismanagement that set in under the weak Charles IV, who was dependent on all kinds of favorites, and which undid all the efforts of his capable predecessor, the Spanish colonial empire could still have had a long life.

However, at the beginning of the 19th century, events occurred in Europe that undermined and destroyed the supporting foundations of that structure. In the course of his game of world politics, for which he used the unconditional compliance of the Iberian state, Napoleon had found it necessary to intervene in the family quarrel of the Madrid royal house, to force both father and son, the incompetent Charles IV and the equally incompetent Ferdinand VII, to abdicate, elevating his own brother Joseph to the throne. This fall of the Bourbon dynasty in 1808—that was the axe that felled with one blow the tree of the Spanish Empire, which had already become rotten in places but was still green! For with this fall, Spanish rule in America lost the consecration of legitimacy without which it could not be sustained.

What kind of inner connections we are dealing with here

becomes clear if we consider what Spanish rule in the New World was actually like. It was a "Spanish" rule in a very special sense! The government of the colonial empire was almost exclusively in the hands of Spaniards native to Europe. For the Spaniard born in the colonies, the Creole, however pure in race and however noble in descent, was barred access to the high offices and dignities. He was just as much a mere subject as all the Indians, Negroes, and half-breeds of the most varied blood and degrees that the mixture of races in Latin America gave birth to. If, nevertheless, a Creole did reach a position of influence, it was rather an exception that proved the rule. In the stately line of viceroys who resided in Mexico, only three colonial Spaniards are to be found. Among the 754 men who occupied the highest posts in the administration and army of New Spain between 1535 and 1813, only eighteen Creoles are to be found!

It is easy to answer the question of why this was so. Right at the beginning, at the time of the conquista, the insubordination of individual conquistadors had alerted the Spanish kings to the danger of colonial secessions. Just as the formation of independent conquistador states was prevented by sending reliable officials, the colonies were kept firmly under the control of the mother country by a regiment of European crown representatives. The overseas possessions were not granted any autonomy at all, and economic development of any kind was not even tolerated. In order to ensure that the officials sent from the Pyrenees Peninsula to America did not become too intimate with the Creoles and consciously or unconsciously become spokesmen for their wishes, strict preventive measures were taken. The duration of colonial tenure was limited, frequent transfers to distant provinces were common, marriage to a colonial was not permitted, and the acquisition of landed property was forbidden. In short, the Spaniards who exercised rule in the colonies formed an upper class that stood out sharply from the mass of the rest of the population, including the Creole.

The question is, how did this small Spanish master caste remain unchallenged in the saddle for so long? How did it happen that the colonial peoples endured their yoke for so long? In the history of Mexico, there has been no lack of attempts at revolt by the Indian lower classes, and dissatisfaction with the Spanish regime was general. The Spaniards, whose military means of power were relatively small, could not have imposed their rule by force alone. Nevertheless, they were masterful at playing off one against the other and balancing the variously intertwined racial and class antagonisms that filled colonial life. The means later employed by the English to secure their rule in India are in many ways reminiscent of the methods wielded by the Spanish in the Americas long before them. "Divide and conquer!"—that was the principle by which action was taken. The men who divided and ruled in the Indies, however, did so in the name of a king by the grace of God. They derived their fullness of power directly from the rights of an anointed monarch; they possessed an authority which was not merely based on external pretensions, but was also fed from the mysterious sources of divine statutes. To revolt against this authority was more than merely a crime of majesty; it was—at least this is how the Catholic-prominent colonialist felt—religious sacrilege.

Such authority could not emanate from upstarts such as the Bonapartes. Joseph, the king by Napoleon's grace, was regarded by the Spaniards as a usurper and foreign ruler, and even worse, as an enemy of Catholicism. No sooner had he ascended the throne than the storm broke out against him. First, people in the mother country rose up in support of Ferdinand VII. This uprising was more than a struggle arising from a feeling of attachment to the rightful dynasty—it was a struggle of the newly awakened national consciousness, which rebelled against French foreign rule. Voices of freedom were raised in Spain in a way that had not been heard there before. Moreover, these voices resounded across the ocean and found a variety of echoes in the colonies. Yet those who listened more closely soon discovered that this echo had a sound that differed markedly from the national cry for freedom in the mother country.

Populist forces also initially stirred in Mexico under the patriotic slogan "For Ferdinand! Against the usurper!" Then, once the question of foreign domination was raised, thoughts took their own course. Was there only French foreign domination? Was there not also foreign rule in one's own country? What was the rule of the Spanish actually other than foreign rule? The political slogan changed. "Mexico to the Mexicans!" the Creoles started shouting, thinking of an empire in which Mexico stood on an equal footing with Spain, united by one and the same king, Ferdinand VII. And the stone, once dislodged began to roll onward, growing into an avalanche that thundered inexorably down the mountain!

The bell of the parish church in the small town of Dolores, in the province of Guanajuato, rang out at the midnight hour that marked the beginning of September 16, 1810. It was the priest Miguel Hidalgo who rang it to announce to his fellow conspirators that it was time to break loose and drive out what he claimed was a Bonaparte-friendly government in Mexico. "El grito de Dolores," Dolores' wake-up call, was the beginning of the Mexican Revolution. "Long live independence! Long live our Lady of Guadalupe!" shouted the men who set out at dawn to march toward Mexico. A banner with the image of Our Lady of Guadalupe, that Madonna with the dark face whom the Mexican Indians venerated as their special patron saint with the same masked dances they had once performed before the idol of the earth goddess Tomantzin, flew in front of the crowd. Indians flocked from near and far, their numbers grew and grew, and after only twelve days Hidalgo was followed by as many as eighty thousand men. Religious fanaticism mixed with terrible racial and class hatred. The Indians did not ask much about the political aims of the uprising. Our Lady cried out, the hour of vengeance had come! "Death to the Gachupines!" Death to the Spaniards! shrilled through the air, a cry that threatened the Creoles as much as the Spaniards. Robbing, burning, murdering, the hordes made their way through the country. Whoever had property to lose from the Creoles or mestizos, whoever was afraid of this volcanic eruption of Indian bitterness, sided with the Spaniards. But the troops that the Viceroy was able to send against Hidalgo's advancing army were too weak to break the force of this onslaught. In order to protect the capital, the Spaniards knew no other way than to bring the image of their patron saint, the gold and pearl laden Madonna de los Remidios, to the Cathedral of Mexico and to lay down the marshal's staff before it. And the miracle happened. The Spanish Madonna, appointed "General", was victorious over the Indian Madonna! In cruelly bloody battles Hidalgo's army was blown apart, the priest himself was captured on the run to the north and shot in Chihuahua. Nevertheless, even if the Spaniards hung Hidalgo's head in an iron cage on a building in Guanajuato as a warning to all who thought of rebelling against their rule, the "Grito de Dolores" could not be stifled. Other men jumped into the breach, reviving the freedom movement, and the Mexican Civil War, arguably one of the most horrific known to world history, continued.

Texas was not spared the pangs of revolution. When the uprising began, Hidalgo had sent one of his followers, Bernardo Gutiérrez, to Washington to seek the support and recognition of the Union government. The legation was unsuccessful, however, and Gutiérrez left for home without having achieved anything. There he came in contact with the American lieutenant Augustus Magee in Natchitotches, and soon the two agreed to make a joint incursion into Texas to help the Revolution prevail there as well. In doing so, Magee will certainly have had his ulterior motives. He had previously considered the possibility of winning Texas for the Union by a coup d'état, and it may have suited him just fine that the Mexican revolutionary now provided him with the pretext to carry out this plan. He handed in his resignation, beat the publicity drum, and organized the "Republican Army of the North" out of American adventurers, bandits of the "Neutral Zone," some Mexicans, and Cushatta Indians. How popular the idea of a draft to Texas was among Americans in Louisiana is evidenced by the fact that Magee was able to enlist close to eight hundred volunteers from the Union states.

The "Army of the North" crossed the border in the summer of 1812. In a short time, Nacogdoches was in their hands and that autumn began the advance on the Spanish settlements in western Texas. The Spaniards were fully aware of the seriousness of the situation. A force of such size as Magee commanded, with new Americans, Mexicans, and Indians pouring in daily, was a tremendous danger given the small military force in the country. Salcedo, the governor of Texas, mustered as many soldiers as he could raise from all the surrounding provinces. Despite his 1500 men, however, he was unable to prevent the revolutionary army from taking La Bahia. The Presidio was besieged by the Spaniards for four months in vain. When at last they retreated fatigued and discouraged to San Antonio, Gutiérrez — Magee had died in the meantime under mysterious circumstances — followed them on their heels and forced the surrender of the city in March 1813. Salcedo and his officers were granted pardon, and a captain named Delgado was ordered to take them to New Orleans. But no sooner were the prisoners out of the city than they were ambushed by the escorting party and barbarically massacred with knives. This act outraged the American participants of the march most intensely, for even if they were privateers, they had not lost their sense of fairness. How had it been possible to entrust the escorting of the Spanish officers to Delgado, whose father had been shot by Salcedo as a supporter of Hidalgo? When the assassin was brought before a field court, it was revealed that it was not only an act of private revenge, but that Gutiérrez himself had ordered the slaughter! As a result, a large number of the American volunteers turned their backs on the "Republican Army". The others deposed Gutiérrez and elected a new commander. However, internal strife damaged discipline, and when the revolutionaries — their numbers, including all the Indian allies, had by then risen to three thousand — tried to invade Mexico in the summer of 1813, they were ambushed. Except for 93 men who found their way back to Natchitotches, the "Army of the North" was hewn to pieces by the Spanish troops. The Viceroy could breathe a sigh of relief! The revolution in Texas—if the strange combination of Mexican "republicanism" and American freebooterism can be called a "revolution" at all —had been put down!

The victorious Spanish troops had a terrible time on their advance to East Texas. Wherever they got hold of a Mexican suspected of revolutionary sentiments, wherever they encountered an American who, given the ban on foreigners entering the country, could only have done so illegally, they made short work of him. A shot, a blow with the butt of a rifle, a rope on the nearest tree branch—such justice was quickly administered! In the city of San Antonio. Three hundred citizens were arrested and crammed so closely together in one room that when the doors were opened the next morning, eighteen were found to have suffocated. Nacogdoches, that Spanish settlement which then maintained the frontier guard, was almost depopulated. Of course, party passion never asked whether it was harmful to the national interest or not!

When the Spanish once again departed, they left Texas in a more pitiful state of defense than ever. It is only in this way that Galveston Bay could have become a haven for gangs of pirates who caused endless damage to Spanish shipping. And here begins the story of Jean Lafitte, the last great pirate of the Gulf of Mexico!

Jean Lafitte, the Buccaneer

Hidden among wild roses and tall grass, on Goose Bayou, twenty-five miles south of New Orleans in the Mississippi Delta, stands an iron cross eaten away by rust, and in front of it lie three dilapidated graves without inscriptions. It is said in Louisiana that the bones of Jean Lafitte, the famous and notorious pirate, are buried in one of them, those of Jonas Paul Jones, the admiral of the American Revolution, in the other, and those of Napoleon I in the third. Jean Lafitte, so the fantastic story goes, was a blood cousin of the Corsican, the illegitimate son of a brother of Jones and Jesse Corsica Bonaparte. Secretly the pirate had brought the body of his uncle, the American national hero, from France to the Mississippi, and some unknown person had been buried in the United States Academy at Annapolis. On January 18, 1819, Lafitte freed the emperor from captivity on St. Helena and left behind a double who played his role to the bitter end and whose mortal remains were later transferred to the Invalides in Paris. The real Napoleon, however, died during the voyage to America and was buried by his cousin on Goose Bayou.

Whoever wants to believe it, may do so! In any case, there is no evidence for these claims, which contradict everything that is known about the three personalities and their fates. Nevertheless, the legend is not entirely without historical background. In fact, in 1821, New Orleans was eager to equip an expedition to get Napoleon out of his island imprisonment. The plan for the daring enterprise originated with French Captain Bossiére, who had come to the Mississippi in a fast clipper ship. It was financed by Nicholas Girod, the rich mayor of the city, who even had a house prepared to receive the emperor. The coup was to be carried out by Dominique Youx, who had once been one of Lafitte's most capable sub-leaders and who was still believed to be capable of such a piratical feat, even though he had already found his way back into civilian life years before. Finally, everything was ready, the hour for the departure of the "Seraphine" was set — when three days before, the news of the death of the Corsican arrived...

There is no shortage of legends about Napoleon and no shortage of legends about Lafitte either. They were two men who, each in his own way, kept the world in suspense but it is much more difficult to distinguish truth from fiction in the stories about Lafitte. Reliable information about this romantic figure of American history is known only for the years between 1809 and 1821, and even then the news is scanty enough. In general, buccaneers are not in the habit of letting the public know too much about their activities. And Lafitte was a pirate. During his lifetime, however, it would have been a mistake to mention this to him, as it would have been badly received. He did not deny that wherever he could, he raided Spanish ships. But he claimed to have the right to do so, and referred to warrants of capture that had been granted to him by the revolutionary governments of the Spanish colonies that were rising up against their mother country. It was nothing but infamous slander, he declared, if he and his men were accused of raiding ships of other than Spanish nationality! Initially, they even believed him. At that time, no one in Louisiana had anything against "honorable" privateering! The most respected citizens of New Orleans were his friends, and when he appeared on the streets, in the coffee houses and wine bars or at the balls of the mulatto women, he was greeted with frank cordiality.

Thus, the question of whether Lafitte was a pirate or just a privateer remained open at this point — it was obvious that he was unabashedly violating the laws of the United States through all kinds of smuggling. Only the American authorities resented him for it, however. The people of

A LONE STAR ARISES IN TEXAS

Louisiana at that time still considered smuggling a good old custom, with which one could at least make up a little for the stupidity of the Yankee government in making imports more expensive through tariffs and damaging trade and commerce. Hadn't smuggling been rife during the decades when the country was first under French and then under Spanish rule? And hadn't the customs officials turned a blind eye to this with appropriate gratuities? It was difficult for the French and Spanish Creoles to understand why the Americans were so unenthusiastic about smuggling and they were only too happy to play a trick on them. When Lafitte sent out flyers in New Orleans saying that he would be auctioning off goods and Negro slaves on such and such a day at such and such an island in the water network of the Mississippi delta, he did not have to worry about being betrayed. Merchants and farmers turned out by the hundreds, and each auction went according to schedule. When the American governor demanded money and troops from the state parliament to finally root out Lafitte's nest of smugglers at Barataria Bay, one could be sure that the deputies would reject the requests. Firstly, they were pleased that they could annoy the governor and secondly, they were in favor of "cheap importation" for the sake of the common good, and thirdly, there were enough men of honor among them who earned considerable sums of money through business connections with Lafitte. Finally, when the governor offered a reward of 500 dollars for the capture of Lafitte, notices could soon be read in New Orleans in which Lafitte promised 1500 dollars for the capture of the governor. The whole city was deliciously amused by this impudence.

Jean Lafitte is believed to have been born in France around 1780. There are only unverifiable rumors about the first decades of his life. In 1809, he is found in New Orleans running a blacksmith shop with his brother Pierre but word had already spread around town that there was more to the Lafittes' workshop than just hardware. The brothers had good relations with the affable fishermen who came up from the coast with fish and oysters and were happy to broker all kinds of deals that the customs authorities didn't necessarily need to know about. If the supply was too scarce or the price too high on the slave market, one could turn with confidence to the Lafittes, who were able to help out with cheap, fresh imports from Africa—they had been strictly forbidden in the United States since 1808. When disputes broke out between the various smuggling groups, putting the business in jeopardy, Jean Lafitte took over the leadership himself. That was in the fall of 1810. With iron energy he created order. He established a fortified settlement on Grande Ile in Barataria Bay, and soon he was joined by hardy, sea-experienced pirates alongside the harmless fish smugglers who scoured the Gulf with ten or twelve ships. In the end, Lafitte was the leader of a motley band of a thousand men!

Jean Lafitte's "profession" was not outwardly apparent. An exceptionally handsome man, always well dressed, of impeccable manners, an amiable conversationalist and a brilliant conversationalist, in short, a gentleman from top to toe. No wonder that a lady of New Orleans society, who met him at a party, wrote: "I had heard that Mr. Lafitte did not care for women, which seemed strange to me, and I am convinced that those who told me so were misinformed. He is a tall man of exceptionally good appearance, dark and slender. His hands and feet are small, and his black eyes have a look that few women could resist..." But the men who met Lafitte—and there were many who sought him out at his home on Grande Ile—praised his hospitality, his generosity his helpfulness, reliability and loyalty. And yet this man was a buccaneer!

The governor of Louisiana saw an increasingly serious danger in Jean Lafitte and his men. If in the long run it was intolerable that the authority of the state was so brazenly disregarded, then at the moment when a new war with England broke out and the signs increased that a British attack on the Union would also take place from the Gulf Coast, the presence of a myriad of lawless people in the Mississippi Delta was bound to appear alarming. The number of troops that the federal government could detach to defend Louisiana was small enough in any case. What if, however, the pirates and smugglers of Barataría would turn to the service of the British and pilot English battalions to navigate the delta labyrinth?

On September 3, 1814, an English warship did indeed appear off Barataria Bay, and a white-flagged boat, manned by three British naval officers, headed for shore. Lafitte was not a little surprised when the gentlemen told him that they had come on behalf of the British supreme commander to negotiate with him about an alliance of his people with the English forces. They presented Lafitte with various official letters in which he was promised the rank of captain and far-reaching rewards. The double-cross that Lafitte now embarked upon would be worthy of any diplomat. With committal words that feigned a certain inclination to accept the offer, he asked the English for more time to think it over. At the same time, he informed the American governor of the events, sent him the English letters, and made himself available to him with all his crews to fight the English. The British felt the same way about Lafitte as they did about all the other Louisiana Creoles—

these people could not be stirred up against the Americans, because even if all those who had French or Spanish blood in their veins did not love the Yankees, they certainly hated the English. Lafitte, however, also wanted to take advantage of the situation, demanding from the American authorities what he urgently needed in return for his proposal—an amnesty. For he knew that the governor would not stand by and watch the goings-on in Barataria Bay for much longer, and the time seemed to have come when it would be wise to liquidate the company.

Everything, however, turned out quite differently at first. The governor doubted the authenticity of the documents presented to him and the honesty of Lafitte, and the commanders of the Union forces, probably for very selfish reasons, urged the clearing of Lafitte's hideout. Not wanting to put up a fight, the Baratarians retreated before the advancing American soldiers. The booty that fell into the hands of the Union generals on Grande Ile was worth close to 400,000 dollars, an enormous sum at the time! But even this ignominious raid did not tempt Lafitte to treason. From the hiding place in the river delta, where he had taken refuge with his men, he once again offered his good services to the governor of Louisiana without reservation. And this time he was successful! For in the meantime Andrew Jackson, the frontiersman and militia general of Tennessee, had taken command of New Orleans, and this man knew from his experiences with the rough backwoodsmen how to estimate such personalities as Lafitte. Without hesitation, he let him know that he was welcome to join him and his party at any time. The Barataria Bay pirates soon stood together with the Mississippi Valley frontiersmen in the quickly dug trenches, in the cover behind trees, hedges, and houses. When the British Redcoats advanced against New Orleans in closed formation, as if on a parade ground, on January 8, 1815, it became apparent how well the frontiersmen had learned to shoot and fence in the Indian battles and Lafitte's henchmen in the sea skirmishes. While the Americans suffered only eight killed and thirteen wounded, the defeated English left 2600 men on the battlefield. These losses were all the more tragic because peace had already been concluded in Ghent at Christmas and the battle had only taken place because news of the end of the war had not yet reached America!

All the pirates of Barataria Bay, in gratitude for their loyal and brave conduct, were granted full amnesty by a decree of President Madison on February 6, 1815. Some of Lafitte's comrades, among them Dominique Youx, who later participated in the rescue of Napoleon, gave up their pirate life. Jean Lafitte himself was different! Only for a short while was he able to endure the boredom of bourgeois society, then the adventurer in him rekindled, making him jump into the heart of open piracy. The United States soil was too hot for that, however. It was only a stone's throw from Barataria Bay to Galveston Bay on Spanish territory. He thought he would feel safe in Mexico, which was troubled by revolutionary turmoil.

For some time now, Galveston Bay had been the location of a band of pirates with whom Lafitte had maintained close ties. The leader, a certain Luis Aury, called himself the "fleet commander" of Morelos' revolutionary government, and from Galveston Island he had opened a privateer war against Spanish ships, while at the same time engaging in a vigorous smuggling of Negro slaves across the American frontier. In 1816, however, he joined a revolutionary fantasist, Xavier Mina, who came from Spain and thought he could overrun the conservative government in Mexico with two hundred men.

No sooner had Aury left Galveston Island than Lafitte took possession of it. Campeachy was the name of the new camp he set up. Once again, the old, wild life began. Again he had a strong pirate fleet at his disposal, again there were several thousand bandits who obeyed his orders, and the riches he gathered were perhaps even greater than before. Spanish commerce suffered terribly from his raids, and England also saw many a ship disappear never to be seen again in the nooks and crannies of Galveston and Matagorda Bay. Accomplices and traffickers shifted what Lafitte captured and looted across the Union border. Negro slaves he disposed of by live weight for a dollar a pound. The middlemen resold them at a good profit of five hundred dollars a head, and the Southern planters were glad to have such a cheap slave market.

Lafitte had given his subordinates strict instructions under no circumstances to tamper with American ships. He knew that enmity with the United States would be his undoing. Nevertheless, these orders were not consistently obeyed and the Union intervened! If Lafitte had succeeded the first time in appeasing the Yankees by harshly punishing the wrongdoers—the second time, an American brig appeared and gave him an ultimatum to vacate Campeachy. Lafitte obeyed without resistance. He did not even invoke the fact that he was, after all, in Spanish territory, and that the Americans could only expel him from Galveston Island in violation of international law. As if the Union would have cared about boundary lines and international law in such a case!

After the deadline had passed, Lafitte once again entertained the American naval officers on his ship like a grand seigneur, showing them all that he himself had destroyed, and after animated hours of social gathering, he escorted his guests off the ship. A young lieutenant wrote in his diary at the time, "We shook hands with the chivalrous buccaneer at parting with more affection than one would ever dare confess."

That night, Lafitte set fire to his camp on the Texas coast, and in the glow of the red flames, three sailors were seen gliding seaward into the deep darkness. That was in early 1821, and Jean Lafitte was never heard of again. Legend has it that he died of yellow fever in an Indian village in the Yucatan in 1826.

The Buccaneering Campaigns of James Long

The Union wanted Florida, but the Spanish were reluctant to give up their oldest province on North American soil. The peninsula was no longer of much use to them, but the Yankees' demand offended their pride. The government in Washington tried to negotiate amicably but Spain stuck to its "No!" The government in Washington put Madrid under diplomatic pressure but Spain continued to stubbornly refuse to give up Florida. Andrew Jackson, the Tennessee frontiersman, however, thought very little of negotiation and very much of action. One day he called together his militia, marched south, crossed the Spanish border in the midst of the deepest peace, and in a few weeks drove out the Presidio soldiers along with their Indian confederates. Fluttering over Florida now was the star-spangled banner! This private war, which Jackson had undertaken on his own, was a great coup! The statesmen in Washington assumed their most respectable countenances and solemnly declared that they had not the slightest knowledge of Jackson's action. The Spaniards had no need to see the twinkle in their eyes! However, to bring back the militia from Florida, to take back the Union flag, that was out of the question. Since Spain could not risk an armed conflict with the United States, it had no choice but to "voluntarily" sell Florida for a sum of five million dollars. In 1819, the treaty was drawn up that made the cession of the peninsula legally binding. Simultaneously, it also settled all boundary issues that were in dispute between Spain and the Union. Behold, now that they had Florida in their pocket, the Americans were willing to drop their claim to Texas and settle for a Louisiana that reached to the Sabine River! President Monroe, like so many American politicians, had never seriously believed in the legitimacy of the Texas claim and now gladly gave it up completely in order to come to a quick and smooth trade agreement over all points with Madrid.

The frontier population in the western states of the Union, however, disagreed strongly with their president. When the treaty provisions became known, a storm of indignation arose in those parts of the country. "Texas," wrote one of the frontier spokesmen, "is worth ten Floridas—it is larger, more fertile, and healthier than any State of the Union, and if it had been in our possession but twenty years it would be populous, prosperous, and powerful." Louisiana was too well acquainted with the advantages of the Spanish frontier province to judge it so disdainfully as did the statesmen in distant Washington. The pioneers had long had their eye on Texas, and they were now sorely disappointed that they should be forever forbidden access to the magnificent valleys and forests of the very tract of country between the Brazos and the Colorado.

The question is whether it was politically wise to forego Texas for the sake of Florida. Florida lies wedged between Georgia and Alabama, Henry Clay declared in a great opposition speech before the House of Representatives; it cannot escape the Union, but must fall to it all by itself in five or ten years. Texas, on the other hand, can slip away from the Americans. "Is it not as clear as day," Clay asked passionately, "that it is the will of Providence... that Texas, too, like the whole American continent, should be settled by Europeans? The only question is by what race it will be settled. If the land falls into our hands, it will be inhabited by free men who will bring with them our language, our laws, our liberties, who will erect temples on the prairies of Texas where God will be worshiped simply and piously.... But if Texas falls into other hands, it will possibly become the site of despotism, peopled by slaves subject to the base rule of the Inquisition and superstition."

That was speaking from the heart of the frontier! For nowhere was the belief in the cultural mission of Americanism stronger than on the "frontier". The Anglo-Saxon pioneer might live a life on the edge of the wilderness that was so primitive, so devoid of culture, so much a struggle for bare existence that nothing, nothing at all, remained of "Europe's whitewashed politeness" — but he never lost the old Puritan consciousness of being a citizen in "God's own country". Certainly, the naive arrogance with which the Americans considered themselves the first among all the peoples of the world, their constitution, their laws, their institutions the best possible, this arrogance was to a large extent a self-deception, which saved them the trouble of criticizing all kinds of questionable character traits of their own. Nevertheless, it was also, and especially on the frontier, the inner support that helped them endure all the hardships and deprivations, efforts and dangers, and was able to give meaning and consecration to even the most troublesome existence.

What could be more natural than for Louisiana to imitate the example set by Andrew Jackson in Florida and attempt to create a fait accompli in Texas by a private coup d'état? When citizens and farmers gathered in Natches, a town on the lower Mississippi River, to protest Madison's "unconstitutional" relinquishment of "American" land, the proposal was made to equip a free army and take Texas. The idea met with enthusiastic approval, and Dr. James Long, who had been a merchant in Natches for some years, was chosen to lead the platoon. James Long was then a 26 year old young man. He had studied medicine and had been a military surgeon, but for some reason had preferred to leave the army service and try his luck as a tradesman. He was married to a niece of General Wilkinson, the man who had been an accomplice of Aaron Burr, but who at the last moment had betrayed the enterprise and brought it down. It may be that these kinship ties had something to do with Long's Texas adventure.

In June 1819, James Long crossed the Mississippi with 75 men. Journeymen from the "Neutral Zone" joined his band, and soon a troop of three hundred men entered Nacogdoches. Immediately Texas was declared independent, a constitution was enacted, and a provisional government was formed, in which Bernardo Gutiérrez was also given a ministerial seat. Yes, even its own newspaper was founded, in which laws were published and "state lands" were offered for sale to immigrant settlers. All this meant drawing bills of exchange on a future that was still dark and uncertain. And since Long, too, realized that the "Republic of Texas" would be difficult to keep alive without a major military force, he set out to travel to Galveston to see Jean Lafitte and offer the pirate chief an alliance. But Lafitte had no use for political experimentation. He did not like to be disturbed in his "economic" undertakings and therefore refused to play the role of "Governor of Galveston" and to put part of his crew at the disposal of the "Republic of Texas" for warfare. James Long departed sorrowfully, and already on the way to Nacogdoches he heard that his presidential dream was over. Spanish troops had occupied the site, the army of the "Republic of Texas" was in captivity or had fled, and Texas was once again a Spanish province, as it had been a few weeks earlier. What else could "President" Long do than to flee as quickly as possible and seek safety on the other side of the Sabine River in American territory?

James Long was a man of hot-blooded temperament and the failure he had suffered made his blood boil, and he thought, "Now more than ever!" With some of his men who had rejoined him, he took up an observation post at Bolivar Point on Galveston Bay. Upon learning there that the Spanish troops had left following yet another thorough destruction of Nacogdoches, he hurried to New Orleans to gather, at his own expense, men and material for a new campaign of conquest into Texas. On this occasion he also became acquainted with two leaders of Mexican liberalism, and the three men agreed to work together to drive the Spaniards out of Texas under the green, white, and red tricolor of the Mexican independence movement. Shortly thereafter, events occurred in Mexico that made such an undertaking seem quite promising.

The political development of New Spain had taken a strange turn. When in 1814, after the fall of Napoleon, Ferdinand VII had again ascended the Spanish throne and established the old absolutist regime, the Spanish upper class of Mexico had plucked up new courage. In years of fighting, they had succeeded in crushing the revolution to such an extent that only an insignificant band of rebels in the barren mountainous regions south of the capital needed to be neutralized. Then, in 1820, the Spanish people in the mother country forced Ferdinand VII to restore the liberal constitution that they had given themselves in the times of need of the national struggle for freedom, but which had been lightly pushed aside by the returning monarch. This was now a new storm signal for the Spanish master caste in Mexico! Is this why it had put down with such infinite effort the forces that wanted to wrest sole rule from it by force, in order to now voluntarily grant them a right of political co-determination by the introduction of a liberal constitution? The officer corps and the aristocracy conspired together under the leadership of the bishops, and in these conventicles the plan was hatched to undertake a coup d'état themselves and to declare Mexico's independence in order to secure their own position of power. Agustín de Iturbide, a wealthy landowner who had distinguished himself in the Civil War struggles and was popular with the army, seemed the right man to carry out the conservative revolution. The unsuspecting viceroy was easily persuaded to give the colonel a larger number of troops to clear out the last rebels in the south. Instead of fighting the insurgents, however, Iturbide concluded an agreement with their leader Guerrero at Iguala on February 24, 1821 — the date the Mexican state considers to be its birth — in which they sought nothing less than to bring red and white, revolution and reaction, into harmony. The main points were: Independence of New Spain, guarantee of the Catholic religion, equality of all citizens of any race and establishment of a monarchy under a Bourbon prince. The nation jubilantly acceded to the "Liberator" and the officials loyal to the king soon had to abandon their attempts at resistance. In September, Iturbide moved into the capital to temporarily assume the regency. Mexico was from now on an independent state!

As soon as Iturbide's coup d'état and Iguala's agreement became known in Louisiana, James Long and his Mexican friends entered into Texas in support, as it was said, of the new independence movement. The Spanish troops posted in the province were royalist-minded and opposed the invaders. In October 1821, Long captured Old Fort La Bahia, but was forced to surrender with some of his men soon afterward. The governor of Texas sent the captured leaders of the buccaneering campaign to the capital to receive their due punishment from the Viceroy. By the time James Long was delivered in Mexico, there was no Viceroy, and instead of being punished, he was warmly received as a welcome confederate of the liberated New Spain. A few weeks later, the bullet of a Mexican sentry struck down the American adventurer. According to the story, this happened because a dispute arose over a misunderstanding and Long, in his agitation, hit the soldier. Yet there is another reading of this bloody event, and that is that the Anglo-Saxon had made himself suspicious to the Mexicans and that Iturbide himself or someone else ordered his assassination. Those were turbulent times in Mexico, and a human life was of little value....

James Long, believing in his lucky star, had left his wife and little daughter at Bolivar Point under the protection of twenty-five men when he set out in the summer of 1821 to drive the Spaniards out of West Texas. "Just wait here", he had said at parting, "in a few weeks I will be with you again!" But summer passed, autumn dawned, and Long was still not back. The privateers stole out of camp one by one, and when winter came, Jane Long found herself left alone with her child and a twelve-year-old Negro girl. She had taken it into her head to hold out there on Galveston Bay. She wanted her husband to find at least one faithful person when he returned! The last runaways had taken the remaining provisions with them. However, what was the point of being the wife of a "frontiersman", what was the point of having a rifle and a fishing rod! Jane Long bravely set about providing for the livelihood of her little flock. Unfortunately, the birds became more and more scarce, and a big fish snatched her fishing rod. The three solitary individuals lived on oysters for weeks. Then snow fell, and the white masses weighed down on the tent until it collapsed. Before it was possible to put it up again, Jane went into labor and gave birth to a second baby daughter. Would that the Indians did not come! Every morning, to frighten the savages, Jane fired a shot from the cannon that had been left in the camp. Then came the December day, however, when she saw a sailboat gliding along the bay. She waved and she called and the occupants of the boat became aware of the woman with the two children and the Negro girl, steered ashore and took the forlorn aboard. The schooner was named "Lively" and belonged to a man named Stephen Austin. The people it carried were American emigrants who wanted to move to the Brazos, where Austin intended to establish a colony with the permission of the Mexicans.

The era of privateer raids into Texas was over, and the age of Anglo-American settlement of the land was beginning. Jane Long, wife of the last American privateer, became one of the first American settlers. She lived through the "Americanization" of Texas, the fight for freedom, the Lone Star Republic, the War of Secession, and much more. At 83, she died in Richmond on the Brazos in 1880.

FIFTH CHAPTER

AMERICANIZATION

The governor in 1806 estimated the "white" population of Texas to be four thousand souls: San Antonio had about 2,000 and La Bahia 1,400 inhabitants; Nacogdoches may have had about 500 people. A century had now passed since the colonial government had decided to occupy the lands beyond the Rio Grande, and still Texas was a wilderness inhabited by savages with a few points of European settlement. Then again, the Spanish had made little effort to open up the country any further. It was too far from the colonial heartland to take advantage of its fertility. It was seen only as an outpost that had to be held to protect the Mexican silver mines, an outpost in which any enemy attacks could be intercepted.

One could tell how much Texas had been neglected in the last decades. The Creoles, Mestizos and other half-breeds lived pretty poorly in the three towns that were the only ones there. Their thatched mud huts were wretched and ugly, equipped only with the bare necessities and, like the people themselves, unspeakably dirty and unkempt. They grew only what they needed for their own sustenance, and raised some livestock to sell to the small garrisons. Further work did not seem to be worthwhile. Unfortunately, we don't really know whether it was just the lack of any drive and any trade that made these Mexicans live so dully and sluggishly, or whether it was also that tendency to *dolce farniente* that is in the blood of so many southerners. The Presidio soldiers were even more ragged than they had been at the time when the monks complained about them. Now the city council of San Antonio complained that they slaughtered the cattle in the pasture, stole the corn from the field, and committed the most manifold iniquities. Yet what were the poor fellows to do, when the provision sheds were increasingly empty and the pay was repeatedly not forthcoming! Only the houses and the lifestyles of the Spanish officers and officials were reminiscent of Europe. They tried to imitate the glamorous colonial social life of Mexico City, which they otherwise had to miss here in the wilderness, at least to some extent, with guest parties, balls, games of chance and levées.

Since Louisiana had become American, the Spanish began viewing the question of opening up Texas with different eyes. As long as it remained necessary to avert the threat of military attack, it might have been right to pursue a strategy of leaving the land wild and desolate. Now that Anglo-Saxon pioneers had penetrated the eastern Mississippi basin and frontiersmen were looking covetously to the unsettled ground beyond the Union frontier, the sparse development of the province was a downright danger. If Texas was to be protected from the approaching surge of the Anglo-American frontier, there was only one remedy and that was to raise a dam of living men. Yet where was Spain to get these people? Only a few of her former subjects from Louisiana — most of them were not native Spaniards, but French, English, Irish and even Americans

AMERICANIZATION

—had migrated to Texas. In the central provinces, few farmers were willing to settle in the Texas wildernesses. Not even the inmates of the Mexican prisons, which were truly anything but comfortable and healthy places to stay, could be persuaded to exchange their incarceration for freedom in Texas. The only ones who began to populate the Texas outskirts in larger numbers were the Indian tribes driven out by the Americans from their previous hunting grounds. However, as furiously as these Redskins hated the Yankees and were therefore most welcome to the Spaniards, they could not replace white colonists. The question was discussed in Mexico whether it would not be possible to recruit settlers for Texas in Europe but none of the many projects that came up were carried out, because the colonial government could not get beyond the ifs and buts. In the end, the only measure left was to once again order the provincial government to strictly close the borders of the country to all foreign immigrants. This looked fine on paper, but since the wildernesses were in reality impossible to control, there was nothing to stop American squatters from crossing the Red River and settling in north Texas. To make matters worse, the freebooters weren't going to ask whether or not they were forbidden to enter the land.

Then, one November day in the year 1820, a certain Moses Austin rode into San Antonio on a gray horse, accompanied by a negro slave, and asked the governor for an interview. In order that the Spanish official might know at once what he was about, he sent him a memorandum asking permission to settle three hundred respectable Union families in Texas. Upon hearing that Austin was from the States, however, the governor, without even looking at the papers submitted, issued a deportation order.

A LONE STAR ARISES IN TEXAS

These Americans had already caused so much trouble—one only had to think of James Long—that it was best to keep them at bay!

Moses Austin was very saddened when he was told to get out of San Antonio as soon as possible. He had made a long and arduous journey. Riding from the Missouri across the virgin forests to Texas was no child's play for a sixty-year-old but this colonization plan was his last lifeline. He had recently lost his entire fortune, and was fervently hoping to make some money again as a settlement entrepreneur. In his opinion, the deal would bring him about 12,000 dollars! Yet he was to leave again without any result. As old Moses strode discouraged through the plaza of San Antonio, someone called to him. Was it possible, Baron Bastrop, the old acquaintance from the good old days in Missouri, here in Texas? Moses Austin told Bastrop of his situation and his plan, and the baron promised to intercede for him with the governor, his friend. Three days later Austin was received in audience, and the Spanish official was now suddenly on fire for the settlement project and immediately forwarded it with a warm letter of endorsement to his superior in Monterey for approval.

Austin's case was, after all, quite special. A true Yankee by birth—his father's house was in Connecticut—Austin had gone to Philadelphia at a young age, when the westward migration began and all America was on the move. There he founded a trading company, and later he opened a branch of the business in Richmond, Virginia. Now, Moses was an enterprising man, lively, agile, always with his head full of plans, always bent on speculation, and so it was that he was soon found busily engaged on the frontier in West Virginia, exploiting lead mines and selling lands. One day, however, when he heard that there were silver mines in what was then still Spanish Missouri, he abandoned the lead mines and crossed the Mississippi into the wilderness. The Spanish governor had no objection to Americans coming into the country, provided they converted to Catholicism and swore an oath of allegiance to the King of Castile. As for Moses Austin, who thought that "Paris is well worth a mass"[3] he changed religion and nationality. In fact, he became a wealthy, if not a rich man. That was the time he met Baron Bastrop, a Dutch nobleman who had fled the Netherlands to escape the invading French Revolutionary Army and was trying to make himself useful to the Spanish in Louisiana as a soldier of fortune with all sorts of colonization attempts. When Louisiana became first French and then American at the turn of the century, Bastrop had moved to Texas while Austin continued to work his silver and lead mines in Missouri. This had gone well until a severe economic crisis broke out after the Union's second war against England in 1812/14, and Moses Austin, who had ventured too far with many a speculation, lost all his property. But since he was not at a loss for good ideas even in times of need, he had conceived the Texas plan.

He was still a Spaniard, he had told the Texas governor, and he really didn't want to know anything more about the Union. Besides, there were many men in Louisiana who, like him, longed to live under Spanish rule again. He could vouch for the honesty, the diligence and the loyalty of these people. Why would they deny him, who had so long been a respected Spanish subject in Missouri, settlement in Texas? These arguments did not fail to make an impression on either the governor at San Antonio or the

---

3 Paris vaut bien une messe (French, "Paris is well worth a mass"), an expression of King Henry IV of France when he converted to Catholicism (1593).

commander general at Monterey. What harm was there, these officials might say to themselves, in giving it a try once! Three hundred families—that was not much, after all. If they did well, it was a gain for Texas. If difficulties arose, it was still possible to expel them. In short, the Yankee Spaniard's request was granted.

Moses Austin had not wanted to wait for the general commander's answer in San Antonio. He had ridden away in good cheer, certain that a new future lay ahead of him. As it turned out, however, the old man was no longer up to the rigors of the journey. When he arrived home, he became seriously ill, and not long afterward he died. But the news that his petition had been finally approved reached him before his death, and as the only legacy he had to leave, he laid the execution of the colonization plan in the hands of his son Stephen.

Open Borders

The Americanization of Texas began on the day Stephen Austin accepted his father's bequest. At first, there was only talk of settling three hundred Anglo-Saxon families. Yet it was not to stop there. Mexico declared its independence, and new men with new political views came to the helm in New Spain. Freedom, that was the slogan now, freedom in all areas! Away with those restrictions with which the mother country had gagged its colonies! Freedom of trade, freedom of the economy, but also freedom of immigration! The Mexican state had enough land. Its domain extended from the Panamanian border up to San Francisco and eastward far into the North American continent. After Russia and China, it was the third largest empire in the world! Only the people were missing to settle these huge amounts of land. Yes, the Spaniards, they had been concerned about the security of their overseas possessions and had had to keep the borders of their colonies closed to any foreigner! What, however, did the great, strong, free Mexican nation have to fear from the foreigners? Could she not open wide the gates of her house and invite anyone to enter who wished to acquire citizenship with her? As is always the case when a people throws off the chains that have hitherto bound it, there prevailed in Mexico at that time an excess of pride and self-confidence that lacked any counterweight of sober forethought. It was particularly disastrous that the Mexicans had the example of their North American neighbor, the Union, before their eyes. Tens of thousands of immigrants from all over the world were settling annually in the United States, and the vast "melting pot" of the frontier was remelting them all into Americans. So why shouldn't what succeeded in the Union succeed in Mexico?

One thing the Mexicans did not intend to imitate, however, was the granting of religious freedom! Mexico was a Catholic country, and whoever wanted to settle in Mexico had to be or become a Catholic! The unity of religion seemed to be the best guarantor of the unity of the nation. For centuries, Catholicism had proven its soul-forming power in New Spain. Even more than political power, it had been the cement that held together the tense mixture of races and classes. And the Mexicans were firmly convinced that with the help of the Catholic Church they would succeed in *Hispanicizing* the Anglo-Saxon immigrants as well.

The attempt of the Spanish upper classes to protect their rule from the threat of being undermined by a liberal constitution through secession from the mother country soon failed. After only a few months of reign, Iturbide found himself in such domestic political straits that he gave in to the demands of the army and sought to lend his authority new luster by accepting the imperial dignity. The parliament, which despite all the electoral machinations was not very compliant, was dissolved, and Iturbide continued to rule under a purely military dictatorship. When Emperor Augustine I ran out of money, however, the army's allegiance quickly came to an end. The call of a young officer, the ambitious and unscrupulous Santa Anna, was enough to cause the imperial regiments to go over to the opposite party with flying colors. After nine months of imperial rule, Iturbide declared his resignation in February 1823. Mexico became a republic.

Again, the example of the United States proved to be disastrous. For centuries, New Spain had been administered in a strictly centralized manner. Now, however, the provinces were given independent sovereign rights, and a unitary state was turned into a federal state. Texas, coupled with Coahuila, became one of the constituent states in this artificially constructed political structure. A people undertook to govern itself with the most complicated constitution that could exist, although it had hitherto known limited self-government only in the cities and had otherwise been systematically kept away from any participation in the affairs of state. Politically inexperienced, internally divided, torn by class differences, hostile because of racial antagonisms—the Mexican nation had to go through a hard school of life before it began to realize what it took to master its internal problems!

For the time being, as mentioned above, all parties were in favor of the opening of the borders and the settlement of foreign colonists. A settlement law was already as good as ready under Iturbide, and only the fall of the emperor prevented it from coming into force. It was later adopted almost verbatim by the Republic in 1824. Mexico was more generous than the Union in that it did not sell the state lands, but instead gave them away! Every family man who wanted to settle in Texas received a piece of land approaching 6700 acres in size! In exchange, he had to pay all kinds of fees to the state, survey agency, and so on, amounting to about $200, a sum that could be paid off in installments spread over four to six years. However, in order to speed up the settlement and make the work easier for the state, large areas were given as "grants" to settlement entrepreneurs, so-called *empresarios*, who had to undertake to settle a certain number of families—100, 200, 400 or even 800, depending on the case—there within six years. If the empresarios fulfilled their contractual obligations punctually, they received 35,000 acres of land for every hundred families, up to a maximum of 280,000 *morgen* (one morgen is approx. 1½ acres), in return for their efforts. This may seem like a tremendous amount of money. But how difficult it was to fulfill an empresario contract is evident from the fact that, except for Stephen Austin, only one of the other settlement contractors managed to do it. Then again, what was such a wilderness latifundia worth while the Texas state still had soil in abundance to give away!

Texas thus opened its doors to Anglo-Saxon immigration! Even in normal times, the American pioneers, who were on a constant, restless hunt for the best arable land, would have listened to such a call. How much stronger an echo it must have aroused now, when times in the United States were anything but normal, when there was real need on the frontier! No, the American frontier was no longer the paradise for the land-hungry settler that it had been before! The severe economic depression that had long weighed on the Union had escalated into a panic-stricken convulsion in 1819, and the newly developed settlements in what is now called the "Midwest," which still had little resilience, had been hit especially hard. The farmers groaned under the pressure of debt, a large proportion of them were completely ruined, the bailiff went from door to door and even the resilient optimism of the trappers and squatters were sounding more subdued.

To make matters worse, in 1820 the federal government enacted new land and banking laws that did not take into account the special circumstances of the frontier. Previously, the authorities had charged two dollars per morgen for the sale of federal lands. But the buyer had not had to put the sum on the table all at once, but could pay it off in four annual installments. Then it had been possible for anyone, even if he had only modest means, to purchase a piece of wilderness to clear and cultivate. If he had the necessary money on the due date of the next installment—well! If he was unable to pay, he had two options. Either he sold his farm and moved further west to start over, or he borrowed the amount from one of the frontier banks that sprang up like mushrooms and were very generous in their lending practices. Because these "wildcat banks", as they were called, had the right to print notes, they could create money in a very simple way. For years, the greenbacks, the dollar bills of the private banks with the green back, had financed a tremendous land speculation, which had contributed to plunging the Union into economic crisis. In itself, it was only right that the new banking law deprived the "wildcat banks" of the right to issue notes. But unsound as these banks were, they soon began an endless series of collapses, with the result that there was no more money at all on the frontier, which had hitherto been abundantly supplied with means of payment. On top of this came the new land law, which reduced the price of clearing land to one and a quarter dollars, but demanded immediate cash payment! The question arose as to where the frontier was going to get this cash. How was the farmer, driven from his home and farm by the Depression, to get a new homestead? The American frontier was beginning to feel the horrors of deflation with all its acuteness, and those who know how to read figures will understand what it meant that the sale of Federal lands fell from over five million acres in 1819 to three-quarters of a million acres in 1821!

Such was the situation in the west of the Union when, in the summer of 1821, Stephen Austin appeared in the frontier newspapers calling for emigration to Texas. Word soon spread that this Austin was not one of the speculative project makers so often at play on the frontier, but a serious, capable young man, well acquainted with frontier work and life. Austin's advertising letters made all the more lasting impression because they not only told of a most fertile country with a mild southern climate, but also offered the acre at the amazingly low price of twelve and one-half cents. This seemed like good news to many of the destitute, land-seeking farmers. Nationally rootless as they were, they bore no misgivings about going abroad, which promised the cheap clearing ground that the United States was depriving them of. Inquiry after inquiry was received by Austin, asking for more information about settlement. However, many applicants immediately lost interest when they heard that immigration to Texas meant renouncing all the political and religious freedoms they had enjoyed in the Union, that those who became Spanish citizens would have to submit to an authoritarian regiment, and that sooner or later they would have to convert to the Catholic state religion. But there were enough others to whom democracy and Protestantism did not mean much, provided that they could only make their economic living.

Even if most of the emigrants did not immediately decide to go, and it was initially only a small band that Stephen Austin led to the Brazos and the Colorado in 1821 — behind this vanguard a whole army was waiting to conquer the wilderness of Texas with axe and plow. From 1825, when Austin had overcome the initial difficulties and favorable reports of his enterprise began to arrive in the Union, this army of settlers began to move. The number of foreign colonists in Texas gradually grew to 30000, and before Mexico knew it, Texas was over-freighted, "Americanized". And then came the time when Texas broke away from Mexico politically as well! There is more than one example in the history of the United States of how the economic expansion of the Anglo-Saxon settlers gave direction to the political expansion of the Union, how it began with the clearing of the wilderness and ended with the unfurling of the Star Spangled Banner. The course of events in Texas during the years from 1821 to 1836 is one of these.

Stephen Austin, the "Father of Texas"

"The successful military leader is admired and acclaimed, and monuments immortalize his fame. But like the corn and cotton which he makes grow where they never grew before, the pioneer of the wilderness receives no attention.... Neither thousands slain nor smoking cities testify to the service he renders to mankind, and in the eyes of most he exists only to blaze the trail for others." So wrote Stephen Austin, one of the noblest figures known to Texas history, with grim humor in a reflective hour in 1831.

He has also not escaped the fate of the pioneer, whose work is insufficiently appreciated. Although he stands tall above the mass of all those trappers and squatters, farmers and traders who pushed the "frontier" of Anglo-American settlement westward in the 19th century, his name is little known even in the United States. Only his closer compatriots know what they owe to this man, and aptly they call him, whose striving was directed solely "to redeem Texas from the wilderness", the "Father of Texas".

The image of a "leather stocking", who went alone with rifle and axe into the untrodden Indian land, may seem more romantic than the image of this colonizer, who planted thousands of farmers in a foreign state. Yet, if one researches the sources and biographies, a life unfolds that is absolutely fascinating. It is filled to the brim with work, with the many and varied tasks required to build up and manage a colony—advising and instructing the settlers, distributing and surveying the land, organizing and administering the community, negotiating with the government agencies in Mexico and with the local authorities in San Antonio, drafting petitions and memoranda, and dealing with a correspondence the volume of which can only be imagined by picking up the several thousand printed pages of the papers he left behind. At the same time, however, a personality is revealed who, with a truly statesmanlike talent, steered the settlement enterprise through the manifold dangers that arose from the lurking distrust that the Mexicans, despite their willingness to pursue a liberal immigration policy, harbored against everything that came from the Union states. Without Austin, the Anglo-Saxon immigrants might very soon have been driven out of the Mexican border province, and who knows what the history of Texas and the North American Southwest might otherwise have been.

The task Austin had to solve was by no means easy. Already the trust of the settlers did not fall to him effortlessly, but had to be won laboriously. It would never have been given to him if he had abused his position of power in the slightest way as an entrepreneur and in the first years also as the sole administrative officer, militia commander and judge of the colony. There was no lack of misunderstanding on the part of the settlers against him. Austin held to tight discipline and made his decisions unflinchingly, even if they earned him personal enmity. But he answered openly to everyone about his doings, gave clear, factual reasons for his actions, and in the end even the last colonist saw that nothing was further from this man's mind than greed for gain and domination, and that he meant it sincerely when he said: "I feel the same sympathy for the welfare of my settlers as I feel for that of my own family—and really, I regard them as one big family for which I have to care."

It remains nevertheless doubtful whether Stephen Austin could have become the avowed leader of his rednecks if he had not himself been a son of the rednecks. The people of the American frontier were a special breed—rough and tough, stubborn and self-willed, sometimes hard-working and sometimes whipped up by passions, sometimes childlike and gullible and sometimes malicious and mistrustful. Whoever wished to direct and guide them had to have grown up among them like Austin, who, born in 1793 in a remote district of West Virginia, had spent his youth beyond the Mississippi on the edge of civilization and, after his college years in New England and Tennessee, had run his father's mines in Missouri and later a farm in Arkansas. Austin's own nature, however, betrayed little of his redneck origins. Even with his diminutive stature, his fine-cut face, the high forehead more befitting a scholar, he stood out strangely from his coarse-boned surroundings. Many a pioneer of true grit felt that the keen logic, the chastened temper, the diplomatic smoothness were "Jesuitical", and it was probably said that the obligingness and suppleness of the Canadian coureurs, who still sat in Missouri from the French days, and with whom Austin had been much associated as a boy and man, had rubbed off strongly on him. Whoever senses behind all these qualities the shyly concealed warmth of feeling and enthusiasm, the simple willingness to make sacrifices and fairness, whoever recognizes his tenacious determination and his sober sense of reality, will see in him a representative of the best Anglo-Saxon blood.

Stephen Austin had carefully chosen the most fertile areas of Texas, the lands between the Brazos and the Colorado, for his colony when he came to San Antonio in the fall of 1821 to introduce himself to the Spanish governor as the son and legal successor of old Moses and to discuss with him the details of the settlement. Then he had hurried to New Orleans, where he made the first contracts with immigrants and equipped that schooner "Lively" with food and farming implements, which later rescued the abandoned Jane Long with her children at Galveston Bay. When he returned to Texas in December, he already found the first settlers, and in the spring of 1822 the young community already numbered one hundred and fifty people, who, closely packed together because of the Indian danger, began to break up the virgin soil. Then came the setbacks!

A LONE STAR ARISES IN TEXAS

The Texas coast was so monotonous that the captain of the "Lively" accidentally landed the immigrants at the mouth of the Brazos instead of the Colorado. The merchandise had to be left behind by the inland settlers and was stolen by the Karánkawan. On her second voyage, the Lively was shipwrecked, and again an entire cargo was lost. These were nasty financial losses for Austin! Worse, however, was that the new Mexican provincial officials, who had taken the place of the Spanish ones, did not recognize the settlement agreement and declared the establishment of the colony illegal. Thus the whole enterprise was in jeopardy and, however difficult it was for Austin to leave the young settlement that so desperately needed his guidance and care, he had to decide, willy-nilly, to go to Mexico to persuade the new Mexican government to recognize the treaty his father had made with the Spanish authorities.

Traveling from San Antonio to the capital was a risky business. The roads ran for hundreds of miles through unsettled territory and were made unsafe by Indians and bandits. Stephen Austin had barely left Texas when he was harassed by a band of Comanches. The encounter went well, but one of the Redskins stole Austin's Spanish grammar book (the empresario did not know a word of Spanish at that time and wanted to acquire his first knowledge in the saddle), and when after a few weeks the book turned up among the natives on the Red River and got into American hands, the rumor spread in Missouri that Austin had been murdered by savages. In the meantime, however, the dead man had reached Mexico and had already made all kinds of efforts to make his case heard. That was easier said than done! For in Mexico all people were highly agitated, and Austin himself became an eyewitness of the coup d'état that elevated Iturbide to emperor.

AMERICANIZATION

The American was certainly well received everywhere, and the leading men of the Mexican state showed understanding and sympathy for his wishes. But Stephen Austin was not concerned with private expressions of opinion. What he needed was an official confirmation of his "grant". How indeed would it be possible to obtain it, since the Mexicans had so many more important and urgent matters to attend to? With fine tact and infinite tenacity, Austin began to work the governing authorities. If one path was blocked to him, he took another. One had to be agile, and one had to have the nerve to wait! These months in Mexico were a time of intense political education for Austin, and in them he learned more than how to speak Spanish fluently—he learned the art of dealing with Mexican politicians and Mexican authorities!

Nevertheless, his patience was sorely tried. The parliament had almost been about to approve his request, when it was disbanded by the emperor Iturbide. When the imperial government had at last given its approval, Augustine I abdicated a few weeks later, and all his laws and decrees were declared invalid. At last, in April 1823, the Republican Federal Parliament finally confirmed the "Grant". It was an exceptional law in favor of Austin. The other empresarios who were campaigning in Mexico were told to wait until a general settlement law had been enacted and the Texas state had made its supplementary special provisions. Can there be any better proof of the strong, trustworthy impression Stephen Austin had made on the Mexican statesmen than the fact that a special arrangement was made with him?

Austin had been away for more than a year when he arrived back in Texas. He found the settlers deeply discouraged, indeed, a number of them had returned to the States, where they told so many bad tales about the enterprise that many a willing emigrant was deterred and the influx into Texas was noticeably stalled for some time. The strong hand that should not be lacking when a colony is founded was missing. Some settlers had concluded from Austin's long absence that a new grant could no longer be expected, that the colony would sooner or later be banned, and that any further cultivation work would therefore be pointless. They had suffered much from the thievery and raids of the Karánkawan and Tonkawan, and the first harvest had been all but destroyed by a nasty drought. But now Austin was back and could comfort and cheer, advise and help! He was able to prove to the colonists in black and white that their fears about the imminent end of the settlement were groundless. And those who did not want to believe him could have it confirmed by Baron Bastrop, who had been commissioned by the Mexican authorities to survey the land and issue the title deeds.

The settlers now began anew to plow up the millennia-old turf of the prairies with fresh courage, transforming the wilderness into fertile farmland. Austin's colonists were industrious and there was no denying it! But the empresario also saw to it that there was nothing reprehensible in the character of the settlers he accepted, that each was "a moral and industrious man, and entirely free from the vice of drunkenness." Those who did not meet these requirements were ruthlessly expelled from the colony. Austin did the same with the first three hundred families when he distributed the four additional "grants" that were awarded to him from 1825 to 1831 for another 1700 families. It was no exaggeration when he proudly declared that, all things considered, the people he had brought to Texas were of a better disposition than those on any other frontier in America.

AMERICANIZATION

This did not mean that Austin's colonists were angels! Oh no, they were human beings with all too human shortcomings, they were American frontiersmen who thought that freedom was synonymous with unruliness and obstinacy at any price! "It is innate in Americans," Austin complains in a letter, "that they resent and revile a man who is working for the public good, whether he deserves it or not. I am dealing here with a motley crowd, gathered from all points of the compass. They are strangers to each other, and they are strangers to me, knowing neither the laws nor the language of the land. They come here with all the notions of the American, expecting to be shown the laws by which they are governed, and believing they can readily understand them. Moreover, many, very many, are licentious, insubordinate frontiersmen! By the time they arrive here, the worst of all human passions, greed, has burned to boiling point and is the vanguard in its attacks against me. Jealousy and envy advance from the flanks, and malice lurks in the background, ready to intervene at any favorable opportunity. If I could show them a law that says plainly this is how much land you are to get and no more, if I could put a book in their hands in which the laws to which they are subject are printed, I would have no trouble."

That was the point—in the special law for Austin's first colony, the immigrants were granted a different amount of land than in the general settlement law, a distinction was made between farmland and pastureland, between families and individual settlers. Moreover, the Mexican law codes were written in Spanish, and except for Austin, no one in the colony understood the foreign language. So the settlers had to rely on Austin's translations, and immediately suspicion arose as to whether the empresario was translating correctly, whether he was not changing the law in his favor. Most Mexican laws, however, had no validity at all for the colony! Austin had been expressly granted the right to administer his settlement as he saw fit until it was on a firm footing. To find a way out of the awkward situation, Austin sat down and drafted regulations specifically tailored to the circumstances of his colony, which remained the settlers' civil and criminal code until 1828, when the burden of sole responsibility was lifted from him and a proper Mexican administration was established. Capital offenses, however, had to be reported to the authorities in Monterey. The lesser offenses, however—and among them fell gambling, profane swearing, and drunkenness—could be adjudicated by Austin and the settler-elected district judges, the "alcaldes". In addition to fines, the punishment was expulsion from the colony. Imprisonment was not known, since there was no prison. This was not necessary, as Austin's selection process prevented criminal elements from establishing themselves in the settlement right from the start.

Once the initial difficulties were overcome and the settlers began to realize that no right had been robbed or diminished, the colonization work went quietly on its way, thanks to Austin's firm, purposeful leadership. The workload and worries of the "empresario" did not diminish because of this! Quite apart from the fact that the development of new "grants" always presented him with new tasks—he had become the confidant of all Anglo-Saxon Texans to the same extent that he was the confidant of the Mexican government. Without having pushed himself forward, only thanks to his personality and performance, he was considered "the" representative of the foreign immigrants in Texas. To him the colonists turned for advice as did the Mexican authorities. It was he who had to negotiate, to represent and to solve all the difficult and delicate political and economic questions. He had truly become the "Father of Texas". He devoted himself to this work with such dedication and tirelessness that his relatives admonished him to take more care of himself and to look after his health. Austin wanted to know nothing of such admonitions! The colonization of Texas had become his mission in life. What had once determined him to start the settlement enterprise, the hope of profit, had long since ceased to play a role in his life. The Mexican authorities had forbidden him to collect the twelve and a half cents per acre from the settlers, which he had demanded in order to be able to use them to pay for his own work in addition to the various fees. He had to be content with the land that was his empresario's grant. Nothing was to be gained from the sale of these wildernesses! Austin was happy if he earned enough to pay off the debts that still weighed on him from the time when he had managed his father's lead mines in Missouri.

He once wrote to his sister in later years, "I labored with faithful intentions, and as disinterested views of general good as circumstances and my capacity permitted... For the first time Ambition kindled its fires in my breast, but I think I can with truth say that the flame was a mild and gentle one, consisting more of the wish to build up the fortunes and happiness of others and to realize my dreams of good will to my fellow men than of the overbearing spirit of military fame or domineering power. My ambition was to redeem this fine country — our glorious Texas — and convert it into a home for the unfortunate, a refuge from poverty, an asylum for the sufferers from selfish avarice.

"Here the hand of nature had spread her bounties with such profusion that the most indigent, with moderate industry, could make a support. The poor, but honest, man's cottage would not be looked down upon with contempt from the lofty attics of the lordly palace, for in that particular there would be perfect equality." Another letter says: "If you come here you will find me living in a log cabin—a bachelor's life—poor as to active means, no comforts around me, rather soured with the world, laboriously engaged to serve my settlers, who do not thank me for the care and labor they cost me. When I began this enterprise my ambition was to succeed in forming a flourishing settlement of North Americans, and I sacrificed pecuniary considerations to that object. I shall succeed fully as to the main object and benefit a great many, but no great pecuniary benefit will result to me." Yet Austin also did not want—if only to set an example for his colonists—to live in prosperity. When his mother intended to join him in Texas (she died before that plan could be realized), he wrote to her, "I wish everything in our home to be plain and simple, much like our neighbors. Here in this country we are all poor and therefore all equal, and as long as this is so we shall all keep good, friendly neighborly relations, and our industriousness will soon overcome our poverty, if we know how to economize properly. In the position I occupy here, everything that any of my family members do is closely watched, and we must be kind to everyone, whoever he may be, so as not to offend anyone. The only distinction that may exist here is between the good and the bad, and we must emphatically and firmly make that distinction."

Even a man as clever as Stephen Austin was found it difficult to find the right political path with the perpetual revolution prevailing in Mexico. He was most careful not to get his settlers caught between the millstones of Mexican party infighting. He feared, not without reason, that if the American immigrants intervened in the domestic strife of their host people and took a one-sided stand, they would eventually incur the hatred of the entire Mexican nation. In his opinion, the best thing to do was to make as little fuss as possible about the colony, to let Texas flourish in secret. If there were questions to be settled with the Mexican authorities, he proceeded carefully and cautiously, avoiding every impatient word that offended the national sensitivities of the Mexicans, and masterfully he knew how to present the special interests of his settlers as the total interests of the Mexican people. By his manner he achieved that the leading men in Mexico heeded his proposals and many influential personalities became his friends, on whom he could count when it was necessary.

Austin was only able to maintain his course of calm and quiet and ensure undisturbed development for his settlement work until about 1830. Then came the years when the Mexicans began to distrust the political reliability of the Anglo-American Texans and to counteract the threatening alienation of their northern province with harsh measures, when the colonists resisted the restriction of their liberties and finally raised the flag of revolution. For a long time Austin continued to hope for a peaceful resolution of the tensions, and only reluctantly did he abandon his loyal attitude toward Mexico. Other men, nationalist zealots, hotheads, and daredevils who had labeled him a soft-spoken man, began to raise their voices and dispute his leadership position. When the situation had become so acute that it could only be a question of bending or breaking, it was Austin again who had the decision in his hands and, for the sake of the future of his work, gave the signal for armed resistance. Whether he was offended by the fact that after the victory the Texan people did not elect him, the pioneer, but Sam Houston, the army commander, as president of the newly founded republic we do not know for sure. Hardly though! His pipe dream of settling Texas with Anglo-Saxon frontiersmen had come true. The child he had taught to walk had become independent. For a few more months he served the young republic as secretary of state for foreign affairs. On December 29, 1836, he died, just over 43 years old.

One of his last letters states, "The flourishing of Texas has been the goal of my work, the content of my life—it has taken the form for me of a religion that guides my thoughts and actions." To that religion, Stephen Austin made many sacrifices. From the day he came to Texas, he was caught up in a whirl of the most difficult and grueling public business that would not let him go—and from which he did not escape, even if now and then the longing for the idyll of a simple farm life stirred him. He neglected his own affairs because of all this work, he renounced marriage and the building of a homestead and he lost his health. His reward was that in October 1836 he had to lament, "I have not a house, not a roof in all Texas that I can call my own. The only one I had burned down at San Felipe during the last invasion of the enemy.... I have no farm, no cotton plantation, no income, no money, no comforts. I have spent the prime of my life and worn out my constitution in trying to colonize this country. Many persons boast of their 300 and 400 leagues of land acquired by speculation without personal labor or the sacrifice of years or even days, I shall be content to save twenty leagues or about ninety thousand acres, acquired very hard and very dear indeed. All my wealth is prospective and contingent upon the events of the future, what I have been able from time to time to realize in active means, has gone as fast as realized, and much faster (for I am still in debt for the expenses of my trip to Mexico in 1833-34 and 35) where my health and strength and time have gone, which is in the service of Texas and I am therefore not ashamed of my present poverty." Stephen Austin did not write all this to boast of it but at one time he felt it necessary to tell the forgetful what sacrifices he had made for Texas, because even those who do not expect thanks find ingratitude hard to bear. Sometimes it made Austin bitter to be only the pioneer paving the way for others. Time and again, however, he was carried away by his life for Texas, "my glorious Texas," a life full of restlessness and toil, which he loved because it meant to him the development and fulfillment of his personality.

Mexican Suspicion

The "Americanization" of Texas was by no means the result of a deliberately planned, finely contrived game of intrigue on the part of the Union, as has also already been stated, but was the result of a historical development which was essentially due to the inability of Mexico to assimilate the immigrant Anglo-Saxon element. That Mexico failed to "Hispanize" the American settlers in Texas is no doubt partly due to the fact that it was then wracked by party turmoil and that the number of colonists swelled too much in too short a time. Still, was the task for the Mexicans to be solved at all? It is obvious how they lacked psychological understanding of the peculiarities of the foreign immigrants and how they made one mistake after another in their treatment. Excluded themselves from the political leadership of their country until recently, they did not possess the inner independence to guide the Anglo-Saxon settlers with a light hand. But probably the Mexicans' failure had deeper causes. The Mexican nation was rooted in the older, more conservative of the two cultural worlds that collided in Texas, and of which the younger, active world of Americanism proved the more superior.

Stephen Austin came to Texas in 1821 without the slightest political ulterior motive from the start. His only concern was to create a new existence for himself and his countrymen. He no longer felt bound by anything to his former home, the Union, and he honestly intended to serve his adopted country loyally. His attachment to Mexico was all the more genuine because he lacked altogether that Yankee pride which holds Americanism to be the ultimate, and on his journey to the capital he had gained a great respect for the Mexican nation. Incessantly reminding his settlers of the debt of gratitude they owed to their host nation, he exhorted them to fulfill their civic duties to the last, especially in difficult situations. In short, he was sincere in his efforts to grow into the Mexican state with his settlement work.

Now if Austin's authority was sufficient to induce the colonists in Texas to maintain strict neutrality in the partisan struggles of the Mexicans and to avoid anything that might have drawn disagreeable attention to them, he failed to transfer to them the same affection for the Mexican people that he himself felt. The simple "frontiersman" was too "American" not to be haughty, and what Mexicans he met were the old-established Creoles and half-breeds who lived dull and humdrum lives. No wonder the industrious, upwardly mobile Anglo-Saxon settler despised them abysmally! And he transferred this contempt to everything Mexican. Even before the first friction with the Mexican state authorities, the American colonists were in an inner defensive position against their host people, and even if they were initially prepared to give to the state what was the state's—they refused to become "Mexican" beyond that, which in their opinion meant descending the ladder of civilization.

The immigrants in Texas were left to fend for themselves for a long time. The rapidly changing Mexican governments had more pressing concerns than what was going on in the distant northern province, especially since there was no immediate reason to do so, as the colonists went about their work quietly and peacefully. Nothing was even done about the religious question, the importance of which the Mexicans had so often emphasized. Stephen Austin, who did not want to miss the moral strengthening influence of spiritual care on his settlers, had already asked in vain for the dispatch of an English-speaking priest in 1823. The colonists themselves were undoubtedly quite pleased that they were not bothered by any Catholic priests. They were almost all Protestants, though not very zealous for the faith, as is evident from the fact that they could very well endure many years without a priest or a church service. But the Puritan prejudice against everything "Roman" was still present in the most religiously indifferent among them, and if they nevertheless sometimes wished for a clergyman, it was only because a priest was the only one who could conclude legally valid marriages, and the marriages performed by the "Alcaldes" were mere makeshifts. But it took until 1831 before the first priest appeared in Austin's colony, a jovial Irishman who took the strange "orthodoxy" of his subjects humorously and did not examine their consciences too strictly. He left after only one year, without a successor having been found.

A LONE STAR ARISES IN TEXAS

The immigrants did not come into contact with the Mexican authorities in the beginning, just as they did not interact with the Mexican church. They dealt exclusively with Austin in the early years, as has been previously mentioned, and it was not until 1828 that the state-legislated "Ayuntamientos" were formed. These district councils were self-governing bodies to which the inhabitants of each district had the right to vote. Naturally, the Americans filled the posts with their own countrymen, and although the powers of the "Ayuntamientos" were limited, they were generally sufficient to handle the mostly simple affairs of the colonists on their own. What there was to settle beyond that with the "jefe politico," the Texas provincial governor, and the state and federal governments, was in any case left to Stephen Austin's tried and true diplomacy. In other words, the Anglo-Saxon settlers administered their commonwealth in the spirit of that frontier democracy which was commonplace on the American "frontiers," and life in Texas was not very different for them from that in the Union. Here as there they had to go through the same hardships and privations of pioneer life, here as there they had to wrestle with nature and fight with the Indians. And here as there, the same feeling of personal independence developed, the same consciousness of freedom, the same aversion to any state coercion. Even under the green-white-red flag of their adopted country, the immigrants remained the Americans they had been under the star-spangled banner. There was not even the slightest sign of their becoming part of the Mexican people!

Who knows how long the Mexicans would have kept their reins locked on Texas if they had not been roused from their carelessness by the Washington administration.

AMERICANIZATION

In the western states of the Union, the complaints about the treaty of 1819, about the "renunciation" of Texas, could and would not be silenced, and under the spell of this popular sentiment, President John Quincy Adams instructed the American envoy in 1825 to sound out the Mexican government to see if it would be willing to cede the province in return for appropriate monetary compensation. Mexico's answer, as might have been expected, was a flat and unequivocal No! Nevertheless, Adams ordered the purchase offer to be repeated in 1827, and when Andrew Jackson, the old frontier captain, had succeeded him in the White House, the inquiries became more urgent, more insistent, and almost assumed the tenor of a demand. The Mexicans now seemed to be becoming concerned after all about the heavy immigration of Anglo-American colonists, and suspiciously they associated the steady influx of settlers with the Union's covetous insistence on border revision. Truly, it would not have taken the warnings and diatribes of the English envoy to bring the Mexican government to the decision to change its overly permissive immigration policy. The report made by General Terán, the first senior Mexican official to inspect Texas in 1828, spoke a clear language. After all, this was not how the conditions in the northern province had been imagined!

"When you travel from San Antonio to Nacogdoches," Terán's letter said, "you will notice how the Mexican influence is dwindling more and more until it becomes almost nothing in East Texas. And from whence could that influence also be coming? Hardly from a numerical preponderance! For the ratio of Mexicans to foreigners is one to ten. Certainly not through a spiritual superiority of the Mexicans! For the exact opposite is true, and the Mexicans of

Nacogdoches form what in all countries is called the lowest class—the very poor and the very uneducated. The immigrant North Americans maintain an English school in this town and send their children north for further education. The poor Mexicans not only have not sufficient means to open a school, but are not of the kind to think of promoting public institutions and remedying entrenched abuses. There are neither authorities nor judges. All we have at this important place at our frontier is an insignificant little man, to say no more, who calls himself 'Alcalde', and an 'Ayuntamiento' that does not even meet during the whole electoral period... It would cause you as much grief as it does me if you heard what views the foreign settlers express about our nation. But then, with the exception of the few who have visited our capital, they know no other Mexicans than those who live here in the country... Under these circumstances, I ask, can it be otherwise than that enmity arises between the Mexicans and the foreigners?... The whole population here is a mixture of elements alien to each other and living side by side without any relationship, such as does not exist elsewhere in our whole empire." "If the settlement of Texas by North Americans does not cease," the general summed up his opinion, "if the settlements are not supervised, then one is forced to declare that the province is already at the mercy of foreigners."

In 1830, the Mexican government decided to take strong measures to counter the threat of over-immigration and the loss of Texas. A federal law prohibited any further immigration from "neighboring states". A ring of strong garrisons was placed around the Anglo-Saxon colonies—the soldiers for them were taken from the prisons who were to be settled in the country at the end of their compulsory service. Customs houses were erected on the borders and coasts, since the period for which the Anglo-Saxon settlements had been granted freedom from customs duty had expired and the extensive smuggling from Texas to the northern Mexican provinces was no longer to be tolerated.

The American settlers could not have been hit more severely! The economic rise of Texas was, as is the case with every newly opened country, not least dependent on the continuation of the influx of labor and capital. Nothing other than the hope that the colonists would one day be able to live in safety and security, even if it was only a modest prosperity, after the arduous early years had brought the colonists to the Texas wildernesses. When it was said that Texas was heaven for the men and hell for the women, this was intended to mean that the women let themselves be weighed down too much by the burdens and sufferings of pioneer life, while the men took everything more lightly because they believed they could see a promising future ahead of them. And yet, how was this faith to be honored, how was the land to blossom, if its frontier was closed off and its driving energies throttled? The Anglo-Saxon settlers felt cheated out of the prize of all their labors, which made them grow despondent.

Their agitation heightened when they thought of the Mexican convict soldiers who had been placed under their noses. Should they let themselves be commanded by these criminals? Should they merge into one people with these penitentiary vermin? What would have upset any self-respecting man outraged the colonists all the more because, as was the way of the American frontier, they saw in every mercenary the instrument of a tyranny threatening to trample on the inalienable rights of liberty. On top of that, there were the customs houses! Everywhere on the "frontier", the demands for taxes and duties were considered a brazen interference of the state in the private sphere of life, and the Texas settlers were exactly the same—one might say almost anarchistic—frontier individualists as their brethren in the Union.

Stephen Austin tried his best to calm the colonists and to obtain from the Mexican government a mitigation of the brusque measures. He was unable, however, to prevent friction here and there, and the irritation stirred up by the newcomers finally broke out in clashes at Galveston Bay and at the mouth of the Brazos River. It was only fortunate that just then, in 1832, Santa Anna, as leader of the liberal party, began his revolution against the conservative government. For when a Mexican detachment of troops landed on the Texas coast to punish the rebels, Austin managed to fool the commander, a Santanist, into thinking that the settlers had taken up arms only to help the liberal revolution achieve victory in Texas as well. Reassured, the Mexican general departed, and the few conservative officers who remained in Texas were soon afterward forced by the colonists to leave the country with their soldiers.

This success gave the Anglo-Saxon would-be Santanists hope of getting through to the new liberal government with their other grievances as well. In the fall of 1832, they elected confidants who set forth Texas wishes and demands in a series of submissions at a "convention" in San Felipe. Of all the settlements, only San Antonio was not represented at the deliberations. The Mexican citizens, who formed the majority in that city, agreed with the program points in themselves, but did not think the democratic path embraced by their Anglo-Saxon compatriots was viable. Indeed, the colonial Spanish belief in authority was still so alive in the green-white-red republic that the actions of the American Texans almost looked like a revolution in the eyes of the Mexican government! The demands that were made were as follows: Recognition of English as a second official language, expansion of the militia, reduction of customs duties, revocation of the immigration ban and, most importantly: separation from Coahuila, formation of an independent Texan state! What the Texans demanded, to put it clearly, was autonomy within the framework of the Mexican federal empire.

Stephen Austin traveled to the capital at his own expense to represent the Texan wishes before the Mexican government. No matter how insistent he was in his demand for autonomy, the only thing he could obtain from Santa Anna was the lifting of the 1830 immigration ban. Austin was finally satisfied with this rather important concession. He still considered Texas too weak to be able to enforce his demand for autonomy with threats, and believed that time would also bring this fruit to maturity. However, as he was on his way back, he was suddenly arrested in Saltillo, escorted to Mexico, and thrown into a dungeon there. What had happened? Well, Austin had written a letter to the "Ayuntamiento" of San Antonio asking his Mexican friends to secede from Coahuila on their own initiative. If, instead of the Anglo-Saxons, the Mexican Texans were to take the lead in the autonomy movement, he had calculated, the matter would take on a very different face and Mexico would resign itself to the fait accompli. The members of the "Ayuntamiento", however, were not heroes. Not only did they refuse to act on their own authority, but they also sent the letter with the dangerous proposals to the Mexican government. In Mexico, the matter was turned into a major state affair and Austin was indicted for treason. The Texas leader spent ten months behind prison bars. The opening of the trial dragged on because no court seemed to have enough material to charge him with. Austin was then released on bail, but it was not until the summer of 1835, when the prosecution had been quashed under a general amnesty, that he was allowed to leave the capital.

The Mexicans, in the meantime, tried many things to dissuade the Anglo-Saxon Texans from their desire for independence. After the federal government had already lifted the immigration ban, the state parliament of Coahuila allowed the use of English in intercourse with the authorities. New administrative districts were established, and while previously all major civil and criminal cases had had to be settled in writing in Saltillo, eleven hundred kilometers away, from now on there was a court of appeal in San Antonio. Juries were introduced, and a large part of the Texas grievances became obsolete. Had these measures been taken earlier, the Anglo-Saxon settlers would probably have calmed down in the process. It was now too late. After the evil experiences of the previous years, the colonists felt it necessary to protect themselves as much as possible from Mexican arbitrariness. Thus, they held fast to their demand for autonomy.

However, there was still little inclination among the majority of the Texan population to openly break with Mexico over this demand. For the time being, only a small, activist group was prepared to do so, and they were already flirting with the idea of joining the Union. These were mostly young Americans who had not been in the country long, or political hotheads amongst whom national passions were running wild. The old-established settlers, on the other hand, the men who had property to lose and the fathers of families who had to fear for their wives and children, were in favor of an amicable settlement.

AMERICANIZATION

Political events in Mexico were to blame for the fact that things turned out differently. As the leader of liberalism, General Santa Anna had become Mexican president but was concerned less with liberal principles than with his own power, seeing that the liberal party organization and the complicated federal constitution did not allow him to govern as he thought, he secretly sought contact with conservative circles and, at the end of 1834, openly sided with his former opponents. As an unrestrained dictator, Santa Anna began a ruthless fight against all liberal attempts at resistance. It also became immediately apparent that the political course was moving toward the establishment of a tightly centralized unitary state.

The end of the Mexican Federal Republic had to mean the end of Texas' autonomy aspirations. Nobody doubted that Santa Anna, once he was firmly in the saddle, would try with all his might to "Mexicanize" Texas! Already there was talk that "El Presidente" intended to garrison an army of four thousand men in Texas. In spite of the fact that the Anglo-Saxon settlers, to whom as true frontiersmen the commitment to democracy was almost a religious confession, were in themselves committed to the cause of Mexican liberalism — if they wanted to preserve their rights as a national minority, there was nothing left for them to do but to become advocates of the liberal, federalist constitution of 1824 and to stand up to the new dictator of Mexico.

At first, only the radical colonist element was aware that the political upheavals in Mexico made it inevitable that Texas would have to fight for its right to exist. The majority of the settlers felt deeply concerned, but did not know how to judge the development of things and what to do. They lacked a leader who could have helped them out of their perplexity. Stephen Austin, however, was being held in the capital! When the "war party" called for a new convention to discuss the situation, most of the "peace party" refused to participate in the confidence elections. It almost seemed as if Texas would present a picture of internal dissension and powerless indecision at the crucial hour. Already the Mexican commander-general Cós, a brother-in-law of Santa Anna, was beginning to reinforce the garrison at San Antonio. Even now he was gearing up to move into Texas with a larger force.

That's when Stephen Austin landed at the Brazos Estuary on September 1, 1835! The city of Brazoria invited him to a public welcome banquet, and like wildfire the news spread throughout the country that Austin would speak at the banquet on September 8. Everyone knew that this speech would decide war or peace, battle or submission. Moreover, Stephen Austin spoke in favor of the election of trusted men and the convening of a new convention! The colonists, he declared, had to come to a conclusion as to whether they could agree to the change from a federal to a unitary state and what particular form of state government they desired. Unmistakably he had pointed out to Santa Anna, Austin continued, that a military occupation of Texas would lead to armed hostilities. Nevertheless, soldiers were now moving into the country in large numbers without any inducement from the colonists. Now it was up to the Texas people to decide what action to take!

If anyone had ears to hear, he heard! That was the call to arms! That was the signal to rise! That was the cue to begin the fight for freedom!

SIXTH CHAPTER

THE FIGHT FOR FREEDOM

When the Revolution began, there were close to thirty thousand Anglo-Saxon settlers living in Texas, all women and children included. That was a lot, considering that it had been less than fourteen years since Stephen Austin had brought the first American immigrants into the country. It was little, considering that the colonists dared to throw down the gauntlet to the eight-million-strong Mexican nation.

One might wonder whether their boldness in taking on the advancing armies of professional soldiers was not bordering on presumption. There could have scarcely been more than eight thousand men capable of bearing arms in the Texas settlements at that time. These men were scattered over an area estimated at fifty thousand square miles in small communities and individual farms. They were in no way prepared for war. Militias had been formed here and there to protect against Indian raids but there was no trace of a well-organized national army. At best, the weaponry consisted of hunting rifles. There was no military training, soldierly discipline, field-marching equipment anywhere!

One thing is certain, the Texans could never have won their revolution if they had been on their own. They won because the Union was behind them! Not the Union as a government, however! Andrew Jackson, the frontiersman in the president's chair, would have loved to come to the aid of his countrymen on the other side of the Sabine with the federal army. Internal political conditions in the United States, however, tied his hands and condemned him to inaction. The East and the North of the Union wanted nothing to do with a war with Mexico and with a land acquisition in the South. The antagonism between the slaveholding and the "free" states had already become too great for the whole American nation to be enthusiastic about an open policy of expansion on the Gulf Coast. For Texas was a "slave state!" Stephen Austin, though not himself friendly to slavery, had successfully resisted, in the interest of part of his settlers, the application to Texas of the antislavery laws which applied in the rest of Mexico, and when the Mexican government forbade the new immigrants to bring Negro slaves with them, the colonists had fallen back on the resort of concluding life-long "service contracts" with their blacks. In short, the annexation of Texas to the Union would have increased the number of "slave states" and shifted the balance of votes in the Senate in favor of the South. This was fiercely opposed by the North and East. For better or worse, therefore, Andrew Jackson had to declare the neutrality of the Confederacy and instruct the authorities to see that the neutrality provisions were observed.

The people of the West of the Union knew exactly what they thought about the official orders of their Andrew Jackson. They did not care one bit about the policies of the Washington administration. When the first news of the

Texas uprising arrived, enthusiastic sympathy rallies were held throughout the Mississippi basin. In the newspapers, in meetings, in a flurry of word-of-mouth advertising, young men were called upon to volunteer and move across the Sabine. Committees were formed to receive donations of money and goods. Whole shiploads of arms were sent to Texas. So what about the American authorities? When the citizens of Cincinnati sent the Texans two cannons, customs officials let the shipment, declared to be "Hollow Stoneware," pass with a smile and a wink. The prosecutors who brought charges of a violation of the Neutrality Act could be counted on the fingers of one hand. There were no juries that would have found anyone guilty anyway. The District Attorney of East Tennessee announced under his breath to the inhabitants of his district that he would adhere exactly to the letter of the Government's decree and prosecute anyone from within the Union who took up arms against Mexico, but that he himself would lead a company of volunteers to the border where they could cross the Sabine as immigrants and arm themselves on Texas soil without interference!

The Mexican emissary filed complaint after complaint against this "favorable" interpretation of the neutrality provisions. The Washington government shrugged its shoulders and pretended not to know anything. Moreover, it was not alone in this! Jackson commanded a strong detachment of troops under General Gaines, one of his aides in the Florida campaign, to the Louisiana frontier to suppress "Indian disturbances" even on Texas territory if necessary! Union non-intervention, as can be seen, was a peculiar affair. Little by little, about seven thousand freedmen went to Texas, and even if a good part of them arrived only when the decision had already been made—it was quite actually these spirited young fellows, filled with fighting spirit and love of adventure, who won the independence of Texas.

For the time being, however, there was no talk of independence in Texas itself. Certainly, now that the die was cast, there was not a single colonist who wanted to remain a Mexican. There was a consensus of opinion that Texas could not prosper if it remained coupled to a state whose political life, as Stephen Austin said, was as volcanic as its geographic soil, which seemed unable to achieve internal stability and peaceful development. Although many a firebrand would have liked to proclaim Texas independence at once, however, the more thoughtful and politically shrewder elements did not think it advisable to declare that goal openly too soon. As long as the uprising was presented as a struggle for the Federalist State Constitution of 1824, they could count on the support of liberal Mexicans inside and outside Texas, and as yet they felt too weak to do without that support.

Thus the Texas Revolution began under the green-white-red tricolor of Mexico, in the center field of which the year 1824 was inscribed as a sign of defiance against Santa Anna's dictatorship.

Resistance

The first clashes between the settlers and the Mexican military occurred even before the assembly of trusted men that Stephen Austin had endorsed at the Brazoria banquet had convened.

The citizens of Gonzales had been given a six-pounder brass cannon years before, an ancient thing without any combat value, in order to be able to scare and chase away predatory Indians if necessary. Now, all of a sudden, the Mexican provincial commander demanded the surrender of the gun, and this looked suspiciously like the beginning of a general disarmament action. Outraged, the people of Gonzales refused to obey the order. They called together the militia, hid the cannon in a peach orchard, and planted a sign threateningly proclaiming, "Come and get it!" The Mexican colonel sent out a hundred dragoons to have the cannon seized. But the Texans received the horsemen with rifle bullets and, after a short exchange of fire, put them to flight.

Martin Perfecto de Cós, the Mexican commander general, had arrived the day before with an army of several hundred men in the former La Bahia, which was now called Goliad. After the bloody defeat of the liberals in Coahuila, rebellious Texas was now to be brought to heel. Without taking any notice of the skirmish at Gonzales, Cós marched on to San Antonio so that he could take his military measures from there at his leisure. In doing so, he was imprudent enough to leave only a small guard at Goliad. A band of Texans, recognizing the opportunity to cut off Cós's force's line of communication to the coast, swiftly overran the old fort.

This marked the beginning of armed resistance! In Gonzales, the colonists gathered to prevent the Mexicans from advancing into the Anglo-Saxon settlement districts. There may have been as many as eight hundred farmers who gradually arrived. Using all his authority, Stephen Austin tried to bring order into the wild confusion and organize something like an army out of the multitudes. This was a task beyond his strength, however, and the only thing he accomplished was to get the men of each district to form themselves loosely into companies. Such a frontier company, for instance, sometimes consisted of thirteen and sometimes of seventy men. One was content to elect a sergeant as its leader, while would have nothing less than a captain and three lieutenants. In addition, each division elected a representative to the War Council, which was to advise and instruct the higher commands. Even in wartime, in the face of the enemy, the true frontierman gave up nothing of his democratic rights! When it came to electing a commander-in-chief, there was so much resentment, jealousy and partisanship that the whole "army" almost broke up! In the end, it was agreed that Stephen Austin would be the new commander.

To elect a commander-in-chief and to obey him, however, were two different things! The Texan farmers did not know discipline at all. Where should they have learned it from? They were brave and courageous, sometimes even reckless and daring. Sissies had no business on the frontier, and anyone who settled in the wilderness had, of course, already been in a fight to the death with the Redskins. Yet then, everyone had been his own master, had fought as a free man together with his peers, and had done what he thought was right. Now the colonists believed that they did not have to submit to a commanding force! Orders that did not suit them were not obeyed, and when something occurred to them, they acted on their own. If someone felt that he needed to do something at home, well, he just left the camp and came back later, or didn't come back at all, just as he pleased.

Just as much as they lacked manpower, they lacked weapons, money, provisions, clothing, blankets, tents, everything and anything! A reasonably effective opponent would have dealt with these insurgents very quickly, but fortunately for the Texans, the troops commanded by General Cós were not the best. For as well equipped as these soldiers were in comparison to the settlers—a large part of them had been freshly taken out of the prisons and put into uniforms, some of them were holding a rifle in their hands for the first time in their lives, and all of them lacked what no armament and equipment, no matter how brilliant, could replace—courage, patriotism, the will to sacrifice even one's life, if necessary, for the cause of the homeland. This is how Stephen Austin was able to lead his troops to San Antonio and besiege the city from October 1835 without being threatened by Mexican raids.

While the Texas army held San Antonio locked down, the long-planned "convention" convened at San Felipe. Its most important task was to form a provisional government which, it was said, would guide the fortunes of Texas until constitutional conditions were restored to Mexico. The Texas deputies really could not be said to have shown any political talent or foresight. While the situation demanded a tight consolidation of all forces, here, too, the principles of democracy were ridden to death. The radical Henry Smith was elected governor, an honest, upright, but highly choleric man who was in no way suited to the difficult post. He was assisted by a numerous council of district representatives. Without delimiting their powers in any way, both were given the same rights! As commander-in-chief of the regular troops, which for the time being were still on paper, one appointed a certain Sam Houston, who had come to Texas in 1833 and, as it was rumored, was supposed to be an intimate friend of the American President Jackson. The "major-general," however, was expressly deprived of the command of the volunteers who lay before San Antonio. Nobody dared to offend democratic sensibilities—and that included the right to choose one's own commander.

This opened the door to conflicts of authority, and it was not long before the governor, the council, the major general and the volunteer commander were so at loggerheads that one deposed the other. Everything went to pieces and there was no government at all. The only sensible thing that the "convention" decided to do was to send Stephen Austin to the United States to establish relations with the Washington government and to find volunteers, weapons and, above all, funds. Even if Austin proved unsuccessful in persuading the Union to abandon its policy of neutrality, he was at least able to procure a few loans that solved the revolutionaries' most serious financial problems.

Meanwhile, the siege of San Antonio dragged on. The Texans did not dare to attack because they had no artillery with which to storm the city. As winter set in and the settlers in their positions began to suffer from the grim cold, the army command thought it best to break off the siege and take the troops to Gonzales for winter quarters. However, those men who, despite the grueling inactivity in the trenches and bulwarks, had not yet lost their fighting spirit, did not want to hear of that under any circumstances. "Who's going for a walk with old Milam to San Antonio?" shouted a volunteer colonel as the Texans prepared to march. With a sudden flaring enthusiasm, the frontiersmen hurried after the charging swashbuckler. Four days were spent in San Antonio fighting for possession of the city. Carefully avoiding the streets, the Texans forced their way by pounding the thin adobe walls of the houses with heavy wooden beams and advancing from dwelling to dwelling amid cries of terror from the occupants. When Cós saw that the city could no longer be held, he retreated to the old Spanish mission of San Antonio de Valero, popularly known as the "Alamo." A few days later,

THE FIGHT FOR FREEDOM

on December 11, he surrendered with his thirteen hundred men and was given safe conduct to the Rio Grande in exchange for his word of honor never to march into Texas again. By Christmas 1835, not a single Mexican soldier was left on Texas soil!

The revolution seemed to be over for most of the settlers. They took up their shotguns and went home to their farms, where so much work had been left behind. Few colonists believed the warnings that the real fight was yet to come, and had it not been for them and the Union freedmen arriving in ever-increasing numbers, the entire Texan army would have quietly disbanded.

Even the men who remained under arms, however, wasted their time and did nothing to prepare for the coming events. Some loitered in San Antonio, and others planned an adventurous coup d'état against the Mexican port of Matamoras on the Rio Grande.

The only one who understood the dictates of the hour was Sam Houston, the generalissimo of the imaginary regular army. He hastened to East Texas to conclude a new peace treaty with the Indians, among whom Mexican agents had been sighted. After all, that would have been the downfall of the Anglo-Saxon settlements if the Redskins had taken the warpath and raided the defenseless women and children while the men in West Texas fought with the Mexicans!

The Mexicans came once again, with a stronger force than ever before! The colonists were rudely torn out of their self-delusion that the fight for freedom had already been won!

The Alamo

Mexico's forces had been exhausted until they had been bled almost white by the interminable revolutions and civil wars of the previous decades. As soon as the dictator-president Santa Anna heard of the ignominious defeat his brother-in-law Cós had suffered in San Antonio, he did not rest until he had once again drained the weakened masses and gathered new funds and troops. He believed he owed it to his prestige and the honor of the nation to make an example of Texas as soon as possible and driven out the rebellious immigrants. Santa Anna addressed the Mexican public with bombastic appeals full of high-sounding phrases. He solemnly declared the struggle against the Texan settlers a national war and endowed a medal of the "Legion of Honor" specifically for this campaign. Grandly he announced that he himself would ride north at the head of an army of fifty thousand men to restore peace and order in the rebellious province that threatened to slip away from Mexico.

However much he tried, he could not raise more than six thousand soldiers, and for the small loan of 400,000 dollars, which he obtained from the Mexican merchants, he had to grant a monthly interest of four percent. Judging by the confused conditions in Texas, however, it was still a handsome army that marched from Monclova toward the Rio Grande on February 8, 1836, under Santa Anna's leadership. What the Texans had to expect is illuminated by an order that "El Presidente" issued to the troops, "The foreigners who have taken up arms against the Mexican nation in violation of every rule of law deserve no leniency, and no pardon is to be granted them!" All leaders of the rebels were to be executed, all participants in the uprising expelled from the country, and all settlers' assets confiscated to cover the costs of the war. Santa Anna wanted to do away with the precarious Anglo-Saxon element in the Northern Province once and for all!

The news of the approach of a strong Mexican army struck the settlers like a bolt from the blue. Even the more insightful colonists, who were not under the delusion, like the mass of their countrymen, that Santa Anna would quietly accept the San Antonio defeat and let Texas go its own way undisturbed, were surprised by the swift action of the Mexican government. In defense of the country, as has been said, not the slightest thing had been done in the weeks since the departure of General Cós. Of the irregulars, ninety men stood at Corpus Christi Bay, at Goliad some 450 men had assembled under Colonel Fannin, ready to make the attack on Matamoras and about 150 men had remained at San Antonio. That was all that was under arms in Texas.

Governor Smith and Major General Houston had endeavored in vain to raise a regular army. Colonel Travis, who had been ordered to enlist one hundred men to augment the garrison at San Antonio, had to report at the end of January that, in spite of all his efforts, he had not succeeded in getting together more than thirty. "Things are indeed quite sad for our cause," Travis' letter reads, "the people are listless, weary and exhausted with war. As a result of the discord between the leading men, they have lost all confidence in the government. You cannot imagine how discouraged the country is. No more volunteers can be found, and the few that are found can't be relied upon." In a desperate mood, Travis moved his handful of people to San Antonio. The fate of Texas seemed sealed. Soon Santa Anna's troops would flood the land and destroy the Anglo-Saxon settlements! Anyone who would have foolishly predicted a future for Texas would have been rightly scolded!

As soon as Travis took command in San Antonio, however, he knew what he had to do- defend that city at all costs for as long as it was at all possible! San Antonio was the first major town on Texas soil when coming from the Rio Grande, the gateway to the Anglo-Saxon settlements further east. To leave this gateway to Santa Anna without a fight—no, it could not be! Hardly will William Travis have indulged in the delusion that he could succeed in beating back the enemy's advance with the few soldiers and volunteers who occupied San Antonio. But was not an infinite amount already gained by holding up the enemy here for days or even weeks? Travis knew—he says it himself in one of his letters—that "only the thunder of the enemy's guns and the ravishment of their wives and daughters, the cries of their starving children and the smoke of their burning huts" could rouse the settlers from their indifference and apathy. He also knew, of course, that when the danger suddenly loomed large before them, they would courageously take up arms and sacrifice themselves in defense of their homeland. Only the march of the colonists took time, and Travis was determined to buy them that time at any cost.

He found a kindred spirit in James Bowie, the romantic silver miner and wealthy land speculator whom the San Antonio volunteers had elected as their militia commander. "True, we are ill prepared to receive the enemy," Travis wrote to Governor Smith, "for we are not more than 150 men here, who are in a very miserable condition. Nevertheless, we are willing to hold out as long as there is a man left alive. We think death better than the disgrace of abandoning a post that has been so dearly captured." This was not just idle talk but deadly serious. The men who conspired with Travis and Bowie to defend San Antonio in order to save Texas knew that they would be overrun by Mexican superiority and that none could hope to escape with their lives. Certainly, there were greenhorns among them, boys barely out of boyhood who had no idea yet what it meant to die. Next to these boys were the men with graying temples, who had left behind their wives and children somewhere in the East and whose souls were burdened with the responsibility of their decision, the young men who had gone out into the world full of energy and had promised themselves so much, oh so much, from life! However, they all hid their hopes and worries silently in their hearts. What did the individual count for at a moment when people and country, the future of Texas, were at stake! Where a secret fear or wavering wanted to stir, it sank before the indomitable will of the two leaders.

Fate had wrought both Travis and Bowie to be tough. William Travis had seen the woman he loved and who had given him two children become unfaithful to him. Wounded to the core of his being, he had left his home in Alabama in 1831 and fled to Texas to forget the past while living a troubled existence as a lawyer and politician. James Bowie had been able to acquire a great fortune through shrewd speculation of all kinds. By marrying into the distinguished family of the Mexican lieutenant governor, he had become a weighty figure on the Texas frontier. Then, in 1833, his wife, his children, his parents-in-law, and most of his relatives died in three days of cholera, and all at once he was completely isolated. This is not to say that the twenty-seven-year-old army colonel and the forty-one-year-old militia colonel threw their lives away because they were tired of life. Travis was touchingly attached to his young son, and just in his last year he had found the love of a girl who helped him heal old wounds. Bowie had thrown himself anew into the whirl of his business and had been as active as ever before the outbreak of the Revolution. Both of them had just experienced how deceptive personal happiness can be and how life only gains real value when it is selflessly sacrificed to a great cause. As in all the men who had taken up the frontier guard at San Antonio, the flame of manly idealism blazed in them — and surely its glow is the brightest and most beautiful to illuminate the history of Texas.

Had it not been for this idealism, it would probably never have been possible to hold the western outpost of Texas for a single day against Santa Anna's advancing six thousand men. San Antonio was an open city, with only the stone walls of the old Spanish mission, the Alamo, providing some protection. The Texans — there may have been one hundred and eighty men all told, but twenty to thirty of them lay sick in the hospital — were poorly armed. So far they had used their shotguns only in buffalo hunting and in fighting with Redskins. There was a shortage of powder and a shortage of lead. Provisions were meager. The men had not received pay for months, and hardly anyone had a cent left. Initially, there had also been disputes of authority between Travis and Bowie, since the militia would not, under any circumstances, be commanded by a regular officer. The two leaders had been reasonable enough to agree on sharing command. Fortunately, when the Mexicans had left the previous December, they had left behind some thirty gun barrels. About twenty were now hastily mounted and brought into position in the Alamo.

For as soon as the first Mexican cavalry squadrons appeared in front of San Antonio on February 23, the Texans abandoned the actual city and occupied the Spanish mission, whose massive structures were like the enclosures of a small fortress. "To the people of Texas and to all Americans in the world!" read the headline over an appeal that Travis sent out by courier the following day, when the enemy had already begun to encircle Alamo. "Fellow citizens and countrymen! I am besieged by a thousand or more Mexicans under Santa Anna. I have been constantly shelled and bombarded for twenty-four hours and have not yet lost a man. The enemy has demanded an unconditional surrender, otherwise, when the fort is taken, he will have the whole of the garrison killed. I have answered this demand with a cannon shot, and our flag still flies proudly from the walls. I will never surrender or give way. Therefore, I call upon you in the name of liberty, patriotism, and all that is dear to the American being, come in haste to the aid! The enemy is receiving reinforcements daily, and in four or five days his numbers will have increased to three or four thousand. If my call is not heard, I am willing to hold on as long as possible and die like a soldier who never forgets what he owes to his and his country's honor. Victory or death! William Barret Travis, Lieutenant Colonel and Commander. P.S. The Lord is on our side. When the enemy came in sight, we did not have 75 kilograms of corn. Now we have found 200 to 250 kilograms in an abandoned house and have been able to drive 20 or 30 head of cattle into the fort."

How could Travis' hope that his call for help would be heeded! Where were there any Texan troops left in the field? Fannin and his men at Goliad did make an attempt to march to San Antonio. But when they got nowhere with their baggage on the unmade roads, they turned back. Perhaps they thought the defense of San Antonio at all to be useless and insane. It was only from Gonzales that 32 men hurried over. Meanwhile, the ring of siege closed tighter and tighter around the Alamo and its two hundred and ten heroic defenders! Once again, on March 3, a courier managed to steal through the enemy lines. He took with him, with many farewell greetings, this last letter from Travis to a friend: "Take care of my little boy! Perhaps I shall be able to work up a rich fortune for him if the country is saved. On the other hand, if Texas is lost and I perish, I can leave him nothing but the proud remembrance that he is the son of a man who died for his country."

James Bowie had been stricken with severe typhoid fever on the day the siege began. From then on, William Travis alone commanded the Alamo. At first, the small crew had been able to make sorties to burn down nearby houses that provided cover for the enemy, blocking the field of fire. Soon even that was no longer possible. Little by little, five thousand Mexican soldiers had gathered around the Alamo, and the days passed for the Texans with the dreadful waiting for the moment when the enemy bugle would sound for the assault. At that point, yes, the only thing to do was to sell one's life as dearly as possible! The men stood behind the walls of the old mission feverishly nervous and tired from all their guarding duties. Twelve days had already passed, twelve hard days, each of which Travis nevertheless blessed for giving the colonists in the rear time to arm themselves and rush to the front. Perhaps the hope of relief, of rescue, still smoldered in one or two of the young men. It was a faint spark, however, and they did not kindle it—their lives were over.

On the morning of March 6, at four o'clock in the morning, the Mexican troops stormed in from all sides. They

THE FIGHT FOR FREEDOM

were met by a hail of bullets and shells. For a short time the lines faltered. But the courage of the officers pulled the Mexican soldiers forward again. Already the enemy was so close to the walls of Alamo that the Texan guns could no longer find a target. Then the end came, as it had to come. In furious bayonet fighting, the Texans were cut down to the last man. Only a few women and children who had taken refuge in the church were spared. Santa Anna's capture of Alamo cost him close to fifteen hundred dead and wounded, and a large proportion of the wounded died because they were not given medical attention! He probably could have achieved his objective more cheaply if he had not had the fort attacked from four sides at once—many of the bullets intended for the Texans hit Mexicans rushing in from the other side. "El Presidente" did not care much about that—the main thing was that he had San Antonio in his hands and the way to the Anglo-Saxon settlements was open in front of him!

Then on March 1, when the doomed men in the Alamo waited with final tension for the hour of the Mexican attack—when the people, seized by wild panic, began to flee on foot and on horseback and in ladder wagons toward the protective American frontier—when there was no Texan army anywhere to oppose Santa Anna's advance. On March 1, the representatives of the people assembled at Washington on the Brazos to declare independence for Texas and to give the country a constitution. Now, at this moment, when the collapse of the Revolution seemed only a matter of a few weeks, to launch a "Republic of Texas" verged on the grotesque! Even the external setting in which the meeting of this "National Constituent Assembly" took place did not exactly suggest that it was more than an emergency baptism! "Washington on the Brazos," recounted a visitor, "is in the middle of the woods. The whole town consists of about a dozen shabby shacks and sheds, not a single real house is there, and there is only one road, a lane hewn out of the woods, with tree stumps left in it." Only a few deputies found shelter in a carpenter's workshop; the others had to camp out in the open. With a wintry temperature approaching freezing, the people's deputies began their sessions in a half-finished house where there were neither windows nor doors and where cloths had to be hung in front of the openings to break the violence of the icy north wind.

Congress was reminded almost hourly of the dubious nature of the constitutional edifice they were about to construct. More and more alarm calls arrived from West Texas, more and more reports of the alarming number of Mexican troops. There was no thought of calm deliberation and reflection. When Travis' call for help became known, one of the congressmen made the suggestion that Congress should adjourn and hurry united to the front. To this Sam Houston passionately objected. It was too late to save the men in Alamo, he said. It would be all the more treasonous to break off the deliberations. For the threatening situation in which they found themselves had been called into existence because there was no government capable of action in Texas, and to create one was the most urgent patriotic duty.

Houston was right! If Texas was to be saved at all, then only if the unworthy and disastrous spectacle that the so-called "provisional government" had presented with its personal disputes was put to an end as soon as possible and if a firm and unified leadership was established in which the people could once again have confidence. It was therefore not at all as inappropriate as it might have seemed at first glance to give the country a constitution at this time. However little what the deputies in Washington achieved at the Brazos can be compared to what the heroes of Alamo accomplished. Boldly and defiantly, in the midst of the worst adversity, to effect the final separation from Mexico and to found a new republic was no less a stirring, encouraging sign of unshakable faith in the future of the country! The Constitution of March 1836 proclaimed to the colonists, "See, this is the house in which you will live when you have driven the Mexican soldiery from your land! It is worth fighting and bleeding for!"

More important than the creation of a constitution at that moment was the establishment of a new government and the appointment of Sam Houston as commander-in-chief of all land forces. The question was whether these men could make a difference. At two o'clock in the morning of March 17, the "National Convention" dissolved, and immediately the deputies dashed off in all directions. "A general panic seemed to have seized them," reported an eyewitness. "Their families were endangered and defenseless, and thousands were already fleeing eastward.... The farm families and merchants of Washington, too, packed up their belongings and hurried away.... The new government has decided to move to Harrisburg on the Buffalo bayou."

The Victory at San Jacinto

As soon as the "National Assembly" had confirmed his position as commander-in-chief, but this time with the authority to command the volunteers, Sam Houston had ridden from Washington on the Brazos to Gonzales to organize the Texan resistance. When he arrived there on March 11 — not yet knowing that the fate of the Alamo defenders had already been fulfilled—he found 374 colonists and freedmen who had flocked on word of the renewed Mexican incursion. To face Santa Anna's superior force with this completely undisciplined force would have been folly. But in Goliad there was still the militia colonel Fannin with about 450 men. Houston immediately instructed him to blow up the old fort, send a third of his crew to Gonzales, and retreat with the rest to Victoria. It was, after all, impossible in this state of affairs to hold the forward chain of Anglo-Saxon establishments. It was a matter of massing the existing forces while retreating.

Fannin hesitated to obey the order, allowing precious time to pass. He had sent a detachment of 150 men under Colonel Ward to relieve the small garrison at Refugio, which had been surprised by a 600-man Mexican corps marching up the coast and had already cut down Johnson and his 90 men at San Patricio. Fannin did not want to abandon Goliad without waiting for Ward's return. In the meantime, however, Ward had been attacked by the Mexican advance party and had been forced to flee all the way to Victoria. When Fannin finally received word of these events and left with his 300 men, it was too late. No sooner had he left the fort than he found himself surrounded by the Mexicans. Bravely, the volunteers defended themselves on the open prairie behind a quickly assembled wagon train. When ammunition ran out, when thirst became more and more agonizing and when a breakthrough would only have been possible if the wounded had been left behind, the men decided to surrender. It was an unconditional surrender, even if the prisoners expected to be deported to the Union. Along with Ward's men, who had been overpowered at Victoria, Fannin's force was taken by the Mexicans to a camp near Goliad.

THE FIGHT FOR FREEDOM

"After a week, on the morning of March 27," related one of the privateers, "a Mexican officer came to us and ordered us to prepare to march. We were to be released, he told us, on our word of honor, and sent on ships from the port of Cópano to New Orleans. This, as you may imagine, was joyful news to us, and we hastened to get ready quickly to leave the unfriendly prison camp. Then we were divided into three detachments and marched away under heavy guard.... When we were half a mile out of town, halt was ordered and the guards all moved over to one side. No sooner had this happened than I heard volley shots from the direction in which the other two detachments had marched. One of the men next to me shouted, 'Boys, they are going to shoot at us!' and already I heard the repeating of the Mexican rifles. I turned, and at that moment the Mexicans fired at us. Perhaps a hundred of our 150 men dropped dead." The rest tried to flee, the Mexican soldiery giving chase in wild pursuit. Those whom they reached were mercilessly massacred, and only a few of the privateers managed to save themselves. Incredible though it was, it was true that the Mexicans were attacking the defenseless prisoners of war! Santa Anna himself had given the order for this bloodbath. Had he not issued a decree a few weeks earlier that any Union volunteer found with weapons in his hand was to be considered a pirate and treated as such? Only about 30 men who had been held prisoner in Goliad had been spared, other 30 escaped — but about 390 young Americans lay treacherously slain on the ground!

Alamo, Goliad and Sam Houston's retreat with his troops, which in the meantime had grown to 600 men, to the other side of the Colorado with the Mexican corps advancing, was it surprising that the Texan people left home and farm and fled eastward? This was no orderly flight, however; it was a case of leaving things behind, of gathering up what one could and running away with a swarm of people filled with fear and terror. The masses of wagons piled up at the fords of the rivers as people lay in the marshy grass, hardly able to wait for the time when it was their turn to cross the stream. For were not the Mexicans, the brutalized, debauched Mexicans close on their trail? These were the uncontrollable rumors that were wrenching the fugitives farther and farther to the east! A Texan officer who roamed the country shortly after the escape gives the following account:

"The sad sight of the country we rode through defied description. The houses stood open, the beds lay unmade, the breakfast dishes still stood on the tables, pots full of milk molded in the kitchens. There the cribs were full of corn, the smokehouses hung full of ham, the gardens were full of chickens running after us for food, nests full of eggs were found at every fence corner. Young corn and young vegetables sprouted in the rain, cattle ate the glorious grass, fat, lazy pigs rolled in the mire. Everything was abandoned. Lonely dogs roamed around the abandoned houses, their howls making the sad sight seem even more sorrowful. Hungry cats ran meowing toward us.... There were so few wagons that it was impossible to transport all the household goods. Many women and even many children had to walk. Some had only heavy carts as vehicles, whose screeching only increased the frightfulness of the situation.... And as if the arch-enemy had broken loose, there were men—or rather devils—bent on robbery. They galloped after the fugitives, shouting at them that the Mexicans were following at their heels, in order to induce the unfortunate victims to throw away even the few valuables they had tried to save. All along the way lay broken wagons and discarded household goods..."

Sam Houston and his men camped on the Colorado for a week, while across from him on the right bank of the river was a detachment of Mexican troops that felt too weak to attack. The Texan army grew to 1400 men during these days. The Settlers, determined to defend their homesteads and cover the flight of their families, streamed in. When news of the carnage reached Goliad, however, Houston ordered a further retreat all the way to the Brazos. A mutiny almost threatened to break out among the colonists and volunteers. Why did the general not dare to offer battle to the Mexicans? Why did he cowardly abandon the oldest and most flourishing Anglo-Saxon settlements to the enemy? Did he intend, as was rumored, to retreat as far as Sabine? The Generalissimo kept silent and did not reveal his plans to anyone. "I consulted no one, I held no council of war, if I am wrong, I alone am to blame!" he wrote to the government. Surely Houston had a different judgment of the combat value of the untrained, undisciplined Texas army than the battle-hardened enlisted men with their overconfident frontier self-awareness had! Perhaps he hoped he would be joined at the Brazos by new bands of colonists from East Texas and new volunteer troops from the Union. Perhaps he wanted to gain a backstop from Union General Gaines with his regiment, who was just looking for an excuse to cross the Sabine and invade Texas. Perhaps he fled to deceive Santa Anna about the Texans' will to resist in order to achieve the very thing that actually happened — a fragmentation of the Mexican forces. By now Sam Houston had lived long enough in the wilderness among the Redskins to be well versed in the wiles and stratagems of Indian warfare. He possessed a natural strategic aptitude and did not intend to let the enemy dictate the law of action.

The colonists knew nothing of this! Grumbling and grousing, they finally complied with their commander's order to retreat, but the settlers who had made their homes between the Colorado and the Brazos left the force in droves to hurry back to their farms and help their families escape. By the time the Texas army arrived at San Felipe, it numbered only six hundred men. Now, however, everyone expected Houston to try to halt the Mexican advance here at the Brazos. But calm and unmoved, the general gave the order to march upstream, away from the settlements, into the wilderness. What was the point of this new evasion? Louder and louder were the voices among the Texan warriors demanding Houston's removal. Two companies refused to obey. Sam Houston pretended not to have an ear for this apparent mutiny and "ordered" the detachments to remain at San Felipe to guard the river crossing. He led the rest of the army halfway to Washington and stopped there for nearly two weeks. He knew why! The men were march-weary and discouraged, in dire need of rest and recuperation. More importantly, they still lacked the necessary military order and discipline. The fortnight's rest off the trail offered the best opportunity to organize and drill the frontiersmen and irregulars at least to some extent. Newly arriving squads of young Union boys brought the number of enlisted men back up to thirteen hundred. Finally, on April 14, Sam Houston and his army moved off to the southeast, this time to meet the enemy.

When Santa Anna saw Houston's "band of robbers" and the entire Texas population fleeing eastward after his successes at San Antonio and Goliad, he believed he had already broken the resistance of the rebellious country. What remained to be done, in his opinion, was a "pacification" of Texas down to the last Anglo-Saxon settlement. So then he disbanded his army into five separate corps, which he sent out in different directions. He himself marched with nearly 750 men as far as San Felipe, considered for a moment whether he should not attack the Texan "hordes" encamped under the "pirate" Houston some forty kilometers above the city, but then decided to move in haste to Harrisburg in order to surprise and capture the Texan government there. The President and Minister, however, fled in time to Galveston Island, and when Santa Anna entered Harrisburg, he found the place deserted, and was only able to arrest three letterpress printers who had stood to the last in front of their typesetting trays to finish one more newspaper number. Disappointed, "El Presidente" moved on to Galveston Bay. There he remained until he heard that Houston was approaching with his men by way of Harrisburg to cross the San Jacinto at Lynchburg to flee on to Trinity.

Santa Anna set out with his corps on April 19. He wanted to get to the ferry before the Texans and cut them off. Little did he know that he was marching just where Sam Houston wanted him to go. For here, in the angle between the San Jacinto and the Buffalo bayou opposite Lynchburg, the frontiersman general was going to force the decisive battle. And Santa Anna, the fox, fell into the trap. The "Napoleon of the West" had met his match!

This geographically complex area on the San Jacinto was indeed a trap. Sam Houston had reached the ferry that led across to Lynchburg before Santa Anna. With about eight hundred men—the rest he had left in Harrisburg to protect the sick and the baggage—he stood under cover of an oak grove, a prairie stretching for a mile before him. Santa

Anna made camp at the far end of the grassy steppe, on a small knoll that afforded a good view across the plain. Yet did "El Presidente" know that swamps were hidden behind him, making any retreat in a southerly direction impossible? Did he know that the Texans had destroyed the bridge over the Vinces Bayou that led to Harrisburg? Did he know that there was only one way out, southeast across the prairie toward the Brazos? The Texans knew this way out and would probably have found the opening to safety if they had to. Santa Anna, on the other hand, was as sure of his cause as ever, especially after General Cós had joined him on the morning of April 21 — the same Cós who had promised on his honor six months ago, when leaving San Antonio, never to fight Texas again — with five hundred men in reserve. The Mexican army could now be as strong as twelve hundred men.

"El Presidente" did not make any battle plans for the time being. There was plenty of time for that! The Texans would not escape their fate! His brother-in-law's troops had had an exhausting march and were overtired. They should rest first to be fresh for the battle! At the moment there was nothing to fear from the enemy anyway. Or did anyone think they would dare an attack across the prairie in the bright sunlight, where every man offered a visible target from afar? Such an attack would be complete madness. After a good midday meal, Santa Anna lay down for a siesta, and with him slept his officers. A large part of the soldiers also lay down, the others ate, chatted, and broke branches in the nearby woods to protect themselves from the piercing rays of the sun. The horsemen led the unsaddled horses to the watering trough. The Mexican camp presented the peaceful picture of a maneuver bivouac, the carelessness even going so far as to forget to post guards.

THE FIGHT FOR FREEDOM

It was about half past four in the afternoon when suddenly a still sleepy bugler heard a suspicious sound, and looking out over the prairie he saw the Texans creeping up nimbly and quietly, Sam Houston in front of them on a magnificent white horse, and already close to the foot of the hill where the Mexican camp stood. A bugle call—a warning signal! Some officers jumped up, saw the danger, tried to bring their soldiers to defensive positions. In vain! Already the rifle shots of the Texans rattled into the surprised crowd, the two cannons that the citizens of Cincinnati had sent to the freedom fighters spat their shrapnel. The little Texan band of musicians intoned a sentimental love song as a battle cry, "O come to my bower that I built for thee, on roses I will bed thee, on roses all dewy!" But louder than this song rang out the wildly threatening cries, "Revenge for Alamo! Revenge for Goliad!"

Santa Anna's midday nap came to a rowdy end. "I saw," reported a Mexican eyewitness, "His Excellency pacing about like a half-madman, wringing his hands and unable to give any order." Already the Texans had leaped the low breastworks and were charging the headlong fleeing Mexicans with bayonets, rifle butts, sabers, and knives. What followed was not a battle, but a slaughter! Seized by bloodlust, the Union volunteers cut down whatever came in their way. Might a Mexican kneel before them pleading and crying out in fear, "Me no Alamo! Me no Alamo!", they knew no pardon. "Revenge for the Alamo! Revenge for Goliad!" The fugitives sank into the swamps by the dozen and the corpses covered the surrounding prairie by the hundred. By the time evening fell, half the Mexican army was dead, the other half, wounded or unwounded but trapped, and only a few had managed to escape. Two dead and twenty-three wounded-these were the losses the Texans suffered!

Yet where was Santa Anna? The victors searched for him in vain among the prisoners, and fruitlessly among the dead. Had he perished in the swamps? Had he escaped? No Mexican was able to give information about the whereabouts of the president. But mounted patrols still searched near and far across the terrain to track down even the last fugitives. "As we approached the ravine," recounts one of these horsemen, "we discovered a man standing close to a copse on the prairie! He was wearing middle-class clothing, a blue blouse and long pants. Being the only one of us who understood Spanish, I asked the prisoner several questions, which he readily answered. When we inquired where Santa Anna and Cós were, he explained that they had probably escaped to the Brazos.... A comrade took the man on his horse and rode him a mile to the road. There he ordered him to dismount, which the prisoner reluctantly did. He walked slowly and it was obviously difficult for him to walk.... Finally, the Mexican asked permission to ride, saying that he belonged to the cavalry and was not used to walking.... In the end, I was compassionate enough to take him behind me on horseback.... I remember asking him why he had come to Texas and fought us, to which he replied that he was an ordinary soldier who had to obey his officers. I asked him if he had any family, which he confirmed. Nevertheless, when I asked him, "Do you expect to see them again?' he just shrugged his shoulders. We rode to the part of our camp where the prisoners were, to deliver our catch to the guard. How astonished we were when we heard the Mexicans shouting: 'El Presidente! El Presidente! Suddenly we knew that the "Napoleon of the West" had fallen into our hands. The news spread like wildfire through the camp.... Some officers immediately took charge of the illustrious prisoner and led him to General Houston's tent."

THE FIGHT FOR FREEDOM

It took Santa Anna's capture to complete the Texas victory at San Jacinto. Houston received the president lying on a blanket. He had been badly wounded during the fight, a bullet having struck his lower right leg. There were some smooth words from the Mexican and some nasty remarks from Houston about the Alamo and Goliad! Then Santa Anna offered a truce. Houston accepted the offer, demanding that the President immediately instruct his subordinates to retreat to San Antonio. Willingly Santa Anna complied with the demand, and without objection the Mexican corps commanders obeyed the order of their captured commander-in-chief.

When later "El Presidente" concluded a peace with the Texan government in Velasco on May 14, which provided for the immediate evacuation by the enemy troops from Texas, the Mexican soldiers marched to the last man across the Rio Grande. By early June 1836, Texas was free! Settlers could return to their old farms and begin to rebuild what the war had destroyed and devastated. "The first thing father did after breakfast," a Texan recounts in her memoirs, "was to go out into the field. He had planted corn on March 1, and it was high time to plow it. He didn't wait until Monday, nor did he get the house in order first, but first he started working the land." Is there a better example of a farmer's spirit than the farmer who returns to his home after a battle for freedom and takes up the plow on a holy Sunday because the growth and prosperity of his seed demand it?

However, the bodies of the Mexican soldiers were decomposing back at San Jacinto. No one paid any attention to their burial. At night the wolves took their share, although one Texan had crudely scoffed that even the hungriest wolves did not dare to touch the flesh of people who would have eaten as much pepper as the Mexicans did during their lifetime. Did they forget to bury the enemy in the joy of victory and homecoming? Or was this, too, revenge for the Alamo, where Santa Anna had denied the defenders a Christian burial and had thrown them on a pyre and burned them? It was only in the fall, when the cows gnawed the bones and their milk spoiled, that the farmers gathered the bones and buried them in large ditches...

SEVENTH CHAPTER

THE REPUBLIC

There were three battles of world historical significance after Waterloo, according to American historian Clarence Wharton: the one at San Jacinto in 1836, the one at Gettysburg in 1863, and the one at the Marne in 1914. "Had Santa Anna been victorious," Wharton writes, "the Texan settlements would have been destroyed and Mexican rule would have been re-established over the territories north and east of the Rio Grande. The antislavery movement in the Union North, however, so strongly opposed the acquisition of land where the spread of slavery was to be feared that these states would have been the allies of Mexico against any further expansionist efforts of the Union South. We were writhing in the throes of our Civil War twenty years later, and European statesmen were doing all they could to prevent our westward expansion. The vast territory gained at San Jacinto, and the much greater still which fell to us through the Mexican War which with inevitable necessity followed, might have remained Mexican or passed into the possession of European states. A million square miles, from which were cut the present states of Texas, New Mexico, Arizona, California, Nevada, Utah, and parts of Wyoming, Colorado, Kansas, and Oklahoma, were conquered by us at San Jacinto on April 21, 1836."

Although it may be argued against these views that, in view of the natural expansionism of the United States, even without the victory of the Texas revolutionaries, a military conflict between the Union and Mexico would have occurred at some point, and that the star-spangled banner would have begun its advance to the Pacific coast, if not before, then after the War of Secession, they cannot be completely dismissed out of hand. It remains a historical fact that the breakaway from Texas was the beginning of the end of Mexican rule in North America, and that the annexations of 1845 and 1848 brought the United States that continental sweep of territory that became the basis for its rise to world power. Thus, it is not an overestimation to count the meeting at San Jacinto as one of the decisive battles in world history.

The victory at San Jacinto marked the conclusion of the Texas struggle for freedom and the confirmation of the Declaration of Independence that the Texan representatives had proclaimed in the hour of greatest danger. It still remained to be seen, however, whether the Republic of Texas, which the strategic talents of Sam Houston and the bravery of the colonists and Union volunteers had saved from falling into the abyss at the last moment, was at all viable. The country remained in a state of hopeless confusion for many months. It took quite a while for the fugitive farmers and their families to return to their old settlements, and the fears that Mexico would equip a new army and take revenge for the defeat at San Jacinto would not abate. Hence there was no venture to deport the irregulars, who continued to pour from the United States across the frontier in large numbers, and were so unruly an element in their burning thirst for action that the Texan government was unable to cope with them. Even those American men who arrived when the last shot had long since died away felt themselves the real saviors of Texas and arrogated to themselves the right to have a weighty say in the political affairs of the country.

When the Texan government—thinking correctly that the overthrown Santa Anna, as soon as he was back in Mexico, would strive anew for power, and that the party struggle which would ensue would frustrate all intentions of revenge against Texas—decided to release the Mexican president and send him to Vera Cruz, volunteers who had just landed brought the prisoner down from the ship and forced his further detention. In the opinion of the Texan army, now composed only of young American adventurers, Santa Anna had forfeited his life because of the outrages at San Antonio and Goliad, and demands to execute the "Napoleon of the West" were increasingly being heard. Other disputes sharpened the antagonism between the confident army and the feeble government. The volunteers wanted to shorten their boredom by invading the Mexican northern provinces, while the Texan president rightly thought it wisest to keep quiet and not irritate the enemy unnecessarily. When the government, in order to regain any influence at all over the army, which had completely slipped out of its control, appointed a new commander-in-chief, the irregulars summarily sent this general home. Indeed, it almost seemed as if a military coup was about to take place. Even then a company was on its way to East Texas to depose the civilian government.

The interim government, which had been set up by the "National Assembly" in Washington at the Brazos, finally called new elections, and Sam Houston, the victor at San

Jacinto, was elected president with an overwhelming majority. No matter how much the Anglo-Americans pretend to be opposed to soldierly leadership, when it comes down to it, natural instinct breaks out in them too, real war glory finds true popular appeal, and in the history of the United States there has been more than one successful general who has been entrusted with the political leadership of the Confederacy without much inquiry as to his political ability. The Texans, nevertheless, were fortunate. In Sam Houston. They gained not a political failure, but a gifted statesman who knew how to master the special circumstances of a frontier state, as Texas was. No sooner had Houston taken office as president than the country felt the hand of strong leadership. An administration was established, judges appointed, a currency created, the recalcitrant volunteers sent to the Union on "furlough", and the blue banner with the gold star rose from the flagpole to proclaim to the world far and wide that Texas was an independent state, entitled to be recognized by the other nations and admitted into their fellowship.

Sam Houston, the "Raven"

American democracy has undergone many a profound transformation in the more than one hundred and fifty years that have elapsed since its inception, although the constitutional framework in which it is set has remained almost unchanged. One of the most important changes occurred in the 1920s, when the rugged frontiersman of the West vied with the bourgeois Yankee of the East for authoritative political influence. At that time, frontierism gradually forced the introduction of universal suffrage in all parts of the Union, and in the end the United States had that government "by the people, for the people" which suited the primitive democratic sensibilities of the common frontier settler.

Frontierism was led in its struggles by men who embodied in their very nature the American pioneer with all his toughness and passion, prowess and vigor, unboundedness and boorishness. With Andrew Jackson at their head, who presided over the Union from 1829 to 1837 with almost dictatorial authority, these frontier politicians so deeply stamped their imprint on American democracy that it can still be seen in many individual traits today. It is therefore more than historically appealing to trace the life picture of a man like Sam Houston, who, along with Jackson, is undoubtedly one of the most important frontier leaders of those days. It is the picture of a personality as strong as it is bizarre, with a life course shrouded in the wild romance of being on the frontier, with life paths that are at times shrouded in a mysterious darkness. But as the victor at San Jacinto and the first president of the Republic of Texas, Houston etched his name with great letters in the annals of American history.

Sam Houston was born in Virginia, in a valley of the "Blue Ridge," in 1793, the fifth child of a landowner of Scotch descent. His father, however, preferred to devote himself to the duties of a militia inspector rather than to his business, so much so that at his death the plantation was completely overindebted and had to be sold. Resolving promptly, the widow, a courageous, energetic woman, moved with her nine sons and daughters to East Tennessee and settled immediately on the border of Indian Territory. There, thanks to her industriousness, the family soon regained its prosperity.

Only Sam, then fifteen years old and probably more like

his father than his mother in character, had no taste for the hard work of clearing and cultivating the land, but instead was a real good-for-nothing wandering around in the woods, dreaming of the heroic deeds of the Greeks and Romans. Since he did not seem at all suited to farming, he was apprenticed to an uncle in the nearby frontier town of Maryville. In the counting house. Sam felt like he was in prison, and one day he disappeared without a trace. After a long search, his brothers finally discovered him in an Indian village, lying under a tree and reading Homer's Iliad. The runaway could not be persuaded to return! He stayed with the Cherokees, and only after a year, when his clothes were tattered, did he reappear at home. As soon as he had a new shirt on his back, he ran away again to the Redskins. Again he lived two years as an Indian among the Indians. Under the name Co-lon-neh, the "Raven", the handsome, tall lad with chestnut brown hair and bright blue eyes, whom the chief Cherokee had taken into his wigwam as an adopted son, spent a time of carefree youth with the savages. Old Houston's heart still warms at the recollection of those days when he "took part in the merry games of the happy Indian boys, wandered along the banks of the rivers with some Indian girls under cover of dense woods, and talked to them in that universally understood language which is sure to find its way to the heart."

Sam was a merchant, between gambling and love, and he must have had some skill in it, small as his business was. For when he reappeared in Maryville in the spring of 1812, he had in his pocket the still considerable sum of one hundred dollars. He answered the anxious question of the worried relatives in an amazing way, about what he, who had learned nothing, was now going to embark upon. He was going to start a school! A crude log house, five miles from town, in which gaps in the beams replaced the windows, was soon rented, and since Houston demanded only a small school fee, he did not need to be at a loss for pupils. Wielding the willow whip, with much dignity and little knowledge, the nineteen-year-old ruled his flock of children through the summer until the winter cold put an end to the jest. Feeling that he now had some gaps in his education after all, the teacher turned into a student who let himself be initiated into the rudiments of mathematics by his more accomplished rival in the town. Alongside this, he wasted his money in wild cavorting in the saloons.

By March 1813, Sam had not a penny left to his name, and the war drums were beginning to sound in the country. War with England had broken out, and the Union was looking for soldiers. So Houston enlisted in the American army. After four months he was an ensign and moved into the field with his regiment—but not against the British, but against the Creeks, who had allied themselves with the British. Andrew Jackson, the militia general from Tennessee, was in command in this campaign of extermination. At the "horseshoe" of the Tallapoosa River in Alabama, the Redskins were surrounded. During the assault on the entrenchments of the Indians, an arrow penetrated Houston's thigh; he allowed it to be torn out despite the barb, and he remained lying with a gaping wound as a result. But later, when Jackson called for volunteers to take the last stand of the desperately struggling Creeks, the ensign rushed to the fore. A bullet shattered his right arm and he never was able to use it again.

The wounded man's life was in danger for weeks. When he finally recovered, he received a lieutenant's commission as a reward for his bravery. More importantly, Jackson, the great frontiersman leader, had taken notice of him. On his recommendation, the young officer was appointed official Indian agent in 1817 and given the task of inducing the Cherokees to emigrate to upper Arkansas. There the "Raven" now sat again in the wigwam of his adoptive father, and around him the chiefs of the tribe wrestled with the heavy decision to look for new hunting grounds beyond the Mississippi. Co-lon-neh advised them to yield with honest conviction. He knew that if the Indians did not voluntarily vacate the land, the Americans would take it by force. Nevertheless, there were many questions and complaints that the Cherokees wished to present to the "great father of the whites". Dressed in Indian costume, the "Raven" accompanied their delegation to Washington as an interpreter. After one of the audiences, the Secretary of War reproached him on how he, as a lieutenant of the army, could dare to walk around the federal capital as a savage. This deeply wounded Houston's pride. Wasn't the confidence the Cherokees had in him, because they regarded him as one of their own, the secret of why the negotiations with the tribe had gone so quickly? Now came a minister who knew nothing of frontier life and thought he could rebuke him! Let the gentlemen in Washington see where they could get suitable Indian agents. Houston did not play along any longer. He took his leave, removing his colorful attire!

Thus it was time for a change! After six months of study in a lawyer's office, Sam Houston settled as a lawyer near Nashville, the capital of Tennessee. When he visited his clientele, his path often took him past the "Hermitage", Andrew Jackson's country estate, soon he was a permanent guest at the "Hermitage", and in the course of time his relations with the powerful frontier captain became closer and closer. Houston began his political career as a retainer and protégé of "Old Hickory", which was Jackson's nickname on the other Frontier.

He was first elected colonel, then major general of militia, and later district attorney. In 1823 Nashville sent him to Congress. Publicly, however, the congressman did not distinguish himself much during his four years in the House. He rendered all the more valuable service in backstage politics. Jackson could be quite satisfied with this "young man," who was also happy to help him with private errands and, when it came to the crunch, shot his way about in duels on his behalf. Houston was offered a new opportunity in 1827: the governorship of Tennessee was up for grabs. He was put forward as the candidate of the "Democratic Party," winning the election.

To become Governor of Tennessee, the most important state in the Mississippi basin was something indeed! Already there were whispers of further advancement, naming him as the coming Vice President, yes, even President of the Union. The frontier was on the rise politically and Andrew Jackson was elected head of state with an overwhelming majority, and there were notable circles on the frontier who were convinced that Houston possessed the abilities to succeed the idolized "Old Hickory" in the White House. As a son-in-law of the distinguished and noble family of the Allens, he was more than welcome. True, Eliza had hesitated to say yes when the governor tempestuously asked her to marry him—her heart was probably otherwise bound. Yet the eighteen-year-old girl could not withstand the pressure of the family council, and in 1829 the wedding was celebrated in the midst of preparations for the new election for the governorship.

Again, Houston's election seemed safe. Then, a few days before the vote, the scandalous news spread around the country that Eliza had left her husband and returned to her parents. What had happened? People whispered and gossiped—as always in America, the people took sides with the woman. Only an explanation by Houston could save the situation. In a chivalrous spirit, however, Houston said only as much as was necessary to protect Eliza's honor. Otherwise he was silent, silent then and throughout his life. He did not like to owe his political career to the slight of a woman. He declared his resignation from the governorship and fled Nashville secretly at night. It was not until much later that news reached Tennessee that the ex-politician was living out his life in the West, somewhere in the wildernesses beyond the Mississippi....

Many an ox had to be slaughtered by the supreme Cherokee chief on the Arkansas to feed the many guests who came to greet the return of the "Raven". It was not only guests from their own tribe. Delegations from neighboring tribes arrived from near and far. They all wanted the advice of the experienced Co-lon-neh, who had been such a great chief among the palefaces. There was unrest and discontent among the Indians. The Washington government once again had failed to keep its promises and they had bitter complaints to make about the shady dealings of the government agents. Sam Houston began to travel around from one tribe to another in Indian country, became the spokesman for the Redskins, watched the agents so that none of the money they had to pay out to the Indians on behalf of the federal government would remain in their pockets. People in Washington were paying attention and had the ex-governor watched. What was the man planning? Was he trying to incite the Redskins to revolt? Houston wrote to the government authorities that they need not worry, that he was only concerned with making peace among the Indians.

Years passed by without the fears of Washington's official circles coming true. In the meantime, Houston was looking after the rights of the Cherokees. He proudly declared that his tribe was a free nation and not subject to American jurisdiction. He thought of a novel way to make this fact a matter of judicial necessity. He bought up a large stock of liquor barrels, saying. If the Cherokees were a free nation, then he could not be forbidden to sell them firewater. On the other hand, if they were subject to Union law, then he was forbidden to deal in liquor with them. A major lawsuit ensued, in which Houston was defeated. What was the "Raven" supposed to do now? Pour away the liquor? Houston set about drinking up the hooch all by himself! After all, he had so many bad memories to drown! He, who could have been president of the Union, had built his wigwam among the Cherokees and taken a former playmate, Tiana, as his wife! It was well that there was a remedy to make one forget quite a few things! Soon Sam was no longer called Co-lon-neh by the Indians, but the "Great Drunkard"!

Houston arrived in Washington in early 1832 with a delegation of Indians to negotiate with the U.S. government. He beat up a member of Congress who had spread slander about him in the open street. This caused a huge scandal, and Parliament assembled as a tribunal to investigate and expiate the case. Houston appeared before Congress in Indian costume and so skillfully presented his case that he was fined only pro forma. Then President Jackson invited him to the White House! No one knows what the two talked about but in February 1833, one Don Samuel Houston crossed the Mexican border at Nacogdoches. Texas had one more new immigrant.

It is not known if Houston has been sent by Jackson. Some claim it, others deny it. Even at the Arkansas, Houston had boasted in drunkenness that he would one day be enthroned as emperor in Montezuma's halls. Jackson had heard of this and had given the military authorities the sharpest instructions to prevent any attempt by the ex-governor to join with the Indians in attacking Mexico and embarrassing the Union. On the other hand, Jackson's unscrupulous expansionism, the robust manner in which he annexed Florida, again suggest some political back channels. In any case, Jackson wanted Texas, now almost entirely populated with Americans. This is clearly demonstrated by his various offers to buy it from the Mexican government.

Houston skillfully knew how to play to the fore among the Anglo-Saxon Texans. He participated in the various "conventions" as Nacogdoches' emissary, and when it came to open combat with Mexico, he was appointed commander-in-chief of the Texan army. How he forged a powerful force out of the untrained colonists and during a demoralizing retreat, how he defiantly assumed sole responsibility for military decisions and asserted his authority with calm self-assurance over recalcitrant officers and enlisted men, and how, with cool calculation, he maneuvered the Mexican enemy into an unfavorable position and finished them off by a daring, lightning-quick attack—all bear testimony to Sam Houston's leadership qualities. The victory at San Jacinto was his victory, and it was rightful that the grateful settlers should entrust to him the leadership of the Texan republic as its first president.

Sam Houston was a statesman after the heart of the common frontiersman. No one who met him on the road would have suspected the president of Texas in this man with his unkempt, sometimes outlandish clothes, who frankly shouted a greeting to every wagoner and engaged in conversation with every farmer. But the broad-shouldered, tall figure, the erect, toned posture, the facial expression that reflected an iron will, the manly beauty that even in his later years earned him the affection of women, radiated a natural dignity. And Houston's reputation did not even suffer from the fact that everyone knew what a heavy drinker he was, just as he could afford to preside over the meeting of a temperance-loving itinerant preacher, to rail against excessive drinking in his closing address, and to dismiss the audience with the admonition to follow "follow his words and not his deeds!"

However, there were also enemies who hated Houston. Nowhere else in political life did petty squabbling, gloating jealousy and personal intrigue play a greater role than in American frontier democracy. Houston also knew how to return hatred with hatred. For all his intellectual superiority, he was a man riddled with wild passions, who took unrestrained revenge for the wrongs done to him, who pursued his political opponents with merciless criticism and, as a popular orator, was able to pull out all the stops of unscrupulous demagogy. However, with all his good and bad character traits, he was a full-bodied man of exuberant strength and vitality, the kind of man that only the American frontier could have produced. This was the secret of his popular character, that he never wanted to be more than a frontiersman. Nothing characterizes Sam Houston better than the early morning audiences, when he appeared at the back door of his house, dressed only in shirt and trousers, soaped up and began to shave without a mirror, while at the same time the business of state and administration was being discussed with ministers and officials, politicians and petitioners....

There was only one fundamental difference between Sam Houston and the typical American frontiersman—his attitude toward the Indians. The Anglo-Saxon pioneer hated but Houston loved the Redskins. Co-lon-neh never forgot that the Cherokees had taken him in and treated him as their son and brother. He was one of the few whites who had lived in Indian wigwams and had come to know the humanity of these brown people. He also conceded the Redskins the right to live and was convinced that Americans and Indians could coexist in peace and friendship, if only the white man sincerely wanted it. That was it—the pioneer denied the Indian the right to occupy and possess the land he intended to claim for himself. The Cherokees, having been driven out of the Union, had settled in Texas, in the lands north of the Camino Real between the Neches and Sabine. It had been easy for Houston to conclude a peace treaty with his adopted brethren in early 1836 and spare Texas Indian unrest during the freedom struggle. He had taken an oath of allegiance on behalf of the Texas government at that time that the Anglo-Saxon settlers would keep this treaty and the Cherokees would remain in possession of their new hunting grounds undisturbed. In December 1836, Houston submitted the treaty to the Texas Congress for confirmation. "If we treat them well, and if they find they can trade with us, and learn by experience that we are not their enemies, they will become our friends. It has never come to my knowledge that any treaty made with an Indian tribe was first violated or broken by the Redskins." The Texas Senate refused to recognize the treaty claiming that the Cherokees' assertion that they owned the land on the Neches was false, and that if they had been promised possession by Texas representatives, they had exceeded their authority. Well, Sam Houston found ways and means to see that the agreements with the Indians were honored even without the consent of the Senate. As soon as he had completed his first term, however, his successor, Lamar, began a furious campaign of extermination against the Cherokees, and on this point his policy was undoubtedly more popular than Sam Houston's.

Part of Houston's character portrait is the observation that he remained faithful to his Indian squaw, Tiana. It wasn't until 1840, when Tiana had died and a court had granted him a divorce from Eliza Allen, that he married Margaret Lea, the daughter of a wealthy Alabama plantation owner. And this woman, with her devoted love and pure piety, was able to tame the wild jungle bear. Sam not only gave up the vice of drunkenness, gradually he began to assume outwardly and inwardly something of the attitude befitting his position as ex-president and Union senator, and though it took a long time and his defiant soul also wrestled hard with the decision, in the end he knelt beside his beloved Margaret as a devout Christian in the houses of worship of the Baptist Church.

Sam Houston represented Texas in the U.S. Senate from 1846 to 1858. As the Southern states became more passionate about their right to secede from the Confederacy, he was the only one of their representatives who fully embraced the idea of the Union. In order to keep Texas in the Union, he presented himself as a candidate in the gubernatorial election of 1859. So great was the impression of his personality, even now, that he was elected, although all parties were working against him. Yet he was too weak to prevent the annexation of Texas to the Confederacy in

1861. His plan to prevent the impending fratricidal war by setting before the American nation a common foreign policy goal in a campaign of conquest against Mexico evaporated before the first steps toward its realization could be taken. Houston manfully refused to swear an oath of allegiance to the Confederacy of secessionist Southern states. The Texans deposed their wayward governor and sent their troops to the Civil War battlefield. Houston's eldest son was also among the soldiers who went out to fight the Union!

Sam Houston lived quietly on his estates from then on. There he died in loneliness in 1863.

The Lone Star

After the victory at San Jacinto, when the Texans raised a flag showing a solitary golden star on an azure background, they wanted to express by this beautiful emblem nothing other than their ardent wish to see this star as soon as possible included in the starry wreath of the Union banner. The referendum, which had been held in 1836 at the same time as the new presidential elections, had brought the clear result that all the colonists, with the exception of a vanishing minority, longed for the immediate annexation of their country to the United States. The establishment of an independent republic had been only an embarrassment arising from the necessities of the struggle for freedom. Independence had been declared only to get away from Mexico—if the Texans had had their way, it would have been immediately exchanged for dependence on the Union.

Things did not go according to the Texans' wishes! The recognition of the Texan Republic under international law already met with difficulties in view of the attitude of the anti-slavery movement in the American Congress. Only by Andrew Jackson's authorization to send a diplomatic representative to Texas as soon as the country had a stable government, had it been possible to achieve this through the back door. When the question of Texas annexation came up for discussion, however, the Senate rejected the Texas offer by a vote of 24 to 14, and in the House of Representatives former President John Quincy Adams, who had himself sought the acquisition for sale of the lands beyond the Sabine twelve years earlier, made a three-week obstructionist speech, at the end of which the House went on vacation without a vote. In his diary Adams recorded, "The annexation of Texas to the Union means the first step toward the conquest of all Mexico and the West Indies, the establishment of a seagoing, colonial, slaveholding monarchy and the destruction of liberty." Texas was no longer spoken of in the United States for years to come. The matter was considered a hot potato that no one dared touch for the sake of peace. When forces began to stir again in the southern states to bring about the annexation of Texas, Garrison, the antislavery apostle, declared in the north, "It is unthinkable that any decent man should wish Texas success. Those who sympathize with this pseudo-republic hate liberty and wish to dethrone God."

Thus, the independent Republic of Texas, which was intended as a stopgap measure, became, willy-nilly, a permanent institution, and the Texans, who were refused annexation to the United States, were forced to manage on their own. In more ways than one, the Republic of the Golden Star was in an exceedingly vulnerable position.

Texas had to be prepared for a new Mexican attack at any moment. Mexico did not think of recognizing the independent Texan state. In its eyes, the Anglo-Saxon settlers were and remained rebels who had to be put down as soon as a favorable opportunity presented itself. That this opportunity did not arise for the time being was due to the internal unrest that had broken out anew in Mexico. Basically, however, open war still prevailed. Neither the Mexican government, which succeeded Santa Anna, adhered to the "extorted" armistice that had been concluded on the battlefield at San Jacinto, nor Santa Anna himself, who had been released by Sam Houston in November 1836 and since 1840 had once again played the almighty dictator in his homeland. Smaller and more serious "border incidents" constantly reminded the Texans of the danger that threatened them from the Rio Grande and could one day suddenly escalate like an avalanche.

In the early days, Texas looked in vain to the European powers for support. It is true that France recognized the Texan Republic as early as 1839 but this was based more on animosity against Mexico, whose coasts were at that time blockaded by a French fleet in order to force the payment of arrears on bond interest, than real interest in the young state. England followed with its recognition in 1840, really only so as not to miss out on possible trade advantages, and ratification of the treaty was postponed until mid-1842. It took a long time before British policy realized that its traditional friendship with Mexico, which it wanted to see preserved unweakened as a bulwark against the expansionism of the United States, could very well be reconciled with a sympathy for Texas. In other words: the golden star that was emblazoned on the state flag of Texas was indeed a "lone star" in the years until 1842!

Despite this delicate situation, the Texans claimed boundaries for their new state, for which there was not the slightest justification in history. In Spanish and Mexican times, the province extended only to the Nueces and Medina in the west and to the headwaters of the Red River in the north. What concern, however, was historical lore to a true frontier politician! Andrew Jackson, who had just suffered defeat on the question of Texas annexation, but who nevertheless did not give up hope for a Greater America, thought it best to make provision for the future. When, on the eve of the end of his term in 1837, he received the Texan envoy to inform him of the appointment of a diplomatic representative for the young republic on the Gulf Coast, he advised him, "Texas must lay claim to the territories as far as the Pacific, must demand and hold California. Then in the Northern States resistance to annexation will be crippled, since the North and East of the Union have large fishing enterprises on the Pacific coast." Well, the Texans were after all not quite as bold as Jackson wished. They declared "only" the Rio Grande from its mouth to its source and then a dead-straight line up to Oregon to be the western boundary of Texas, while to the east the boundary agreed upon in 1819 between Spain and North America was to be the dividing line. Viewed in the light of day, the Texans were claiming for themselves the good half of New Mexico, which no Anglo-Saxon settler had yet entered and was still firmly in Mexican hands! The claim remained a claim, indeed: the Texans never occupied these lands. Only such exaggerated territorial claims had the consequence of increasing the hatred of the Mexicans. Nevertheless, the Texan immodesty had its "good" side in the long run! For in 1846, after the annexation of Texas to the United States, the Union president was able to declare war on Mexico on the grounds that Mexican soldiers who appeared on the east bank of the Rio Grande had unlawfully entered "American" soil. It should not be forgotten that in 1850 Texas "ceded" the New Mexican and northern "territories" to the federal government in exchange for tens of millions of dollars, thus getting rid of its debt burden from the republican period.

The "Lone Star Republic" had not been able to survive without incurring debt, and the vexed question of money was always one of its most pressing concerns. The taxing potential of the newly developed land was minimal. The settlers fed themselves from the fruits of their fields, wove their own cloth and sewed their own clothes, and it was considered a sign of prosperity to wear proper shoes instead of homemade moccasins. What the self-supporting farmer had to buy in addition was only marginal, and even these "purchases" were mostly barter transactions. Accordingly, little was imported, and customs revenues were modest, despite a tariff averaging 25 percent of value, measured in absolute terms. Nevertheless, more than half of the total revenue flowed into the state budget from customs duties!

Texas was rich only in land, which, insofar as it was still wilderness, a law had declared to be state property. Adding the New Mexican territories, the government could offer over 180 million acres, or nearly 730000 square kilometers, for sale. Houston was mistaken, however, in thinking that this wealth could be monetized, even in part, and that the state treasury, which looked alarmingly empty, would soon be filled. He overlooked the fact that Texas had already spoiled the deal for itself. The bond and loan lenders—there was a debt of one and a quarter million dollars when Houston took office—had been given land warrants, an acre for fifty cents, as surety, and wild speculation was carried on with these "scrips", which were rapidly sinking in value. It was not very much different with the gifts of land which the Texas Legislature distributed with lavish liberality to the Union volunteers and to the old-established colonists (each family was allotted 4605 acres!) after the close of the struggle for freedom. The result was that there was no market at all for government lands, although immigration from the Union was growing year by year and Texas may have had a population of about 100,000 in 1846. In order to make the wildernesses saleable at least for the future, one even went over to making lands available to immigrant entrepreneurs for settlement free of charge, according to the old Spanish-Mexican model, in such a way that one reserved a section for the government next to each settlement site. Many European immigrants were placed on such "grants", most notably Germans brought to Texas by a German company called the "Mainz Adelsverein" in the years between 1844 and 1846.

The "grant" was a policy for the long term, which initially did not generate any revenue. Since a state cannot be administered and governed without money, Texas too resorted to the remedy that every Secretary of the Treasury has resorted to in times of need — money was issued and banknotes printed. Sam Houston began with the honest intention of issuing paper money only to the extent that the economy had a need for a means of payment. Yet even the road to the hell of inflation is paved with good intentions! Houston himself already had to use the printing press more often than he originally intended, and his successor Lamar unscrupulously financed his various high-flying enterprises by issuing banknotes. When the "star money", for which the government even promised to pay interest, and the "redbacks" were completely devalued, treasury notes were issued, but after a short time they too were worth only thirty percent of their face value. The state lands and the government guarantee did not prove to be sufficient collateral in any case! It was only the treasury that accepted this paper money in payment at the full rate —and the Secretary of the Treasury, for example, received a whole three dollars of silver money in 1842, which he guarded as a rare treasure.

It is possible that the financial situation would not have been quite so disastrous if Sam Houston had been able to remain in power for longer. He certainly left a deficit of two million dollars at the conclusion of his "term" in 1838, but one must give him credit for the fact that the settlement of the freedom struggle and the establishment of the administration had caused extraordinary costs. The extent to which he strove for the utmost austerity is shown by his own lifestyle. "As we approached the President's house," recounts a visitor from Houston's first term, "we had to wade through water up to our ankles.... The house is a small log cabin with two rooms.... We were led into a room which in other countries would be called the antichamber. Well, the floor was dirty and filthy, a large fire was burning, a small table on which paper and stationery lay stood in the middle, cots, trunks, and all sorts of utensils were to be found in this corner and that." As for the bachelor president's private room, that was not much different!

Sam Houston had to move out of this "White House" after only two years. Two years in office for the first president, three years for the following presidents, with a ban on immediate re-election—that was the rule of the Texas constitution, which in these provisions, as in the fixing of the election period of the representatives to one year and of the senators to three years, reflected the typical distrust with which the American frontier persecuted the men whom it appointed to public posts from its own ranks. It was just the reverse of frontier democracy, where everyone felt themselves to be as much worth as each other, that one pettily resented the one who was politically elevated, and thus socially, singled out from the crowd. Without further ado, the backwoodsman presupposed that a politician or a civil servant would be afflicted by intellectual arrogance, would be lining his own pockets or would be setting up an anti-freedom "dictatorship" if he remained in office too long. And this was to be countered by the possibility of dismissal at short notice and by tighter control. No one thought about the fact that, by excessively shortening the terms of office, a possible evil was exchanged for an actual one! For it was an evil that the government of the country was constantly changing, that no political line could be maintained, and no political program could be accomplished. It is in the nature of things that the successor, even if only to prove that he is also a man, at least tries to do things differently from his predecessor even if he cannot do them better.

In any case, President Lamar did things quite differently from Sam Houston. In the three years from 1839 to 1841 in which he governed, the national debt increased from 1.8 to 7.5 million dollars, and the Texas currency fell from a rate of between 50 and 85 cents per dollar to a rate of 8 to 11 cents. These were the financial consequences of a big-man policy that took no account of the actual condition of the Republic of Texas and consequently foundered. Inflation of the administrative apparatus, excessive increase of salaries as well as wanton fights with the Indians, militarily senseless incursions into Mexican territory, dispatch of the Texan warships to support the revolution on Yucatan—

these were some of the sins of Lamar's policy, each equally costly.

Crusader and Troubadour

The Lamars were descended from a French Huguenot who had fled Richelieu's persecutions in the 17th century to Maryland, the colony of the English philanthropist Lord Baltimore. Great-grandfather Lamar had then moved further south to Georgia in the mid-18th century, and father Lamar was still living in that state when a second son was born to him in August 1798. On the advice of a cranky uncle, they gave the little earthling, who would later go down in Texas history as the second president of the Lone Star Republic, the two fancy and highfalutin first names of Bonaparte Mirabeau. Now, parents never know at the time of baptism whether the first name they choose for their child will later fit or not. In Lamar's case, it happened by chance that the first names corresponded to his character. This is not to say that he had the disposition to become a Bonaparte or a Mirabeau; that was not to be expected, and it would be fair to scoff at the fact that he did not become one. The fact that the twenty-two-year-old, after failing as a merchant, found his way into politics as a journalist and private secretary to the governor of Georgia should not even be alluded to, nor should the fact that the French ancestral heritage asserted itself in his self-confidence and ambition, his intelligence and wealth of ideas, his stylishness and gift for oratory, his liveliness and restlessness. What is meant is just this, that the same feeling of the unreal, the degenerate, the fantastic, which one feels when one hears the names of the two great heroes of the French Revolution used as epithets, arises when one gains an insight into the nature of this man.

Lamar's character can hardly be more aptly characterized than in the words which a contemporary entered about the Texas president in his diary, and which, in addition to all the criticism, reveal Lamar's endearing qualities, his personal bravery and cleanliness, the sincerity of his convictions and the zest of his idealism, "General Lamar may mean well, but he is altogether a dreamer and a poet, a sort of political troubadour and crusader, and utterly unable to cope with the realities of everyday life with which his present office confronts him."

In March 1836, as the freedom struggle was beginning, this troubadour and crusader came to live in Texas. Lamar had not made much progress in Georgia, despite his briskness. Now he wanted to settle in Texas to try his luck here. Enthusiastic as he was, general patriotic high spirits seized him. In short order, he postponed all his personal affairs. He made his way alone to Sam Houston's army to join the ranks of the fighters as a volunteer. He arrived just in time to take part in the advance against Santa Anna. And like Sam Houston, Bonaparte Mirabeau Lamar won the laurels of glory at San Jacinto that secured him the adoration of the Texas people and opened the way to the presidential chair.

On April 20, when the enemy armies were sighted, the Texan cavalry attempted to gain possession by a sleight of hand of the cannon in the possession of Santa Anna. The attack having failed, the Texans were forced to turn back and gallop away in haste. Then Lamar saw a young lad fall from his horse, wounded. Ignoring the danger to his own life, he rode back, rescued his comrade from the invading Mexicans and dashed off with him. This courageous act, at the same time a fine testimony to personal bravery and comradely spirit, so excited the Texans that they immediately elected Lamar commander of their cavalry. In the decisive attack the following day, the newly minted colonel led his 71 cavalrymen so well that he contributed in no small measure to the success of the victory. His name and performance were duly highlighted in the report Sam Houston prepared on the Battle of the San Jacinto. When new elections were held in September 1836, the Texan people appointed him to the post of vice president.

The Texas Constitution, just as the U.S. Constitution, did not allow the vice president to have any direct influence on the affairs of government. He was simply a substitute in the event of the president's premature death. The only official duty Lamar had to fulfill was to preside over the Senate sessions, and this left him leisure enough to pursue his historical inclinations, which corresponded so well with the basic romantic trait of his nature. For months he traveled about the country gathering material for a history of Texas, and though nothing ever came of this book plan, which was taken up again and again, the number of documents gathered shows with how much earnestness and zeal he set about this work.

However little Lamar was heard of politically in the early years of the Lone Star Republic, it was a foregone conclusion by the time of Houston's presidency that the vice president would succeed him. There were few personalities in Texas at that time well enough known to the public to make them candidates for popular election, and personality was the only thing that mattered. No parties had yet been formed which would have been able, by their organization and agitation, to establish a dark horse. Bonaparte Mirabeau Lamar would undoubtedly have been elected President of Texas by an overwhelming majority in the fall of 1838 even if his two competitors had not taken their own lives shortly before election day—a strange duplicity of events. The heroic feat he had accomplished at San Jacinto weighed more heavily in the judgment of the Texas frontiersmen than all the political pros and cons that were being brought up.

"If we maintain our present independence," said the new President, anticipating his governmental declaration, in his farewell address to the Senators, "if we spread knowledge and education through public schools; if we establish a sound and fixed currency, if we remove all temptations and opportunities for fraudulent schemes and dishonest gain, if we make truth, virtue, and patriotism the guiding stars of our political action, if we make truth, virtue, and patriotism the guiding stars of our political action and if we secure the confidence of neighboring nations by the wisdom of our laws and the sincerity of our will—then I cannot see why we should not succeed, within a very short period of time, in giving to our young republic such political importance and proud status that it will not only command the respect and admiration of the world, but that even those nations which today reject our friendship will be induced to endeavor to establish commercial relations with us, which at the present moment we are vainly seeking to establish with them." And in his Inaugural Address of December 1838, Lamar reiterated that although there was so great a sentiment in favor of joining the Union, he could discover no advantage, social, economic, or political, in affiliating with a country already so torn by internal antagonisms. Toward a great, powerful, independent Republic of Texas—that is where President Lamar was headed from the first day he took office. And at first he had the overwhelming majority of votes in the House of Representatives and the Senate in his favor, until opposition began to stir under Sam Houston's leadership. Lamar would have had to be capable and a master politician to silence these critics and opponents.

Bonaparte Mirabeau Lamar, however, was a "troubadour and crusader". He wanted more, much more, than the political and economic forces of Texas allowed. Perhaps he would have taken more time in this or that had he faced a longer term in office. Yet again the Constitution gave him only three short years in which to carry out his political ideas, and he knew that his predecessor would again succeed him, leaving undone that which he failed to carry out. Thus it came about that he, who in his government declaration had placed so much emphasis on stabilizing the currency and promoting the economy, sought to obtain the means for his policies through inflationary maneuvers and ruined the currency and the economy. Nothing, however, did so much harm to Lamar and turned the initial friendship of the House of Representatives into eventual enmity as the progressive demonetization. Only the people and the congressmen were short-sighted enough not to notice that the very act of the President, to which they gave their unqualified applause, was mostly to blame for the decline of the currency.

Lamar's Indian policy—the ruthless fight against the Comanches, the relentless expulsion of the Cherokees—cost a considerable amount of money. More than half of the money spent in the years between 1839 and 1841 was for this purpose! Lamar had already learned to hate the Redskins in Georgia, and there was no doubt in his mind that the Indian had to give way where the Anglo-Saxon pioneer settled. "The poorest farmer whose cabin stands in the remotest corner of our frontier has the same hallowed claim to be protected by the government as the man who lives in prosperity and comfort in the midst of our most populous city." Lamar was serious about this solemn assurance when the Cherokees began to harass the settlers who had settled in what Sam Houston wanted to be considered Indian territory. In unmistakable language, the Redskins were ordered to leave Texas territory immediately in 1839. No one questioned the fact that the Cherokees had been in the country longer than the first Anglo-Saxon colonists. When the Indians hesitated to obey this order to leave, the president sent out a strong detachment of troops against them, which then succeeded in bloody battles to force the retreat of the Redskins as far as the Arkansas.

Texan troops simultaneously undertook punitive expeditions against the Comanches. In March 1840, twelve chiefs with a numerous retinue of warriors and women appeared in San Antonio to negotiate a peace with government representatives. In the midst of the deliberations, Texas soldiers surrounded the house where the Comanche emissaries were staying, and in a dastardly raid the Indians were massacred. On the frontier, even such treachery and perfidy was considered acceptable! They were only Indians! Yet, when the Comanches with two thousand warriors then raided the settlements of the palefaces all the way to Matagorda Bay to avenge the murder of their chiefs and messengers of peace, the Texas frontiersmen could not do enough to demand new "punitive measures" against the red "murdering rabble". As a result, the West Texas wildernesses were the scene of incessant fighting with the Indians for two years until, with the advent of Houston's second presidency, a conciliatory Indian policy was again adopted and peace and tranquility were once again established on all frontiers.

A LONE STAR ARISES IN TEXAS

The longer the Indian fighting extended, the more difficult it became to raise the money to maintain the troops and the more Lamar warmed to the idea of bringing New Mexico, which until then had only been a part of the Lone Star Republic on paper, under actual Texan rule. The possession of Santa Fé, however, had to be extraordinarily enticing to a president who found himself facing national bankruptcy. For the capital of New Mexico was the most important transshipment point for the commerce of western North America. The turnover of this market, where not least of all gold, silver, and fine furs were exchanged, was estimated at twenty million dollars a year, and it was known that Americans from St. Louis were involved in the Santa Fe trade to the tune of four to five million dollars. Now that San Antonio or Austin, the new capital cities that were beginning to be built on the edge of the wilderness, were significantly closer than St. Louis, it was a plausible thought to attempt to wrest the profits from the Santa Fe trade from the Americans and let them flow into Texan hands.

New Mexico could not be conquered by force of arms. Lamar was not such a fantasist that he would have believed that a Texan regiment could be imposed on a population of more than 150,000 Mexicans against their will with at best a few hundred men. Still, all the reports that came in spoke unanimously of the dissatisfaction of the inhabitants of New Mexico with Mexican rule, and even more recently a revolutionary movement on the Rio Grande had seriously troubled the Mexican government. Lamar firmly believed that the people of Santa Fé would help a Texan expedition to drive out the Mexican authorities. To his chagrin, however, he learned that Parliament did not share his optimism and, under the influence of

Sam Houston, who roundly condemned the whole thing, rejected his plan. Nevertheless, Lamar had become so entrenched in the idea that he equipped an expedition on his own responsibility and set out in June 1841 in the direction of Santa Fé.

The "actual" expedition consisted of fifty government commissioners and merchants, who were joined by George W. Kendall, a newspaperman from the New Orleans Picayune, who later published a detailed account of his experiences that is still impressive today. The leader of the column had received strict instructions from Lamar not to engage in any fighting and to confine himself to establishing trade relations, as far as he saw that the New Mexican population was averse to the establishment of a Texas administration. A company of at least 270 volunteers was added to the expedition as military protection, so that the "peaceful" intentions of the government commissioners could be given a little emphasis if necessary. Laboriously, these 320 persons made their way through the wilderness. The large, fully loaded covered wagons of the merchants caused endless difficulties. At the upper Brazos, they lost their way and wandered around in circles. They had only two months' worth of provisions with them! It was not until mid-September that an advance party reached the Pecos. The food had long since run out. On the vast plains, constantly threatened by the Plains Indians, the Texans hardly found an opportunity to shoot game, and they suffered terribly from the lack of water. So utterly exhausted, famished, and thirsty were the expedition members that they allowed themselves to be captured willy-nilly when the governor of New Mexico confronted them with a corps of a thousand men. The men, who sought to realize Lamar's dream of a Texan New Mexico, had to walk the twelve hundred miles to Mexico City. There they were thrown into the dungeons, and it was only thanks to the intervention of the American envoy that the Mexican government released them at the end of 1842. Immediately, Mexico began to make raids across the Rio Grande in retaliation for the Texan attack on Santa Fé, reaching as far as San Antonio and Goliad, and it would not have taken much for a new open war to have resulted from the ill-fated Santa Fé expedition.

These consequences were felt not by Lamar, whose term expired at the end of 1841, but by his successor, Sam Houston. At any rate, the evil outcome of the New Mexico train did the most damage to Lamar's reputation. It was the most visible sign of the aberrant course that the second president of the Lone Star Republic had steered. For a long time the critics of contemporaries and historians have forgotten that Texas owes Lamar at least one lasting achievement, which proves its worth when, for once in a frontier state where politicians are usually too exclusively concerned with "useful" things, a man comes to the helm who has a sense of the ideal values of human existence.

In 1859, at Lamar's instigation, the Texas Congress set aside approximately 20000 acres of land in each administrative district, the proceeds of which were to be used to establish and maintain schools. 325,000 acres each were designated to fund two universities in a distant future. Lamar thus farsightedly laid the foundations for an educational system at a time when the average settler had not yet thought that a school education might be of value to his children. The high regard for knowledge and education was part of Lamar's political creed, who himself had attended only an elementary school but always felt the urge within himself to broaden his mind. "It is admitted by all," he had declared before the Texas Congress, "that education is the protecting genius of democracy, and, guided and supervised by a true morality, the noblest mark of human dignity. It is the only dictator a free man recognizes, and the only dowry for the struggle of life a free man desires."

Bonaparte Mirabeau Lamar lived far from all political activity as a private citizen in Richmond on the Brazos after his retirement from the presidency. He continued to gather material for the planned Texas History, and perhaps in tracing the past vestiges of Texas events he made the discovery that the history of Texas is great even without the greatness he wished to bestow upon the Republic of the Golden Star. He was once more tempted into seeking success in the political field, in 1857. Through friends he was recommended to Secretary of State Buchanan and sent to Nicaragua as American envoy. His task there was to secure the ratification of the treaty by which the Union intended to secure for itself the right of an ocean-to-ocean transit across the Central American Republic. The fact that he did not achieve this goal was not his fault, but the result of the all too confused political conditions in Nicaragua. At his own request, Lamar was recalled by the American government in the summer of 1859. He died suddenly in December 1859, shortly after his return to Texas.

The Road to the Union

Lamar's dream had been to create a Texas that by its deeds would prove its raison d'être as an independent state and remain for all time to come as a second Anglo-Saxon empire on North American soil alongside the Union. Was this idea so utterly absurd? Was not Texas actually being urged by the dismissive attitude of the Union Order to seek its way in this direction? Were perhaps not the ends but only the means wrong by which Lamar sought to carry out his idea? Was not Sam Houston also toying with the idea of a Greater Texas when he assumed the leadership of the country for the second time in 1842?

From Houston comes the map of a Texas republic, incorporating on the east all those Union states that sided with the Confederates during the Civil War, and claiming on the west those Mexican provinces that fell to the United States in 1848, including Chihuahua and Sonora. This map, drawn up in 1844, anticipates with prophetic certainty the annexations of the Peace of Guadalupe Hidalgo and the constellation of the War of Secession, and who could deny that at that time this solution of the political organization of the North American continent was also still within the realm of possibility — a division of the continent between a predominantly industrial state in the north, with a purely white population and free labor, and an agrarian state in the south, based mainly on the cotton and sugar cane plantation economy and retaining the principle of Negro slavery. How different would the world look today in many respects if history had brought such a division of North America!

Sam Houston would undoubtedly have been the man who could have steered the course of history along these lines. It also seemed as if he wanted to take this political course. The fact that he radically deviated from the line of his predecessor in all areas did not speak against this assumption. For by reducing government spending between 1842 and 1844 to almost one tenth of the previous term and almost balancing the budget, he merely strengthened and invigorated the Lone Star Republic internally. Moreover, the foreign policy that Houston pursued was strange. He sought and found connection with Great Britain, which since 1842 suddenly began to take a burning interest in Texas and won the support of France for this new turn in its American policy. In the Union, the Texan president's willingness to make his country a tool of British policy so alarmed the aged frontiersman Andrew Jackson, who was already near death, that he wrote a letter fearfully and anxiously imploring Houston's friendship, "Surely you cannot be deceived by British machinations and let Santa Anna's gold divert you from your ingrained sense of duty and patriotism." But Houston gave an evasive answer. The English representative continued to come and go in and out of his house.

England had held negotiations with the United States to resolve the disputed Canadian boundary questions early in 1842, and although agreement had been reached on various details, the Americans had stubbornly refused to make any concessions on the most important point of difference, Oregon. The intention of the London statesmen to make a general adjustment of the hitherto rather strained American-English relations and to establish a friendly relationship with the Washington government had thus failed, with the result that they angrily resumed their anti-Union policy. That English attention now turned more than before to the young republic on the Gulf Coast had a number of reasons. Texas had provided evidence, albeit with difficulty, of its viability. Recent reports from British representatives in particular reported increasing stabilization of internal conditions and predicted a bright economic future for Texas. To use this country, too, as a stone in the game of British diplomacy seemed all the more advisable, since Mexico was being weakened more and more by incessant internal turmoil and hardly possessed enough power of resistance to stand permanently against the American will to expand. The idea of making Texas a buffer state, whose security against both Mexican and American attempts to seize it would be guaranteed by the two Western European powers, seemed obvious.

England believed that such an approach would not only benefit its foreign policy, but also its economy. Texas cotton production and exports had been increasing year by year, and it was to be expected that the country would yield ever richer cotton crops as its development and settlement progressed. Now at that time the United States still held a monopoly position in the cotton market, and the prospect of allowing a competitor to grow large under English protection was tempting. This was coupled with another idea. England had abolished slavery in all its colonies in 1851, and since then, for both humanitarian and economic reasons, the persistence of Negro slavery in the Union had been a thorn in its side. Direct action on the United States to free its slaves was also not possible. The Americans would have most vigorously forbidden such interference in their internal affairs. Yet how if Texas were induced to renounce slave labor, thus setting an example that cotton and sugar cane could be planted without slaves? Was this not bound to give new impetus to the anti-slavery currents within the Union. In the end, was it not bound to lead to the disappearance of this inhumane institution in the United States as well in the foreseeable future, and to the re-equalization of the competitive situation between North America and the British colonies with the introduction of free labor?

Such were the plans and ulterior motives with which England began to press the Mexican government to acquiesce in the separation of Texas. The leading men of Mexico finally saw the advantage of having a protective buffer state, but they did not dare to antagonize the passionately nationalistic Mexican people by recognizing the independence of Texas. Thus, at first, the conclusion of an armistice between Mexico and Texas was the only thing the British envoy was able to achieve. However, British pressure on the Mexican government continued unabated, and London believed it could hope to reach the goal of its wishes in the not too distant future.

It turned out differently than Foreign Minister Aberdeen had thought. For there were two great errors in the English calculation from the outset. One was that Downing Street thought that the Union would immediately give up all possible intentions on Texas as soon as it saw that the independence of the Golden Star was guarded by the British lion. The other was to take Sam Houston's assurances that the Union idea was over once and for all at face value.

So little did Aberdeen and the English representative in Texas, Elliot, see through the diplomatic game Houston was playing. Sam Houston felt far too strongly committed to the Union at heart to seriously consider the possibility of a Greater Texas. While British policy makers thought they had the Texas President harnessed to their chariot, in reality Houston had the British working for him. He was not the deceived one, as Jackson feared, but the deceiver who, not for nothing, admonished the Texan envoy in Washington to be as, "bright-eyed as a lynx and as shrewd as a fox." However, Houston was careful to cover his back. After the Union repeatedly rejected renewed Texan overtures in the years from 1842 to 1844, it had to be expected that Texas would remain condemned to being an independent republic for a long time to come. In this case, Houston did not want to alienate English friendship, if only to be freed from the constantly threatening Mexican danger. Nevertheless, he knew his American countrymen too well not to know that they would under no circumstances permit the hated England to gain influence over a North American country. It was well-considered when Sam Houston publicly declared that Texas had nothing more to expect from the Union and must seek its friends elsewhere, when he flirted with England before all the world, when he concealed the true intentions of his policy even from his friend Jackson. A Jackson whom he would so much liked to have let in on the secrets of his diplomatic game would have grinned and let things take their course. A Jackson, however, anxious over the loss of Texas, would muster all he could to inflame public opinion in the Union!

Indeed, thus it was! Texas became *the* American political issue. The Union's South raged when it heard that England wanted to a clause inserted in the coming Mexican-Texan recognition treaty providing for the abolition of Negro slavery. The Union North became agitated when the rumor—which was untrue—was circulated that Great Britain intended to make Texas an English colony. Certainly, the forces that did not want to see the Texas Republic annexed to the United States were still very strong. Even for the opponents of annexation the Texas question began to take on a different appearance, however, when the Washington government reopened the Oregon question and inquired in Mexico about the purchase price for California. This made it seem possible to compensate for the admission of a "slave-holding" territory by acquiring "slave-free" territory. Polk, who was decidedly pro-annexation, won the presidential election of 1844. The annexation of Texas had reached its decisive stage.

THE REPUBLIC

  Aberdeen had only been bluffing when he let it be known that, if necessary, England would stand up for the independence of Texas even by force of arms. The Republic of the Golden Star was not so important for British policy that they would have gone to war with the United States over it, and as soon as London realized that the Americans were bitterly serious about annexation and that they would have spared no means to break English resistance, they quietly withdrew all promises of guarantees. Nevertheless, the English did not give up all hope. Certainly, the American Congress, in a joint session of the House of Representatives and the Senate, had decided to admit Texas as a state in the Union, and an American representative was on his way to the Texan capital, Austin, to negotiate the more detailed conditions of the annexation. The question was, whether the Texans wanted annexation. Dr. Anson Jones, Sam Houston's successor, assured the British chargé d'affaires that he preferred his country's independence to joining the Confederacy, and Elliot thought he could detect a strong anti-annexation sentiment in Texas. Once again the Mexican government was put under the most severe pressure, and this time, frightened by the Union's negotiations, it actually agreed to recognize the independence of Texas. In June 1845, Anson Jones was able to present two offers to the Texas legislature, one American and one Mexican. The representatives of the Texan people had it in their hands to choose whether to remain independent or become American.

  By a vote of 55 to 1, they chose to join the Union. In December 1845, the American Congress approved the treaty of admission. The Republic was surrendered to the American governor on February 16, 1846. Texas, long "Americanized," thus became finally and for all time American.

EIGHTH CHAPTER

AN ATTEMPT AT GERMAN COLONIZATION

After the end of the Napoleonic wars in Germany, when grain prices rose and the small farmer who bought fodder got into increasing difficulties, when the upswing that the Continental Blockade had brought to the rural cottage industry ceased and with the beginning of industrialization the weavers, the small ironworkers, the craftsmen became increasingly impoverished. Then at the beginning of the thirties of the nineteenth century, the German emigration movement began again, having almost come to a standstill at the end of the eighteenth century. The causes that had long caused the peasant population of southwestern Germany to emigrate—the disastrous fragmentation of agricultural property, the unbearable tax burdens, the bad harvests—had a new effect, and the emigrants who left their homeland out of economic need—they were by far the majority!—were joined by those who, enterprisingly, longed for a wider field of activity out of the confines of the small states, and by those who, voluntarily or involuntarily, sought the political freedom outside that did not exist in

Metternich's German Confederation. While the German emigration of the 18th century had taken the easterly and southeasterly direction—to Russia, Hungary, the Banat, Transylvania—its destination from now on was almost exclusively North America, and as it could not be otherwise, some spray of this German emigration wave spread at an early stage across the Red River to Texas. They were German farmers swept along by the stream of Anglo-Saxon settlers that since 1821 had been pouring out of the Union into the Mexican province and the Lone Star Republic, respectively. Only gradually did Germans begin directly moving to Texas from Europe.

There was no lack of plans to settle German farmers in larger numbers in Texas at the beginning of the 19th century. Such ideas emerged even at the time of Spanish rule, since a strong wall of German colonists seemed to be an excellent protection against the advance of Anglo-American pioneers. Nothing came of the Mexican plans, however, any more than of the Spanish ones. Texas was virtually unknown in Europe at that time, and it would have required special advertising and organization to lure German emigrants to Texas. Stephen Austin also entertained the idea of inviting Germans and Swiss to settle in his colony between the Brazos and the Colorado in 1830. The "Father of Texas" thought highly of the character and industriousness of the German settlers, writing that "they do not generally possess that terrible speculative frenzy which is so prominent a characteristic of the English and North Americans, and that they will especially resist slavery." Austin's scheme also went nowhere. The Germans who came to Texas were loners whom some accident had driven off the path to the Ohio Valley, or wherever else the German immigrant was wont to strive, and had taken

AN ATTEMPT AT GERMAN COLONIZATION

them all the way to the Gulf Coast. They settled among the Anglo-Saxon colonists, and just as everywhere else in the Union, got caught up in the melting pot of the frontier, which moulded them into "Americans" by the second or third generation.

Forces began to stir against this loss of German national power in America. In the 18th century, there had not been much question in Germany as to what national damage emigration to foreign countries meant, and if German princes at that time sought to prevent the departure of their national children by means of prohibitions and police measures, then mercantilist considerations had been entirely decisive for this. Now, however, after the wars of liberation, there was a German national consciousness, and in those circles of the German people in which it was already most alive, one began to look at the question of emigration with different eyes. Certainly, emigration as such was regarded as a necessary evil for which there was no remedy. Necessity knows no precept! Yet surely there was a way out for the German "Europe-weary" to preserve their German heritage overseas as well. First, men from the ranks of the national-revolutionary fraternity conceived the plan of founding a German state in America, which would be a member of the North American Union, but would be governed in such a way that the continuation of German customs and the German language would be assured and a "genuine, free and popular life" would develop. The "Giessen Emigration Society" did much to spread this idea. They wanted to establish their German republic, their rejuvenated Germany, in Missouri. Only an area that had been settled as little as possible by the Anglo-Saxons came into question for the realization of this idea.

Texas was still sparsely populated, however, and one day

there was talk of whether the young republic on the Gulf Coast might not be suitable for the establishment of a closed German settlement area. A "Germania Society" had been formed in New York in 1835 with the aim of bringing the Germans living in the United States closer together in order to preserve the German character and culture and to realize the ideas of democracy in the new homeland. After much toing and froing, the association members agreed to build the all-German state they planned to establish in Texas. They bought a brig, and in November 1839 a 130-man expedition set sail from New York for Galveston. But when the bold pioneers arrived in Texas, they heard that a severe epidemic of yellow fever was ravaging the country, the city of Houston was nearly depopulated, and other horrors. Most of them did not want to expose themselves to such danger, and as far as they had enough money for the return trip, they immediately went back to New York. Only a few families and individual settlers stayed behind in Texas and had to struggle hard for a long time for their existence. This was a miserable end to a great project. But it would have been just as difficult to realize if the New York Texans had shown greater personal courage. For to initiate a mass settlement was impossible without money, and that was precisely what the "Germania Society" did not have.

Upon the revolution against Mexico and the establishment of an independent republic, Texas became better known in Europe, and perhaps some remembered reading in a book published by a certain J. Val. Hecke, a departed Prussian officer, had published in 1821, under the title of "Travels through the United States of North America in the Years 1818 and 1819", the suggestion that Prussia, or, if she had not the means, the merchants of the Hanseatic

AN ATTEMPT AT GERMAN COLONIZATION

cities, should acquire Texas from Spain as a colony. Ten thousand veterans of the wars of liberation, Hecke believed, were sufficient to defend the country against all attacks. If the stream of German emigration were then directed to the Gulf Coast, Texas would very soon have a population of a million and be the richest and most profitable possession that could be desired. At that time when Hecke made his proposal no one in Germany or Prussia was thinking of colonies. Even later, the Prussian government rejected the acquisition of overseas possessions, because without a fleet they could not be held against the resistance of the powerful seafaring Great Britain. Prussia was too exclusively a continental power and too preoccupied with European and German issues to see the possibility of colonial political activity.

It was not the German governments that took up the idea of founding a German colony in Texas, but a private association set up by members of the German high nobility. Moreover, with the publicity that the so-called "Mainz Adelsverein" began for emigration to Texas, an enthusiasm for the land between the Sabine and the Rio Grande set in in Germany that probably found its strongest expression in the "Texan Songs" of Hoffmann von Fallersleben, who himself had never seen Texas, but sang with full conviction:

> Off to Texas! Off to Texas!
> Where the star in those blue pastures
> A new world loudly shall proclaim,
> Ev'ry heart for right and freedom
> And joyfully for truth inflame.

A LONE STAR ARISES IN TEXAS

The »Mainz Adelsverein«

It is difficult to say what gave some of the noble Austrian officers serving in the federal fortress of Mainz in the early 1940s the idea of founding an association to promote German emigration to Texas. Probably, as they shortened the boredom of small-town garrison life by reading novels, they had fallen into the hands of Charles Sealsfield's "Kajütenbuch," (The Cabin Book), which was just then making its first rounds through Germany. The vivid, adventurous descriptions that the Austrian hiding behind that American code name, Karl Postl, gave of the Texan frontier, were, if nothing else, very convincing indeed and were able to arouse their interest in a country that had only recently, since its struggle for independence against Mexico, moved into the European field of vision. Whatever the impetus, however, one day the Mainz circle of friends began to discuss in detail the manifold possibilities for development that presented themselves for the Republic on the Gulf Coast. Spurred on by the agile and daring spirit of Count Carl zu Castell, the young noblemen soon got into plotting, until in the end they all became enthusiastic about the idea of settling the vast, undeveloped territories of Texas with Germans. The eager canvassing of the fellows succeeded in winning supporters for their project among their relatives and acquaintances, and the last misgivings about realizing the plan disappeared when, in addition to Prince Karl zu Leiningen, Duke Adolph von Nassau also agreed. In April 1842, a number of members of the German aristocracy met at Biebrich on the Rhine and decided to form a society that would initiate the colonization project.

The idea of settling Germans in Texas may seem astonishing today, but it was no surprise at a time when tens of thousands of Germans left their homeland every year under the pressure of economic hardship in order to find their fortune in North America, which was denied them by their fatherland. Even at that time, people regretted that so many good compatriots had crossed the border. But the emigration movement was viewed as a necessary bloodletting against the threat of overpopulation, which could not be prevented if the poorer classes of the population were to be helped. In any case, the princes and counts who took part in the new colonization enterprise were inspired by the best intentions, and it does not speak against their humanitarian and national motives that they at the same time carried themselves with the hope that the money spent would flow back to them in rich profits. They believed that they could take better care of those leaving their homeland than the other associations that had been founded in Germany since the 1830's and had seldom proved equal to their task. The generous, well-financed and well-organized settlement they planned was finally supposed to protect the German emigrant from the ruin into which he had often enough fallen, because he had formed false ideas about the conditions in the foreign country, because he lacked the means to build up a secure existence or because he had fallen victim to unscrupulous swindlers. They envisioned directing the stream of German emigration, which had hitherto been lost in thousands of rivulets on the other side of the ocean, uniformly toward a firmly defined strip of land where the Germans could enjoy their Germanness undiminished. They dreamed of creating a "second Germania" in Texas, which would later accept the products of German industry in exchange for raw materials, and they thought of their company playing a role similar to that played in England by the East India Company, which had the privilege of mediating overseas trade between mother country and daughter country.

No part of North America seemed better suited for such plans than Texas, which, with dimensions far exceeding those of the German Confederation, had only about 250,000 inhabitants and was an independent state. For if a German settlement in the Union always had to remain a fragment that could never escape the determining will of its Anglo-Saxon environment, here there was the possibility that the Germans, if they immigrated en masse, might be able to gain a determining, perhaps even decisive influence. Moreover, independence from Texas seemed assured to the members of the German colonization society! Perhaps they were aware of England's intentions for Texas. Prince Solms-Braunfels was a college friend of Prince Consort Albert and Prince Leiningen a half-brother of Queen Victoria. They may also have made sure that English policy did not object to German farmers and craftsmen moving to Texas and forming a counterweight to the Anglo-Saxon element of the population pressing for union with the United States. That England's very efforts to achieve Texas independence would arouse the national passions of Americans and that Texas would be admitted to the Confederacy as early as 1845 was not foreseen by anyone in Europe.

Based on the favorable reports they found in the relevant literature, the noble colonizers considered not only the political but also the geographic preconditions for the establishment of a German colony in Texas to be extraordinarily favorable. The question of whether German settlers would feel at home in this country could be answered with the indication that at the beginning of the forties there were already about ten thousand compatriots living there. The letters of satisfaction that the former gardener of the Grand Duke of Oldenburg, Friedrich Ernst, wrote to his friends in Germany, the booklet full of praise about the beauty of the landscape, the fertility of the fields and the health of the climate, which Detlef Dunt published in 1834, had attracted many Oldenburgers, Hanoverians and Westphalians to the hilly prairies and sparse forests of eastern Texas. Of the hundred or so Germans who participated in the Texas fight for freedom, eleven sealed their allegiance to their adopted country with death. Later, when independence was won, numerous Germans followed the train of American settlers to the Lone Star Republic. Before the Mainz Colonization Society had brought the first emigrant across the ocean, Industry, Cat Spring, and Roedersmühle had been established as purely German settlements by Friedrich Ernst, Robert Justus Kleberg, and Otto von Roeder, and Biegels Settlement, Frelsburg, and Blumenthal already existed. In 1841, the Germans at the Brazos joined together to form the "Teutonia Order" and their leading men petitioned the Texas Congress to be allowed to establish a German "Hermann University", a plan that was granted but unfortunately not carried out except for the building later used as a schoolhouse.

The attraction that Texas exerted on the German emigrant was understandable enough. The farmer found the most fertile soils in the tracts of land which first extend level behind the marshy lowlands of the coast and then slowly rise in terraces. Their cost of acquisition was so low that in the western parts of the country it did not exceed from 5 to 10 cents per acre, while the American government was still charging a dollar and a quarter for even the worst clearing land. German emigrants readily believed it when G. A.

Scherpf wrote in a well-received pamphlet that Texas was the land flowing with milk and honey, even if the milk had to be obtained by milking the cows and the honey gathered in the forests. Anyone who thought these exuberant words were exaggerated was impressed by the more matter-of-fact tone of Detlef Dunt, who declared, "Texas is a land where the immigrant who cultivates the land is made as comfortable as he would like to be in any part of the world. It is a land that holds riches in its bosom that can delight thousands and their descendants."

Viktor zu Alt-Leiningen-Westerburg and Joseph zu Boos-Waldeck, provided with sufficient funds and powers of attorney, embarked for Texas in May 1842, in order to form an opinion of their own on behalf of their friends about the conditions of the country and the settlement possibilities and, under certain circumstances, to purchase suitable lands. Like all guests, they will have been warmly received by Friedrich Ernst in Industry, and it was probably this bright, unselfish man who pointed out to them that recently the Texas State President was again authorized to award grants to immigration entrepreneurs. Count Leiningen hurried to Austin, the state capital, and negotiated with Sam Houston for the grant of such a tract of land. Yet, much as the president appreciated the industrious and honest German settler and welcomed immigration from the German states, he found himself unable to accommodate Leiningen's wishes to give him land in central rather than western Texas and to grant tax exemption for several years to the protégés of the gentry. Leiningen was concerned with obtaining the best possible soil for settlement — Houston had the ulterior political motive of settling the new immigrants on the western frontier, where they could help repel any attacks by Mexico. Without any tangible results from the discussions with the president, Count Leiningen returned to Germany. He might have been flattered by the possibility of later being successful with his demands in Texas, or, more likely, he might have seen other possibilities for the cheap acquisition of land—but he strongly advised his friends in Biebrich to immediately start the planned colonization on a large scale.

In the meantime, Boos-Waldeck had remained in Industry and had come to the conclusion that it would be best not to engage in conspicuous settlement experiments, but to begin with the settlement of individual emigrant families in that area where there was still a lot of agriculturally excellent land to be purchased. Close to the estate of Friedrich Ernst he bought a legua of land for 3321 dollars, which meant that he paid the reasonable price of 75 cents for the acre. The farm, which he named "Nassau Farm" in honor of the Duke of Nassau, he established as a cotton plantation, tilled with the aid of thirty negro slaves. He was also back in Mainz early in 1844, where he heard that his friends did not want to know about a gradual foothold in Texas, but were making arrangements to send many hundreds, even thousands of families to the Gulf Coast before long. When his warnings that the available funds were far too small for an undertaking of such magnitude were lightly thrown to the wind, he refused any further participation in the company for himself and his relatives.

The colonization society had already incorporated as the "Verein zum Schutze Deutscher Einwanderer in Texas" (Association for the Protection of German Immigrants in Texas) at the end of June 1843, becoming a joint stock company with a stock capital of 200,000 Gulden. The articles of incorporation were adopted at the general meeting on March 5, 1844, and approved by the Ducal Nassau State

Ministry in May. The shares were held exclusively by members of the German high nobility, and it was a list of illustrious names that the association was able to present to the public. In addition to five reigning princes, the Duke of Nassau, the Duke of Meiningen, the Duke of Coburg-Gotha, the Landgrave of Hesse-Homburg and the Prince of Schwarzburg-Rudolstadt, Prince Frederick of Prussia, Prince Moritz of Nassau, the Princes of Leiningen, Neuwied, Solms-Braunfels, Colloredo-Mansfeld and Schönburg-Waldenburg, Princes Alexander and Carl zu Solms-Braunfels, Count Friedrich and Viktor Alt-Leiningen-Westerburg, Count Neu-Leiningen-Westerburg and Christian Leiningen-Westerburg, Counts Ysenburg-Meerholz, Hatzfeld, Knyphausen, Renesse, Lilienberg, Colloredo-Mansfeld and Castell. While the Duke of Nassau was offered the protectorate, the Prince of Leiningen was elected president and Count Carl of Castell business director. The intention was to keep the spirit of nobility pure in the association, to base it less on legal formulas and clauses than on good faith, noble honor and attitude.

As excellent as these principles were, the "Mainz Adelsverein" — as the society was soon popularly called — would have done better to go to work with less idealism and more realism and to secure the help of some business-savvy merchants and cunning lawyers. Even the choice of Count Carl zu Castell was a serious mistake. The leadership of the association was entrusted to a man who was rich in imaginative plans and speculative zeal, but who had neither knowledge of human nature, nor organizational skills, nor knowledge of financial matters, and who did not learn from his first bad experiences, but thought he could make up for his failures by continuing to chase deceptive will-o'-the-wisps. It was probably primarily his fault that the association successively fell for two "enterprising" speculators who had already approached the Counts Leiningen and Waldeck in Texas but had not come to an agreement with them.

The Frenchman Bourgeois appeared in Mainz in the summer of 1843 and agreed to cede the grant that had been granted to him by the Texan government to the Nobility Association. With a "d'Orvanne" appended to his name, the impostor introduced himself to the German gentlemen as a member of his class and was so skillful in winning their confidence that he was not only admitted as a member of the association, but was also appointed colonial director. A sober examination of the documents should have made the association's management wonder. Bourgeois' colonization contract contained the provision that the entire grant would be null and void unless one-third of the twelve hundred families and individual settlers to be placed in the area between the Medina and Frio Springs had landed in Texas by December 3, 1843. When the Association entered into a tentative agreement with Bourgeois in September, there was no longer any thought that the most important condition of the contract could be fulfilled. Just as it believed the Frenchman's assurances about the good quality of the Grant lands, the association's management believed him that the contract would be extended without further ado by the Texas government. Did Bourgeois not know that the Congress at Washington on the Brazos was already negotiating the revocation of the President's land grant rights and in January 1844 declared all unfulfilled grant contracts to be terminated? By the time the Association signed the final agreement with Bourgeois in April 1844, the grant had been void for two months. That same month, however, Prince Carl zu Solms-Braunfels was appointed commissioner general and sent to Texas with Bourgeois to make every effort to prepare for the reception of the first emigrants expected in the fall.

Even if Castell did not know that Bourgeois' colonization treaty was only a scrap of paper, it was quite reckless of him to address the German public with an appeal in which it was stated as an established fact that the association had large estates in Texas at its disposal, in the hope that the grant would be extended. The notice, after stating the humanitarian and national aims of the Association, promised as a gift to each emigrant, without any obligation on his part, a tract of good land. It assured that the Association would provide at the cheapest rates, passage, transportation, house building, food, farming implements and seed. That churches, schools, doctors and dispensaries should be established for each settlement, and a hospital for the whole colony. "The association will," it says at the end, "in order not to leave the welfare and well-being of German compatriots at the mercy of the coincidences of an experiment, for the time being allow only 150 families to emigrate in the course of this year, and only then, when they have a well-secured settlement, will it assist further emigration in word and deed."

Voices of distrust were raised in some democratic circles in response to this publication, which doubted the idealistic motives of the members of the princely association and even suspected that the emigrants would end up in an evil relationship of fealty and bondage. On the whole the appeal was received quite favorably, nevertheless. The names of the men who supported the association seemed to vouch for the fact that it was a well-funded enterprise and that one could build on the promises made. It did not take long to gather the first group of emigrants who entrusted their fate to the nobility association.

In the meantime, Bourgeois' grandiose assurances in Texas had turned out to be nothing more than hot air. For some time Prince Carl zu Solms-Braunfels had allowed himself to be lulled by the Frenchman into false hopes about an extension of the land grant. Eventually, however, it became clear to him with dismay what the truth was about this grant and that it had lapsed and nothing had been able to induce the Texan Parliament to renew it. The bitterness with which Solms told the Mainz management that he did not have a scrap of settlement land, while in Germany the emigrants were already waiting for the order to leave, can be imagined. Later he wrote that he considered it very fortunate that the agreements with Bourgeois had fallen through; for he had traveled through the Grant area and discovered that the best land had already been occupied, so that the association's protégés would have had to be content with the inferior ones. What was the use of the association's presidency then dismissing the famous French colonial director without notice!

Solms' unfortunate letter had not yet arrived in Mainz when the association's management made a second grant purchase. In the early summer of 1844, a certain Henry Francis Fisher had contacted Castell to thoroughly inform him that an extension of the Bourgeois grant was not to be expected under any circumstances. What was appealing to this thirty-eight-year-old man was not only the title of Texas consul in Bremen, but also the fact that, despite his American-sounding name, he had been born in Germany. Fisher's father was an Englishman who had come to Kassel at the beginning of the century as a valet to the British

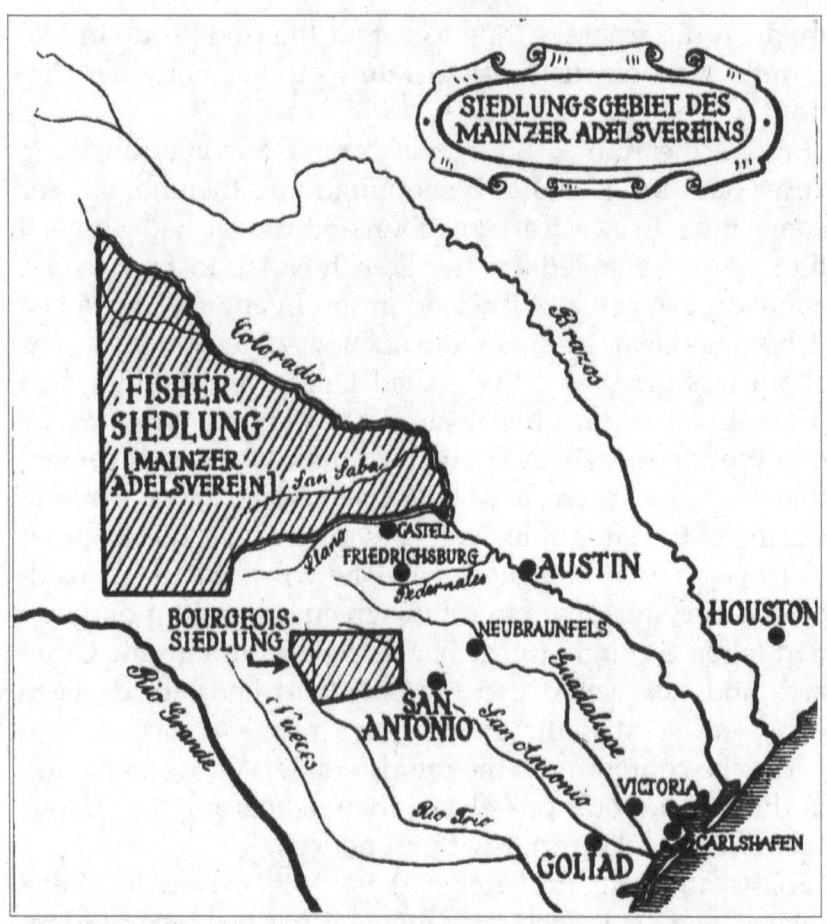

envoy, settled in the count's residence as a language teacher, and married a Hessian. He himself, as a young merchant's assistant, had been driven by a thirst for adventure across the ocean to the United States, where he was eventually sent to Texas. There Fisher had founded the San Sabá Company together with some other speculative minds, which wanted to search in the wildernesses of the upper Colorado for the lost silver mine, which had once been operated there by the Spaniards. As Fisher wrote to his brother in Kassel, "a significant stretch of land — known as the Eldorado of Texas — had been ceded to him by the Texan government," and it was precisely this "Eldorado" that he now offered as a savior in need to the Mainz Nobility Association for settlement in exchange for a sum of eight thousand dollars and a share of one third of the profits.

In Castell's view, the colonization grant that Fisher had made to the Texas government for the vast areas on the Llano and San Sabá was extremely favorable. The grant was for three million acres and the immigrant contractor undertook to bring six thousand families to Texas within three years. For each family a section of 640 acres was to be granted as farmland. This was entirely consistent with the intentions of the association's leadership for immediate large-scale settlement. It remained unclear, however, how Count Castell intended to fulfill the further stipulation that one third of the families should have landed in Texas by February 1845. When he put his name to the purchase contract with Fisher in June 1844, it was not yet foreseeable that the Texas Congress, enthusiastic about the prospect of a strong increase in population, would actually be persuaded to extend the deadline to March 1846.

The details of the grant were of no concern to Castell on this or any other point. Spellbound, he stared at the profit opportunities that seemed to be opening up. The immigration contractor was assured ten sections of land for every hundred families settled under his direction. He was also permitted to keep up to one-half of each section released to the immigrants for himself, if an agreement to that effect was made with the settler. If, the business director reasoned, the association would sell these lands, its expenses would be better and more quickly recouped than if it waited for a long time for the benefits to accrue from commercial intercourse between Germany and the colony.

Castell was now more convinced than ever of the success of the colonization project. He was proud to announce in the newspapers that the association had acquired fertile and climatically healthy land. The only thing that was correct in this report was the healthy location of the settlement area. It formed the last mountainous terrace that leads to the barren Llanos Estacados. Wrong, however, was the legal opinion that the association had become the owner of the land, since it was only a matter of taking over an "Empresario" contract—a very bad mistake, which made the business director neglect to have the emigrants cede to him in writing half of the sections granted to them by the State of Texas. This later resulted in a variety of difficulties and lawsuits. Perhaps Henry Fisher was gullible when he praised his "Eldorado" beyond all measure. He had not yet seen the wildernesses of the upper Colorado himself, where agriculture was only possible in the floodplain, but otherwise only extensive cattle farming could be practiced. Certainly, he also did not give the Mainz gentlemen a clear idea of what it meant that the boundary of the Grant lay two hundred and fifty kilometers from the last Texan settlement without a navigable road, that the area was undisputed hunting ground of the warlike Comanches, and that the Texan government had assumed no obligations whatsoever to drive out the Redskins and protect the settlers.

Henry Fisher was what is called a "smart" businessman. Since he would not have been able to fulfill his colonization contract without the help of the Adelsverein, he painted a far too optimistic picture of the Texan conditions in general and of the Grant area in particular in order to do business with the lords of Mainz. One cannot accuse him of actual fraud. The fact that he demanded a share of the profits and had himself appointed colonial director, i.e., that he was largely interested personally in the success of the enterprise, speaks against it. Nevertheless, there is no doubt that he did not have the sense of responsibility that one would expect from an immigration entrepreneur who is entrusted with the fate of thousands of people, and the worst thing was that the leading figures of the nobility association took his words at face value. After all, it was more than frivolous to want to start settling an area that none of the people involved had yet seen! To make matters worse, Count Castell also believed the naive calculation that Fisher made about the necessary costs of settling the settlers. This led to the fact that it seemed to be sufficient for the management if a not too numerous family brought six hundred gulden of their own money. With this sum they thought they could not only pay for the passage from Bremen to Galveston and the transport from Galveston to the colony area, but also for a house, the farming equipment and the living expenses until the next harvest. How erroneous this estimate was became apparent later when the transportation costs from Galveston amounted to not 10 but 75 gulden and the house construction costs to not 60 but 250 gulden and when the tilling of the land was delayed to such an extent that the immigrants had to be fed not for a few months but for more than a year.

Fisher was back in Texas at the end of September 1844 and introduced himself to Prince Solms as the new colonial director. The Commissioner General was certainly not pleased with the acquisition of the Fisher grant, since a few weeks earlier he had urgently warned the Mainz management against settling in the area along the San Sabá

River. But now that he was faced with a fait accompli, he had to try to do the best he could. Since Fisher informed him that the first immigrants would arrive already at the end of the year, there was no time for a sightseeing trip to the upper Colorado. Solms liked to think that he could rely on the colonial director in this matter. He went to Galveston, where he appointed an agent responsible for the onward transportation of the settlers, and selected a landing place at Matagorda Bay, where the town of Indianola now lies, which he named Carlshafen. Wagons and draft oxen, cattle and food were to be provided by Henry Fisher, to whom Count Castell had trustingly given $11,000, a sum to which Solms added another $2,400. But Fisher cared very little about these matters, instead wasting his time in Washington at the Brazos trying to get the Texas legislature to settle some private matters in addition to the much-needed extension of the term of his contract.

When the first four hundred immigrants disembarked at Carlshafen in mid-December, only 15 of the necessary 50 wagons were on hand, and neither livestock, meat, nor flour were available. Fisher now promised to deliver everything immediately. Yet Solms waited and waited, using the available wagons to get the settlers' party from Carlshafen to Victoria, until he finally realized that he had been shamefully abandoned by Fisher. His reports to the Mainz management are full of indignant accusations against the colonial director, who used every opportunity to enrich himself and his friends at the expense of the association, and had the audacity to incite immigrants and association officials against the Commissioner General. There was soon a complete rupture between Solms and Fisher, and the association was later glad that Fisher renounced his post as colonial director in return for a high compensation payment. The execution of the settlement was now exclusively in the hands of Prince Solms.

Carl zu Solms-Braunfels was then 32 years old—his mother was a sister of Queen Luise of Prussia and in her third marriage the wife of King Ernst August of Hanover. Putting aside his personal wishes, the Austrian cavalry captain had allowed his friends to entrust him with the difficult office of commissioner general: the awareness of opening up a new possibility of existence for the German peasantry and a new field of activity for the German economy and shipping seemed to him, as he wrote to Count Castell with a quiet sneer against Prussia, to be worth more than the decoration with the Fourth Class Order of the Red Eagle. The prince did not lack agility, energy, responsibility and clear-sightedness. If young Friedrich Wilhelm von Wrede, his constant companion in Texas, is to be believed, it would have been difficult to find another who would have accomplished as much as Solms did as commissioner general. The settlers were of the same conviction and felt the idealism of the young officer, the warmth and generosity with which he cared for their welfare, as well as admiring the matter-of-factness with which he shared all their privations. As Wrede wrote, they were devoted to His Serene Highness in love and respect and would have fought the devil for his sake.

The immigrants, under the leadership of this man, finally made their way inland on March 10, 1845—three months after the arrival of the first ship in Galveston. It had long since become clear to the Prince that the Grant area could not be reached in one go and that the establishment of staging posts was necessary. So he rode ahead of the column and bought a two-league property (over 13,000 acres) in San Antonio from a Mexican for 1,111 dollars on Comal

Creek, a small tributary of the Guadalupe. A more scenic spot could not have been found. A fertile prairie stretched along the left bank of the crystal-clear creek, and a dense oak and cedar forest stood on the right, overlooked by rocky cliffs. Nevertheless, the settlers who arrived on March 21 were deeply disappointed when the Commissioner General told them that the road to the Grant was too far, that they would have to settle here for the time being, and that the Association was making them a gift of a half-acre town lot and a ten-acre farm lot.

Most of them accepted this gift reluctantly because they wanted to go to the sections they had been promised at the San Sabá. Solms reassured them, as far as they could be pacified, with the promise that the march north would continue in the fall. Although it was not too late to sow corn and potatoes, only some set to work, the others contenting themselves with erecting simple makeshift dwellings. Further efforts, they thought, were not worthwhile; the association, since it had not kept its obligations, would have to provide for them until next year. For protection against the Indians, the prince formed a guard troop from the young people, and on the "Vereinsberg" they began to build a "fort" — if the elongated blockhouse deserved such a designation — which Solms christened "Sophienburg" in honor of the lady of his heart, Princess Salm-Salm. New Braunfels was founded, and it became, though in a different sense than the prince predicted, the center of German settlement in Texas.

The Commissioner General left Neu-Braunfels in mid-May 1845 to return to Germany. Months before, he had already asked for his recall, since he believed that he could persuade the German governments to join the association through his far-reaching connections and personal influence and expand the colonization work into a national enterprise. As things stood, he was entitled to believe that he had secured a good start for the enterprise. He had mastered all the difficulties arising from the change of the settlement area, from the premature arrival of the immigrants, and from Henry Fisher's unreliability. He had chosen the place of the port and the first area of settlement in a practical way. He had brought the settlers to New Braunfels safely and securely. The foundation had been laid on which they could continue to build.

Nevertheless, it seemed necessary to the prince on the basis of his experiences to change the association's program on various points. Above all, he advised a review of the cost estimate, which was far too low, since it had consumed several times the amount he had taken with him. In addition, he emphatically stressed how important it was, in view of the planned mass settlement of about six thousand families, to provide firm transport connections to the colony area, which had been pushed far into the wilderness. Thanks to his military training in an Austrian cuirassier regiment, he knew that a fighting front could be held only if the supply roads were secured. He suggested that staging posts be laid out along the road from the Gulf Coast to the Grant at intervals of sixty kilometers. He even broached the question of whether it would not be expedient to build a "railroad," which he envisioned at first as a horse-drawn tramway on wooden rails. In a few years, he thought, the problem would anyway arise of how to provide the settlers with a market for their products. As ambitious as the railroad plan was and as inconsistent as it was with the financial resources of the association, it still shows that Solms was thinking seriously about the future of the colony and that it was not so far-fetched.

A LONE STAR ARISES IN TEXAS

Whether he was really as capable as the young Wrede and the settlers, whom he won over with his Chevaleresque generosity, believed, whether he would have been up to the task of the commissioner general in the long run, is nevertheless doubtful. With all his good will, Solms could not make up for his lack of colonizing experience. He had so little understanding of how to manage the settlement of the settlers in detail that he had to leave these matters almost entirely to the officials of the association. To enforce his will with ruthless harshness in all cases did not suit his somewhat soft character, and in financial matters he was too much of a grand seigneur to be considerately thrifty, indeed, he cared so little for administrative correctness that at his departure the accounts were in a state of hopeless confusion. His greatest fault, however, was that he was unable to establish a good understanding with the Anglo-Saxon population. Nor did Solms show the slightest empathy with the peculiarities of the shirt-sleeved Texan frontier life. He despised the Americans for their crudeness and their greed for money and let this contempt be felt openly. Gruffly, he rejected the proposal to allow Americans to settle in the German settlements. He feared that the good-natured German farmers would only be cheated by the wily Anglo-American merchants. Most importantly, he antagonized the Texans by forming a uniformed guard force.

How he was to deal with the Indians was a question that occupied the prince keenly even during his passage to America. The fact that Prince Frederick of Prussia donated two cannons to the association, which were brought up alongside the "Sophienburg", proves how great the Indian danger was considered to be in Germany. Solms had no confidence at all in the border police of the Texan state, the

Rangers, and so he just decided to raise a company of twenty young people to provide military protection for the colonists. Such a measure was incomprehensible to the Texans. Their pioneers protected themselves when they went to the frontier, and needed no special guard force. It was not long before all sorts of nonsensical rumors began to circulate. People began to accuse the Prince of having "aristocratic and monarchist tendencies" and of wanting to introduce German military rule, and there were whispers of the establishment of a "feudal system". Moreover, there were rumors that the German settlement enterprise was a new obstruction of the English, who at that time were trying so hard to prevent the annexation of Texas to the Union. With wounded democratic feeling, people ridiculed the Serene Highness, who was never to be seen without an entourage, had his bodyguard dine at an adjoining table, and had other "aristocratic airs and graces". In short, there was an abundance of misunderstandings that the commissioner general could have avoided with a little more psychological tact.

At the bottom of his heart, Carl zu Solms-Braunfels was an idealist with many romantic tendencies. His successor, Baron Ottfried Hans von Meusebach, born in Dillenburg in Nassau in 1812 and previously a Prussian government assessor in Trier, was a different kind of man. Gifted with a sober sense of reality, he possessed all the qualities indispensable for a leader of colonization—an iron will to discipline, organizational prudence, ruthless thrift and administrative precision. When the new commissioner general arrived in Neu-Braunfels—his arrival had been expected weeks before—Prince Solms had already left in order to reach the next crossing to Europe in time. Meusebach had already been harassed by the association's creditors on the way to the settlement, and so the first thing he did was to check on the state of the finances. The treasurer was not able to tell him how high the liabilities were, since not only he, but also the Prince, the doctor, and the engineer had incurred debts for the association without keeping an exact account of them. Immediately, Meusebach hurried back to Galveston, met the Prince there, who, however, could not answer his questions any more than the cashier, but considered the rough estimate of twenty thousand dollars in debt to be correct and promised to see to it that the shortfall was transferred in Germany as soon as possible. In August, however, Meusebach had to report to Mainz that the association's obligations were one-half greater than he had originally assumed, that he had not only had to use the ten thousand dollars he had been given to settle the debt, but that another twenty-four thousand dollars still had to be cleared up.

Meusebach introduced a regiment of strict thrift in Neu-Braunfels—no wonder that the colonists were not very fond of him. Yet he managed to ensure that the settlers no longer hung around idly, but finally got to work, and he also managed to restore the confidence of the creditors through his tight management of the business. As soon as Meusebach had brought order into the administration of the settlement, he equipped a small expedition to search for a place where a second settlement could be established for the further emigrants that the association intended to send over. Again, the path through the wildernesses proved too difficult and too far to advance to the Grant area. Therefore, the Commissioner General decided to make another stopover at Pedernales, Friedrichsburg, for which he purchased on credit a 10,000 acre tract of land and had it surveyed into town and acre lots like New Braunfels.

AN ATTEMPT AT GERMAN COLONIZATION

He returned from his trip in early November to find a letter from the Mainz management with the news that four thousand emigrants had been embarked and would arrive in Galveston between November and February. Much more distressing than the unbelievable omission that this transport had not yet been registered at all, and thus that in Texas not the slightest preparations had been made for its receipt, was the incomprehensible fact that the letter was accompanied only by an order for 24,000 dollars and that not a word was said about whether a further shipment of money would follow. Since the banker in New Orleans had the entire amount at his disposal to cover the debts of the association, Meusebach was in the desperate position of having to receive an entire army of immigrants without a cent in his pocket.

I wonder how he felt when he supervised the disembarkation of the new settlers. Never for a moment, however, did he lose his head. He did not reveal the true facts to anyone, not even to the officials of the association, and, aware that the fate of all these people depended on him, with dogged energy he set about solving the almost impossible task which confronted him. Soon he was among the settlers, who were housed in makeshift tents and barracks near Galveston and Carlshafen asking with ever-increasing excitement when they would finally be transported to the colony, when they would receive their monies, which they had faithfully paid into the association's treasury and were to receive back in Texas. Soon he was traveling around the country buying food from the German settlers at the Brazos and, through their agency and surety, from the wealthy American farmers on promissory bills. Despite all the help he found, he was only able to raise the bare necessities of flour, corn, and meat.

A LONE STAR ARISES IN TEXAS

In February, Meusebach went to New Orleans to persuade the banker to grant him a larger loan against pledging the Nassau farm. His words fell on deaf ears, however and the banker had been warned against granting further loans by the Frankfurt banking house with which the association cooperated in Germany. Meusebach wrote one inflammatory letter after another to Mainz. He calculated to the gentlemen that he would have to have at least $1,400,000 to settle such a large group of immigrants. Nevertheless, the management refused to listen to him. Finally, the baron had no other advice than to get an agent of the association to write a letter to the mayor of Bremen, to describe the misery of the association's protégés in Texas and at the same time to hand this letter over to the German press for publication. At long last this proved successful. The German governments demanded an account from the association's management, and in July general meetings were held at which the Duke of Nassau took over the guarantee for a larger loan. In September 1846, almost a year after the arrival of the first emigrant ship, Meusebach had sixty thousand dollars in his hands, a first installment that gave again gave freedom to move.

The question of how Count Castell was capable of sending four thousand emigrants to Texas without providing the necessary funds has never been resolved. It is likely that the members of the association only learned through the press publications what a catastrophe the recklessness of their business director had brought about, and they must have been horrified to see their good reputation put at risk in this way. They immediately set about repairing the damage done, as far as possible. However, the financial sacrifices made by the shareholders of the Mainz Adelsverein were not enough to make up for so much damage! Perhaps Meusebach's efficiency and drive alone would have succeeded in dealing with the money difficulties but he was powerless against other obstacles. It seemed as if everything had conspired against the settlement enterprise. Never had it rained so much in Texas as in the winter of 1845/46. The four thousand immigrants lay in the wet and cold in inadequate dwellings and with insufficient food on the Gulf Coast. There was hardly any way to transport them to New Braunfels or further up to the newly founded Fredericksburg. The sodden roads through the prairies had become unroadworthy and could be traveled only at a huge loss of time, if at all. Nevertheless, Meusebach sought in vain to hire wagons and teams. Texas had joined the United States, war with Mexico loomed, and whenever the indefatigable commissioner general succeeded in persuading a wagoner to make his vehicle available to him on the promise of later payment, the American military administration came along, offered a higher price, and put cash on the table. Diseases, especially dysentery, broke out among the immigrants and in the end a fever epidemic raged and death reaped its harvest among the weakened people. The disease was brought to Neu-Braunfels and Friedrichsburg by the small groups of people who were able to leave on their own wagons and by the settlers who left their families and luggage behind and set out on their own. The association doctors were helpless in the face of the disease and at least 850 people, if not more, died in those months.

It was not until September 1846 that the last immigrants were brought from the ports to the colony. But not all of the association's proteges went to the settlements on the Comal and Pedernales. Many, tired of waiting and the misery, had scattered and tried to find work in Galveston,

Houston, or with the Germans at the Brazos. Still others enlisted by the Americans for the war against Mexico, and an 88-man volunteer company was formed under the leadership of Augustus Buechel, a native of Mainz who had served as an instructor in the Turkish army and later participated in the Carlist struggles in Spain. All the same, the population of Neu-Braunfels and its surroundings swelled to fifteen hundred, and about a thousand settlers established themselves in Friedrichsburg.

In 1846 the Mainz Adelsverein brought another 2400 emigrants to Texas. Their settlement, too, was still directed by Meusebach, as it was he who, at the beginning of 1847, advanced into the Grant area and concluded a treaty of friendship with the Comanches, which was so well kept by the Indians that not only did surveying work begin and the first settlements, if only sparsely occupied settlements on the Llano River-Castell, Leiningen, Schoenburg, Meerholz, and Bettina-could be established, but also that the German settlements suffered least from the thefts and raids of the Redskins of all the localities on the Texas frontier. In July 1847, Baron von Meusebach, now an ordinary American citizen under the name of John O. Meusebach, resigned his post as commissioner general. "I have now spent two years in a position," he had written to the Mainz Association leadership six months earlier, "which by its very nature is apt to heap hatred and unpleasantness of all kinds upon a responsible head. Daily and hourly distressed by wretched money matters, struggling with opposition and lack of understanding on all sides, exposed to public criticism, and unable to state the motives for the actions, I did not want to abandon the cause of the association.... To pacify the drunken carters with their demands, to put off pressing creditors, to put up with the coarseness and inconvenience that occurred in the process, was my daily business.... Thus, for almost two years, I led a life that I would not wish even on a dog.... Every emigrant to whom I have had to refuse the distant grasping of commissions becomes my personal enemy, every colonist who finds himself deceived here in his expectations—aroused perhaps by inaccurate publications in Germany, and naturally believes me to be the cause of the non-granting of his wishes—feels hurt." Aware that he had worked for the Mainz Nobility Association to the best of his ability and with all the strength he could muster, Meusebach was allowed to retire to private life. Like most German immigrants, he became a farmer. Married to Countess Agnes Corath of Tyrol since 1852 and the father of eleven children, he served the Texas people as a senator, justice of the peace, notary public, and postmaster, dying of old age near Fredericksburg in 1897.

There were still general commissioners of the Adelsverein in Texas until 1852, but they only had to deal with the administration of the property or better the debts, and they tried to make sure that the immigrants received the legal titles to the sections in the Grant area to which they were entitled. Many German settlers, however, did not settle on the Llano and San Sabá, most preferring to remain in more civilized and fertile areas and then to sell their entitlements. The Association did not attempt any more settlements of German emigrants in Texas after the last transport of the fall of 1846. The events of 1845/46 caused understandable commotion and indignation in Germany, and it would not have been easy to find anyone who would have been willing to entrust themselves to the association's leadership. The revolutionary movement of 1848, which began shortly thereafter, completely paralyzed the activities of the Adelsverein. The attempt to transfer the rights and liabilities to a new "Deutsche Kolonisationsgesellschaft für Texas in Biebrich" (German Colonization Society for Texas in Biebrich), founded by Count Castell and the Freiburg lawyer Ludwig Martin, failed. At the beginning of the fifties, the Adelsverein still offered German emigrants sections in the Grant area for sale. In Texas, however, the loss of property could not be halted. Seizures of the properties took place more and more frequently, and finally all official actions of the association ceased. Silently and unnoticed, the line was drawn under an enterprise that had begun with much momentum and great hopes. The fact that the princes and counts who had ventured in the experiment of settling Germans in Texas lost a total of one and a half million gulden was certainly not the greatest casualty that had occurred.

The Mainz Adelsverein has often enough been sharply criticized by contemporaries and posterity, and it cannot be denied that this criticism is in many respects quite justified. The picture was distorted, on the other hand, when democratic writers tried to turn the failure of the association into political agitation material. Today we know that the colonization attempt did not fail because the counts had a hand in it. The lack of experience and means at that time made the most beautiful plans everywhere come to nothing. Like every nation, the German people had to pay a bitter price for their first overseas settlement attempts. It remains, however, the merit of the men who came together in the Mainz Adelsverein to have dared to found a German colony at a time when only forward-looking dreamers thought that the German colors would one day fly in lands beyond the seas. Later, the acquisition of colonies was to be successful in the Bismarck Empire, when the whole nation mobilized all its political and economic power. Before then it would have been a miracle if a private association would have succeeded. The Mainz Adelsverein was a private association after all, even though it was made up of five ruling princes.

A problem had become urgent for these princes, one that appears again and again in German history in different forms, the problem of the "people without enough space". Their states had too many people, the fields had become too small to feed the peasants, there was still no industry that could absorb the abundance of people and poverty was overwhelming. Was it not better for them to put the excess people in foreign countries on land that might one day become German, than to let it get as far as it did in Baden, where lots were drawn in individual communities to determine who had to emigrate? The fact that those princes supported the Mainz Adelsverein was a practical social policy that grew out of the hardship of those days and is to be understood from that perspective.

Whoever wants to judge the Verein zum Schutze deutscher Einwanderer in Texas" (Association for the Protection of German Immigrants in Texas) fairly, must consider that the sons and grandsons were not the first to learn to love the beautiful country between the Sabine and the Rio Grande, to which their fathers, German farmers and craftsmen, students and officers, had moved. And even today there are descendants in Texas of those first German immigrants who are mindful of the words once exclaimed by Prince Solms to the society's protégés:

"Always remember that you are Germans! Leave your homeland with the thought, with the firm resolution, to always remain worthy of your fatherland, to belong to it, even if far away."

A New Homeland

What became of the protégés of the Mainz Adelsverein? How did they find their way into their new home after the association dissolved and they found themselves left to their own devices?

Two eyewitnesses, Carl Blumberg, who settled in Schumannsville near New Braunfels, and the Swede Frederick Olmstedt, who visited the German settlements in Texas in the late 1950s, provide an account of this.

Before Carl Blumberg made the difficult decision to emigrate to America in 1845, he had served as a faithful public servant and God-fearing Christian in the West Prussian village of Kokocko near Kulm for 26 years. Before long, however, he no longer knew how to support his large family. He did not have to worry about his eldest son, who was offered a job as a teacher. Yet it would be a long time before the other seven children would be able to earn their own bread. So, he wondered how he would raise them. Devastating floods had often hit the Kulm region in recent years, and now the harvest had been destroyed twice in a row by floods. Blumberg also saw his cash income severely reduced without the yield from the school field—the distressed community could no longer afford the previous salary, as meager as it was. One day, the schoolmaster saw one of the advertisements of the Mainz Adelsverein, and since he got the impression that he could entrust himself and his family to this association without any worries, he joined the Texas emigrants at the end of 1845. Like the other thousands of society protégés, Blumberg also had to wait in vain at the assembly camp at Indian Point for transportation to Friedrichsburg. Since he had some money with him, in the spring of 1846 he bought a yoke of oxen, hitched them to the ladder wagon he had brought with him, and drove up to the Pedernales at his own risk. The conditions he encountered in Friedrichsburg, however, were so depressing and the cost of living from the association's store so high that Blumberg parted ways with the Mainz Adelsverein and tried to advance on his own. Looking back, he wrote to an acquaintance in West Prussia in 1853:

" Imagine my situation quite vividly, friend, how desperate it must have been, in a country that had only been snatched from the wilderness, where nothing had yet been cultivated and nothing had yet grown, without shelter, continually exposed to the hot rays of the burning sun and the influence of adverse weather, where all the necessities of life were very difficult to obtain at an enormously high price, helpless and destitute to support a numerous family of eight heads, for which each meal, however meager and simple, required the expenditure of half a dollar. Friend, I tell you, even the firmest trust in God is shaken and made to waver at such magnitude of need, misery, and want of all kinds. And yet, God has helped us wonderfully. He deserves honor, glory and praise for it! None of my dear ones, whom I took with me from Europe, has been taken away by death. His fatherly kindness has also provided me with external prosperity and blessed me in such a way that my and my family's future is assured. Even if I only farm on a small estate of 25 acres, which I bought here six years ago, paying three dollars for the acreage, which is currently worth six hundred dollars and for which I still had to borrow the money, I am now not only free of debt, but also free of worries. At present I have thirteen cows and as many calves of this year, an equal number of calves from the previous year, as well as some older young cattle;

also a beautiful riding horse, ten mules and three very good wagons. One wagon, harnessed with six mules, which is worth $500 altogether, and is almost always driven for hire by my son, brings in $300 net annually after deducting all expenses. Now I intend to purchase a second mule-drawn vehicle, which my second son is to operate for profit. Of my land I have only 15 acres in cultivation and fencing; for all fields here must be fenced, as all cattle roam freely wherever they please without supervision or herdsmen. This year I have planted half of it with cotton, for sale, and the other half with corn grain, sufficient for my household needs. I should therefore be ungrateful to kind Providence if I were to complain of my present condition, or reproach myself for having migrated from Europe; for never could I gain there, in whatever situation I might be and over a much longer period, what I have acquired here in so short a time."

However, Blumberg emphatically warns his acquaintance not to take the step of emigrating lightly. Gaining a foothold in Texas would be infinitely arduous and difficult:

"First of all, you have to create a shelter for your family that will protect them from the sun's rays as well as from the rain. Then one must devote all one's strength and attention to clearing and fencing the land one intends to cultivate, and this is no small matter! It is almost impossible for a single person to clear even a small piece of land of five acres of shrubs and wood, to fence it, to break it up with a plow and to plant it. At the same time, one must not forget the fact that unaccustomed to the local climate, in the first year after his arrival he feels quite weak, enfeebled and quite incapable of such strenuous gigantic work, especially if from home he is not accustomed to arduous physical labor as well as lack of all comforts of life, deprivations and hardships of all kinds, which are added to his efforts in abundance.... Here under a strange sky, in the midst of a plant world quite unknown to us, surrounded by many dangers threatening us, brought about by an unfamiliar climate and by many poisonous animals surrounding us, as rattlesnakes, moccasins, scorpions, tarantulas and so on, troubled by the exhausting glow of the sun's rays and with a meager diet of black coffee and cornbread three times a day, as well as a little bacon, which is often lacking, and which does not please a spoiled European palate in the beginning, to do the most difficult work.... is truly no trifle, is an almost insurmountable affliction, to which very many must succumb and perish in this way."

Not only did the teacher Blumberg survive these initial difficulties, but so did many thousands of other German immigrants. Where these settlers had solid ground under their feet, they created a "German" home for themselves in the middle of Texas. This is clearly shown by the report of Frederick Olmstedt, who traveled from Austin to Neu Braunfels:

"In front of a small brown-painted house with a turret and cross, we met a butcher from New Braunfels. The building was the Lutheran church. The man had ridden out early to slaughter pigs on a large farm, had finished doing so, and was now riding home.

"This man had been in the country for eight years, where he liked it quite well, he did not long to go back to Germany, but wanted to stay here. 'The Germans are doing well on average, and they are content. At the beginning, of course, they have to allow themselves to go through a lot of hardship, but soon they achieve prosperity. I know only one German who has bought a slave. My countrymen are not fond of slavery and think that all men should be free, nor does a Negro ever work as well as a German. In the last two years my countrymen have made very good progress. Down on the coast it is unhealthy, but up here it is very healthy; I am as comfortable here as in Germany and have never been ill. Catholics and Protestants live side by side. For my part, I don't like any priests, neither Catholic nor Protestant, as I already had my fill of them in Germany, they can't tell me anything new and I never go to church.'

"The butcher showed us the ford through the Guadalupe. When we reached with him the high bank on the other side, we found ourselves on a flat plain on which, between the river and the prairie hills, lies New Braunfels. We still had about half a mile to go to the town, and on this route we met about eight or ten large wagons drawn by five or six yoke of oxen or three or four pairs of mules.

"Each animal had a bell hanging from its neck. The drivers, all Germans, were not exactly graceful, but warm and cleanly dressed. They all smoked tobacco, were in a lively mood and called out a good morning greeting to us. I noticed that the wagons were all so durable and strongly made—they were of German workmanship. The butcher said, 'The Germans make better ones than the Americans. We have seven wagon factories in Neu-Braunfels.'

"We rode into the main street. It is more than three times as wide as Broadway in New York. On the stretch of a mile, houses stand quite close to each other on both sides, mostly small, low buildings without elegance. However, they look very nice and cozy. Some had second floors and gardens. Most of them were painted or rendered. We saw many workshops and general stores with signs that were more often in English than in German. Bare-headed women and pipe-smoking men in caps and short jackets were busy everywhere.

"We now spent a day that made us completely forget that we were in Texas. Not a single person in town was known to us. We therefore wanted to go to an inn and not, as had been our habit since then, to eat a cold noon sandwich in the saddle. The butcher said, 'There's my shop.' He pointed to a small house with pieces of meat and sausages hanging on the door. If you want to stay here, I will direct you to my neighbor Schmitz. The 'Guadalupe Hotel of J. Schmitz' was a one-story house, the roof of which protruded, forming a veranda.

"Never in my life, except, say, when waking from a dream, did I see myself transported to such a different world as when I entered this German inn. I didn't see walls of loosely joined boards or logs, with cracks and holes stuffed or spread with mortar, didn't find four bare walls like I had seen a few times in Texas among aristocratic Americans. Rather, I was in Germany in the flesh. Nothing was missing. There was nothing too much and nothing too little. I found myself transported to one of those delicious little inns so fondly and gratefully remembered by all who have ever walked in the Rhineland. A long room took up the whole front of the house. The walls were handsomely and neatly painted with pleasing patterns, and on all sides hung lithographic pictures in glass and frames. In the center was a large strong table of dark oak with rounded corners. Benches ran along the walls, the chairs were of oak and carved, the sofa was covered with flowered furniture calico. In one corner there was a stove, in another a small mahogany sideboard with bottles and glasses. The room was full of tobacco smoke. At the large table sat four men with strong full beards, smoking and saying a friendly good morning to us as we entered and lifted our hats.

"In a moment the landlady enters the room. She doesn't understand our English well, but one of the smokers gets up and does the interpreting. We should be having lunch in a minute. She takes a tablecloth and spreads it out at one end of the table, and just as we have taken off our coats and warmed our hands a little at the stove, the woman is already back and asks us to sit down. She serves us an excellent soup, followed by two dishes of meat—no roasted pork!—two bowls of vegetables, salad, preserved fruits, wheat bread, coffee with milk, and with it splendid unsalted butter, butter such as I have never found in the south of the Potomac, where people always told me it was not possible to make good butter in a southern climate. What therefore is the secret difference? In diligence, in attentiveness, and in cleanliness!

"We talked with the gentlemen in the inn for an hour after dinner. All of them were educated, well-bred men, friendly, respectable, talkative, all born in Germany. They had lived in Texas only a few years. Some were traveling and residing in other German settlements, others had lived in Braunfels for some time. It was so very pleasant to us to meet with such people, and they gave us such interesting and satisfactory news about the Germans in Texas, that we decided to stay. We went out to look after our horses. A man in a cap and neat jacket was rubbing them down. It was the first time that such a thing had happened to them without their asking. Otherwise we had had to do it ourselves or pay a Negro dearly for it. In the manger lay the best mesquite hay, the first that they had ever eaten in Texas, and the animals liked it so much that they seemed to beg us with their eyes to leave them there overnight. Was there a room for us in the little inn? Guests were already there, but we could sleep on the flat ground if necessary and were still better off than we had been before. We asked if we could have a night's lodging. Yes, with pleasure. Wouldn't we like to take a look at the room? We thought it was probably in the rooster beam, but that was a mistake. There was an outbuilding in the courtyard; in it was a small room with blue-painted walls and oak furniture. We found two beds. Everyone should have his own bed, so enjoy the luxury of sleeping alone! This had not happened to us in Texas before! The two windows had curtains and were covered with an evergreen rose bush outside. No window pane was missing—for the first time since we were in Texas! There was also a sofa and a bureau with a complete conversation dictionary next to Kendall's Santa Fe expedition, a porcelain statuette, flowers in pots, and a brass study lamp. A well-appointed washstand complete with clean towels was not lacking either. How it all seemed to us! Of course, we were happy to spend the night in such a house.

"We visited the Protestant clergyman in the afternoon, who received us very kindly. Although he did not speak English fluently, he willingly gave us information about the conditions of his fellow countrymen in Texas. We also visited some workshops and stores and talked with a merchant about the quality and quantity of cotton produced by the Germans. Toward evening we met about a dozen very intelligent men at the inn and spent the last hours of the day at the home of one of our new acquaintances. Everything I saw and heard confirmed the pleasant communications the butcher had given us. When I returned to the inn at 10 o'clock at night, I stopped in front of a house and listened to the singing. For a long, dear time I had not heard such good singing, and the voices were excellent. The next morning I saw a tame deer running around in the open road not far from the schoolhouse. It wore a ribbon on its neck so that it could be distinguished from the wild ones if it got lost. The dearest animal was so unafraid that it came up to me and licked my hand. In what other Texas town could such a thing have happened?

"In the morning we found that our horses had had a litter, likewise for the first time in Texas. And as we rode out of town we were again met with a most gratifying sight. Groups of children, all chubby and full of life, were going to school. They carried slates, satchels of books, and little pouches in which they had their midday bread. The girls, in particular, looked lovely with their slicked-back hair and uncovered heads. Everyone called out a friendly good morning to us as we passed. We had never seen such a pleasant sight in all of Texas. This was our first encounter with the Germans in this country."

CONCLUSION

RANGERS AND RANCHES

"The lone star of Texas, which ten years ago rose among gloomy clouds over bloody battlefields, shining silently for a while, has passed through its orbit, has been transformed, and will now forever take its place in that wonderful constellation which every free man and every lover of liberty must respect and revere—the American Union. May it unite its rays with those of its sister stars and allow its light to shine forever, may a benevolent heaven bless the fulfillment of the wishes of the two republics which have now merged into one! May the Union be of perpetual duration and bestow benefits and blessings upon the people in all the States—this is my fervent prayer. The closing act of this great spectacle is now over: the Republic of Texas no longer exists." These were the parting words of the President of the Republic of Texas when, at the beginning of 1846, the star-spangled banner of Texas was lowered and the star-spangled banner of the Union rose up the mast. The longing of the Texas settlers had been fulfilled: Texas had become a member of the North American Confederacy. Its history was henceforth absorbed into the history of the United States of America.

A LONE STAR ARISES IN TEXAS

For many decades to come Texas remained a frontier state. Indeed, the period of which the Wild West novels have so many adventurous and exciting tales to tell, only began when the country became a part of the Union. If one studies the map and learns that the settlement of Texas still barely extended beyond the boundary drawn by the Camino Real, the old Spanish royal road between San Antonio and Nacogdoches around the year 1845, one sees how little had been settled and how much had yet to be developed. Having said that, this further occupation of the land no longer had any political significance. The struggle for North America, in which Texas had played its part for a century and a half, was over, and what followed was exclusively a struggle against the American wilderness, against virgin forest and prairie, and its inhabitants, the Indians. At the same time, however, and this must not be overlooked, it was also a struggle for the betterment of the people who had gone out west to conquer the American wilderness in the interest of European culture. For these pioneers and settlers, who occupied the frontier and drove it ever onward, had sunk back into the hard, deprived struggle for existence in which they found themselves daily, to a simplicity, not to say primitiveness of existence, so that sometimes one found hardly any traces among them of that spiritual and moral culture which constitutes the nobility and pride of the white race. The culture which they brought into the wilderness was the culture of agriculture and animal husbandry, no more, therefore, than the economic prerequisites for a culture of the spirit and of the soul. It was the beginning, but not the goal, of a true cultivation.

The old Texas settlements, the places once founded by Spanish monks and soldiers, the lands to which Stephen

Austin had led his colonists, had long since ceased to be a frontier in that sense. Even then, at the end of the Lone Star Republic, it was still possible to feel at every turn how young this country was, but year by year life was becoming more like that in the old southern states of the Union. This part of Texas had already experienced a tumultuous boom in the fifteen years between 1845 and 1860. Cotton production increased tenfold, as did the number of cattle, trade and commerce flourished, and the population rose from 103,000 to 421,000, of whom, however, 181,000 were Negro slaves.

This was not, however, the real problem of developing these areas. The task that had to be mastered beyond the taming of the mountain ranges that rise in terraces to the endless prairies, was the development of the plains themselves. For a long time to come, this frontier lay so close to the old settlement areas that its influence was felt even in the cities. At the same time, however, Texas was a frontier state in another sense. It had Mexico as its immediate neighbor in the southwest, and even if the "Americanization" of the country left only names, ruins and a few special legal institutions from the Spanish-Mexican period, Mexican influence continued to penetrate the country via the Rio Grande.

The fight with the Indians was particularly difficult on the Texas frontier. Here the Americans had to deal with the warlike prairie tribes, who resisted the advance of the palefaces into the plains to the very last. Until the middle of the 19th century, these Redskins, in union with nature, formed a barrier that the American pioneer was unable to break through. What was involved in coping with the Plains Indians and in protecting the frontiers of the country against those tribes which, from Indian Territory, from

Oklahoma, made their raids into the most densely populated areas, is shown by the fact that the Union was unable to break through the barrier until the eighties of the eighteenth century and the Union maintained nineteen or more forts in Texas, had two to four thousand soldiers, nearly the third part of the Federal army, posted on that frontier. In 1851, for example, it had to spend over six million dollars for the military protection of the Texan settlers alone!

Texans didn't think much of the performance of American troops. They thought a few hundred Rangers would do more for a fraction of the cost than all the federal soldiers. This was certainly exaggerated and dictated by local patriotism. After all, the Rangers were a Texas institution. It was not entirely inaccurate, however. Experience taught that the Indians—and not only the Indians, but all the riffraff that prowled the frontier—had more respect for a frontier mounted patrol than for a whole company of soldiers. The Rangers—they still exist today, transformed into a kind of constabulary—were the Indian fighters for the books. "They ride like a Mexican, they shoot like a Tennessean, and they fight like the devil incarnate," it was said of them. They knew every corner of the wilderness, they knew all the wiles of the Redskins, they could read the tracks as well as any Comanche scout, they were infallible gunners, they were accustomed to act independently even without command, and above all, they had courage, were daredevils and dauntless, and it did not matter to a Ranger to take on a horde of Indians or a band of bandits even alone. The number of their feats of bravery and heroism is uncounted, and if the frontier was cleansed of the Redskins and the Mexican borderlands of the desperadoes, if the Texan unlearned the all too easy grasp of the Colt revolver, if Texas, the disreputable wild west country, became a state of order and law, it owed this in no small measure to its "frontiersmen".

The Comanches and other prairie tribes had been gradually pushed off the Texas plains since the 1860s, and the herds of buffalo that had roamed the vast grasslands by the hundreds of thousands and millions fell under the rifle shots of the columns of hunters sent out by a profit-seeking leather industry. The face of the prairies changed, the plains became pasture land, cattle made their entrance and with cattle the cowboy. The number of cattle grew into the millions, the cattle ranches expanded into principalities, into duchies. They didn't know what to do with the wealth of cattle. In 1865, the slaughterhouses opened in Chicago, and now the cattlemen of West Texas drove the slaughter-ready animals in herds of tens of thousands up to the North, and on the long train the cattle, eating the grass of the winter steppes, could put on the last fat they still lacked. In the years between 1867 and 1890, over ten million head of cattle were led from Texas on the "trails" to the slaughter benches of Chicago, and this does not include the cattle shipped by rail. It was not until the lands west of the Mississippi were also settled by ranchers and the farmers resisted the damage that the passing herds of cattle were doing to their fields and pastures and not until the northern states enacted strict quarantine regulations out of fear of the "Texas fever" that was repeatedly introduced into their livestock by diseased animals, that the "trails" slowly became deserted. The cowboy, that romantic realist figure of Texas ranches, no longer appeared on the long roads that ran north. From drover he became herdsman, but he still lives, still throws his lasso, still sings the old songs.

A LONE STAR ARISES IN TEXAS

The American government declared in 1890 that there was no longer a frontier in the Union, that there was no more free land, that the "Winning of the West" had come to an end. The last Indians had been driven out of Texas ten years earlier, and the ranches had long since reached the uppermost tip of the state, the Panhandle, through which a Spanish conquistador had passed 440 years earlier in pursuit of the fairy-tale kingdom of Quivira, which was to be joined by the no less gold-rich Kingdom of the Tejás. Gold was never found in Texas, and the wealth that the land held did not open up to the rapacious grasps of Spanish conquistadors. It was not until the American immigrants moved into the wilds of Central Texas and plowed up the fertile soil and until the sweat of toilsome labor fertilized the fields that the wealth of Texas could be grasped and harvested. Looking back over the history of Texas and seeing how Spaniards and Frenchmen, Mexicans and Americans wrestled with each other for this land, the answer to the question of who remained the victor in this global political struggle will perhaps be: the pioneer, the settler, the farmer, the man who set out to wrest Texas from the wilderness.

THE END

BIBLIOGRAPHY

An indication of all books, pamphlets and journal articles used would go beyond the scope of this section. Nevertheless, the most important literature should be mentioned, first to express to which works the author is most indebted, and then to give a hint to those who would like to deal more closely with one or the other epoch or personality.

There has not yet been a German work dealing in depth with Texas history. Most can be found in the fine study by Ernst Daenell, "Die Spanier in Nordamerika 1513-1824" (Munich/Berlin 1911). Emil Kimpen, "Die Ausbreitungspolitik der Vereinigten Staaten von Amerika" (Stuttgart/Berlin 1923), instructs on the Texas policy of the Union government.

Unfortunately, there is no summary account of Texas history, even in English, that processes the rich results of the special studies and monographs of recent decades. A good overview is given by Newton-Gambrell in their "A Social and Political History of Texas" (Dallas 1932), intended as a textbook for college instruction. Otherwise, one must rely on the older works, of which, in addition to H. Yoakum's book, "History of Texas" (Redfield 1856), which is still worth reading, the excellent writing of George P. Garrison, "Texas, A Contest of Civilizations" (Boston/New York 1903).

Under the leadership of Herbert E. Bolton (University of

California) and Eugene C. Barker (University of Texas), a host of younger historians has been in the process of opening up the rich material of the Mexican and Texas archives for some time. In addition to many special publications, essays in the Southwestern Historical Quarterly acquaint readers with the results of this work.

Regarding the first chapter: A German translation of Cabeza de Vaca's report was published by Franz Termer (Stuttgart 1925). The material is treated in detail by Morris Bishop, "The Odyssey of Cabeza de Vaca" (New York/London 1933). The standard work on the Coronado expedition is by George P. Winship in "Fourteenth Report of Bureau of Ethnology" (Washington 1896). Equally valuable are the studies by A. F. Bandelier, "The Gilded Man" (New York 1893). A general overview of the period is given by Herbert E. Bolton, "The Spanish Borderlands" (New Haven 1921).

On chapter 2, A. Rein devotes a penetrating study to the "Kampf Westeuropas um Nordamerika im 15. und 16. Jahrhundert" (Stuttgart 1925). The most important American works for this period are W. E. Dunn, "Spanish and French Rivalry in the Gulf Region of the United States 1678-1702" (Austin 1917), and Herbert E. Bolton, "Texas in the Middle eighteenth Century" (Berkeley 1915).

Regarding Chapter 3, the authoritative work is Herbert E. Bolton's two-volume work, "Athanase de Mézières" (Cleveland 1914), a publication of Mézières' letters and archival material relating to his activities.

Concerning the 4th chapter: A most interesting biography "Jean Lafitte, the Pirate" (New York/London 1930) has been written by Lyle Saxon.

Turning to chapter 5, the basic biography of Austin was written by Eugene C. Barker published, "The Life of

Stephen F. Austin" (Nashville/Dallas 1925). Valuable are the lectures Barker had published under the title "Mexico and Texas 1821-1835" (Dallas 1928).

On Chapter 6: A monograph on the Battle of San Jacinto was written by Clarence Wharton, "San Jacinto, The Sixteenth Decisive Battle" (Houston 1930).

Concerning the seventh chapter: In addition to the scholarly work of Ephraim D. Adams, "British Interests and Activities in Texas 1836/46" (Baltimore 1910), mention should be made of the biography of Sam Houston by Marquis James, "The Raven" (Indianapolis 1929), and the biography "Santa Anna" by Hanighen (New York 1934).

Regarding chapter 8: The best work on the Germans in Texas has been published by Rudolph L. Biesele, "The History of the German Settlements in Texas 1831-1861" (Austin 1930). There is also given the rich pamphlet material that appeared on this side and the other side of the ocean on the occasion of the Texas emigration. A good overview of the activities of the "Mainz Adelsverein" is given by G. Smolka in Freeden-Smolka, "Auswanderer" (Berlin 1937).

In conclusion, an instructive overview of the economic development of the North American Southwest can be found in Richardson-Rister's work, "The Greater Southwest" (Glendale 1934).

www.ingramcontent.com/pod-product-compliance
Lightning Source LLC
LaVergne TN
LVHW032203070526
838202LV00008B/303